Richard Anthony Proctor

Our Place Among Infinities

A Series of Essays Contrasting our Little Abode in Space and Time...

Richard Anthony Proctor

Our Place Among Infinities
A Series of Essays Contrasting our Little Abode in Space and Time...

ISBN/EAN: 9783337187880

Printed in Europe, USA, Canada, Australia, Japan

Cover: Foto ©Thomas Meinert / pixelio.de

More available books at **www.hansebooks.com**

OUR PLACE AMONG INFINITIES.

A SERIES OF ESSAYS

CONTRASTING OUR LITTLE ABODE IN SPACE AND
TIME WITH THE INFINITIES AROUND US.

TO WHICH ARE ADDED ESSAYS ON

THE JEWISH SABBATH AND ASTROLOGY.

By

RICHD. A. PROCTOR,

AUTHOR OF "SATURN AND ITS SYSTEM," "THE UNIVERSE," "THE EXPANSE
OF HEAVEN," ETC., ETC.

"Nous n'avons point la mesure de cette machine immense; nous n'en pouvons calculer les rapports; nous n'en connaissons ni les premières lois, ni la cause finale."—
J. J. ROUSSEAU.

"Freue dich, höchstes Geschöpf der Natur, du fühlest dich fähig,
Ihr den höchsten Gedanken, zu dem sie schaffend sich aufschwang,
Nachzudenken."
GOETHE.

NEW YORK:
D. APPLETON AND COMPANY,
549 AND 551 BROADWAY.
1876.

PREFACE.

This work takes its name from the essays occupying the first seventy pages of the book; but the later essays, as shewing the nature of those parts of the universe which lie nearest to us, are properly included under the same title. Even those on Astrology and the Jewish Sabbath belong to the discussion of our place among infinities; for it was their ignorance of the earth's place among infinities, which led the ancients to regard the heavenly bodies as ruling, favourably or adversely, the fates of men and nations, and to dedicate the days in sets of seven to the seven planets of their astrological system.

It will be seen, that my views respecting the interesting question of life in other worlds have changed considerably since I wrote the work bearing that title. I still consider that work a sound exposition of the theory of the plurality of worlds, though I consider that the weight of evidence favours my theory of the (relative) paucity of worlds.

RICHD. A. PROCTOR.

Sept. 27, 1875.

CONTENTS.

	PAGE
PAST AND FUTURE OF THE EARTH,	1
SEEMING WASTES IN NATURE,	35
NEW THEORY OF LIFE IN OTHER WORLDS,	45
A MISSING COMET,	71
THE LOST COMET AND ITS METEOR TRAIN,	91
JUPITER,	109
SATURN AND ITS SYSTEM,	128
A GIANT SUN,	156
THE STAR DEPTHS,	182
STAR GAUGING,	218
SATURN AND THE SABBATH OF THE JEWS,	290
THOUGHTS ON ASTROLOGY,	314

NOTE.—Most of these Essays have been reprinted from current periodicals.

OUR PLACE AMONG INFINITIES.

THE PAST AND FUTURE OF OUR EARTH.*

> " Ut his exordia primis
> Omnia, et ipse tener Mundi concreverit orbis.
> Tum durare solum, et discludere Nerea ponto
> Cœperit, et rerum paullatim sumere formas."
> VIRGIL.

THE subject with which I am about to deal is associated by many with questions of religion. Let me premise, however, that I do not thus view it myself. It seems to me impossible to obtain from science any clear ideas respecting the ways or nature of the Deity, or even respecting the reality of an Almighty personal God. Science deals with the finite though it may carry our thoughts to the infinite. Infinity of space and of matter occupying space, of time and of the processes with which time is occupied, and infinity of energy as necessarily implied by the infinities of matter and of the operations

---

* This essay presents the substance of a lecture delivered in New York on April 3, 1874, being the first of a subsidiary series in which, of set purpose (and in accordance with the request of several esteemed friends), I dealt less with the direct teachings of astronomy, which had occupied me in a former series, than with ideas suggested by astronomical facts, and more particularly by the discoveries made during the last quarter of a century.

affecting matter,—these infinities science brings clearly before us. For science directs our thoughts to the finites to which these infinites correspond. It shows us that there can be no conceivable limits to space or time, and though finiteness of matter or of operation may be conceivable, there is manifest incongruity in assuming an infinite disproportion between unoccupied and occupied space, or between void time and time occupied with the occurrence of events of what sort soever. So that the teachings of science bring us into the presence of the unquestionable infinities of time and of space, and the presumable infinities of matter and of operation,—hence, therefore, into the presence of infinity of energy. But science teaches us nothing about these infinities, as such. They remain none the less inconceivable, however clearly we may be taught to recognise their reality. Moreover, these infinites, including the infinity of energy, are material infinities. Science tells us nothing of the infinite attributes of an Almighty Being; it presents to us no personal infinites, whether of Power, Beneficence, or Wisdom. Science may suggest some ideas on these points; though we perceive daily more and more clearly that it is unsafe to accept as her teaching ideas which commonly derive their colouring from our own prepossessions. And assuredly, as respects actual facts, Science in so far as she presents personal infinity to us at all, presents it as an inconceivable, like those other inconceivable infinities, with the finites corresponding to which her operations are alone directly concerned. To speak in plain terms—so far as Science is concerned, the idea of a personal God is inconceivable,* as are all the attributes which religion recognizes in such a Being. On the other hand, it should be admitted as distinctly, that Science no more disproves the existence of infinite personal power or wisdom than she disproves the existence of infinite material energy (which on the contrary must be regarded as probable) or the existence of infinite space or time (which must be regarded as certain).

So much premised, we may proceed to inquire into the probable past and future of our earth, as calmly as we should inquire into the probable past and future of a pebble, a weed, or an insect, of a rock, a tree, or an animal, of a continent, or of a type—whether of vegetable or of animal life. The beginning of all things is not to be reached, not appreciably to be even approached, by a few steps backward in imagination, nor the end of all things by a few steps forward. Such a thought is as unfounded as was the fear of men in old times that by travelling too far in any direction they might pass over the earth's edge and be plunged into the abyss beyond, as unreasonable

---

* I mean these words to be understood literally. To the man of science, observing the operation of second causes in every process with which his researches deal, and finding no limit to the operation of such causes however far back he may trace the chain of causation, the idea of a first cause is as inconceivable in its relation to observed scientific facts as is the idea of infinite space in its relation to the finite space to which the observations of science extend. Yet infinite space must be admitted; nor do I see how even that man of science who would limit his thoughts most rigidly to facts, can admit that all things *are* of which he thinks, without having impressed upon him the feeling that, in some way he cannot understand, these things represent the operation of Infinite Purpose. Assuredly we do not avoid the inconceivable by assuming as at least possible that matter exists only as it affects our perceptions.

as was the hope that by increase of telescopic range astronomers could approach the imagined "heavens above the crystalline."

In considering the probable past history of the earth, we are necessarily led to inquire into the origin of the solar system. I have already sketched two theories of the system, and described the general facts on which both theories are based. The various planets circle in one direction around the sun, the sun rotating in the same direction, the satellite families (with one noteworthy but by no means inexplicable exception) travelling round their primaries in the same direction, and all the planets whose rotation has been determined still preserving the same direction of circulation (so to speak). These relations seem to point, in a manner there is no mistaking, to a process of evolution by which those various parts of the solar system which now form discrete masses were developed from a former condition characterized by a certain unity as respects the manner of its circulation. One theory of this process of evolution, Laplace's, implies the contraction of the solar system from a great rotating nebulous mass; according to the other theory, the solar system, instead of contracting to its present condition, was formed by a process of accretion, due to the indrawing of great flights of meteoric and cometic matter.

I need not here enter at length, for I have already done so elsewhere, into the astronomical evidence in favour of either theory; but it will be well to present briefly some of the more striking facts.

Among the various forms of nebulæ (or star-cloudlets) revealed by the telescope, we find many which seem to accord with our ideas as to some of the stages through which our solar system must have passed in changing from the nebulous condition to its present form. The irregular nebulæ,—such, for instance, as that wonderful nebula in the Sword of Orion,—shew by their enormous extension the existence of sufficient quantities of gaseous matter to form systems as large and as massive as our own, or even far vaster. We know from the teachings of the spectroscope that these irregular nebulæ do really consist of glowing gas (as Sir W. Herschel long since surmised), hydrogen and nitrogen being presumably present, though the spectrum of neither gas appears in its complete form (one line only of each spectrum being shewn, instead of the sets of lines usually given by these gases). An American physicist has suggested that hydrogen and nitrogen exist in the gaseous nebulæ in an elementary condition, these gases really being compound, and he suggests further that all our so-called elements may have been derived from those elementary forms of hydrogen and nitrogen. In the absence of any evidence from observation or experiment, these ideas must be regarded as merely speculative; and I think that we arrive here at a point where speculation helps us as little as it does in attempting to trace the evolution of living creatures across the gap which separates the earliest forms of life from the beginning itself of life upon the earth. Since we cannot hope to determine the real beginning of the earth's history, we need not at present attempt to pass back beyond the earliest stage of which we have any clear information.

Passing from the irregular nebulæ, in which we see chaotic masses of gaseous matter occupying millions of millions of cubic miles and scattered as wildly through space as clouds are scattered in a storm-swept air, we come to various orders of nebulæ in which we seem to find clear evidence of a process of evolution. We see first the traces of a central aggregation. This aggregation becomes more and more clearly defined, until there is no possibility of mistaking its nature as a centre having power (by virtue of the quantity of matter contained in it) to influence the motions of the matter belonging to the rest of the nebula. Then, still passing be it remembered from nebula to nebula, and only inferring, not actually witnessing, the changes described,—we see a subordinate aggregation, wherein, after a while, the greater portion of the mass of the nebula outside the central aggregation becomes gathered, even as Jupiter contains the greater portion of the mass of the solar system outside the central sun.* Next we see a second subordinate aggregation, inferior to the first, but comprising, if we judge from its appearance, by far the greater portion of what remained after the first aggregation had been formed,—even as Saturn's mass far exceeds the combined mass of all the planets less than himself, and so comprises far the greater portion of the solar system after account has been taken

---

* The mass of Jupiter exceeds, in the proportion of five to two, the combined mass of all the remaining planets.

of Jupiter and the sun.* And we may infer that the other parts of nebulæ contain smaller aggregations not perceptible to us, out of which the smaller planets of the developing system are hereafter to be formed.

Side views of some of these nebulæ indicate a flatness of figure agreeing well with the general tendency of the members of the solar system towards the medial plane of that system. For the solar system may be described as flat, and if the nebulæ I have been dealing with (the spiral nebulæ with aggregations) were globular we could not recognise in them the true analogues of our solar system in the earlier stages of its history. But the telescope reveals nebulæ manifestly corresponding in appearance to the great whirlpool nebula of Lord Rosse, as it would appear if it is a somewhat flattened spiral and could be viewed nearly edgewise.

And here I may pause to note that, although, in thus inferring progressive changes where in reality we have but various forms of nebulæ, I have been adopting an assumption and one which no one can hope either to verify or to disprove, yet it must be remembered that these nebulæ by their very figure indicate that they are not at rest. If they consist of matter possessing the attribute of gravitation,—and it would be infinitely more daring to assert that they do not than that they do,—then they must be undergoing processes of change. Nor can we conceive that discrete gaseous masses in whorls spirally

* The mass of Saturn exceeds, in the proportion of nearly three to one, the combined mass of all the planets smaller than himself.

arranged around a great central aggregation (taking one of the earlier stages) could otherwise change than by aggregating towards their centre, unless we admit motions of revolution (in orbits more or less eccentric) the continuance of which would necessarily lead, through collisions, to the rapid growth of the central aggregation, and to the formation and slower growth of subordinate gatherings.

I have shown elsewhere how the formation of our solar system, in the manner supposed, would explain what Laplace admitted that he could not explain by his theory,—the peculiar arrangement of the masses forming the solar system. The laws of dynamics tell us, that no matter what the original configuration or motion of the masses, probably gaseous, forming the nebula, the motions of these masses would have greater and greater velocity the nearer the masses were to the central aggregation, each distance indicating certain limits between which the velocities must inevitably lie. For example, in our solar system, supposing the central sun had already attained very nearly his full growth as respects quantity of matter, then the velocity of any mass whatever belonging to the system, would at Jupiter's distance be less than twelve miles per second, whereas at the distance of the earth, the largest planet travelling inside the orbit of Jupiter, the limit of the velocity would be more than twice as great. Hence we can see with what comparative difficulty an aggregation would form close to the central one, and how the first subordinate aggregation would lie at a distance where the quantity of matter was still great but the average velocity of motion not too great. Such an aggregation once formed, the next important aggregation would necessarily lie far outside, for within the first there would now be two disturbing influences preventing the rapid growth of these aggregations. The third and fourth would be outside the second. Between the first aggregation and the sun only small planets, like the Earth and Venus, Mars, Mercury, and the asteroids, could form; and we should expect to find that the largest of the four small planets would be in the middle of the space belonging to the family, (as Venus and the Earth are actually placed), while the much smaller planets Mercury and Mars travel next on either side, one close to the Sun and the other next to Jupiter, the asteroids indicating the region where the combined disturbing influences of Jupiter and the Sun prevented any single planet from being developed.

But I should require much more time than is now at my command to present adequately the reasoning on which the theory of accretion is based. And we are not concerned here to inquire whether this theory, or Laplace's theory of contraction, or (which I hold to be altogether more probable than either) a theory involving combined processes of accretion and contraction, be the true hypothesis of the evolution of the solar system. Let it suffice that we recognise as one of the earliest stages of our earth's history, her condition as a rotating mass of glowing vapour, capturing then as now, but far more actively then than now, masses of matter which approached near enough, and *growing* by these continual indraughts from without. From the very beginning, as it would seem, the earth grew in this way. This firm earth on which we live represents an aggregation of matter not from one portion of space, but from all space. All that is upon and within the earth, all vegetable forms and all animals forms, our bodies, our brains, are formed of materials which have been drawn in from those depths of space surrounding us on all sides. This hand that I am now raising contains particles which have travelled hither from regions far away amid the northern and southern constellations, particles drawn in towards the earth by processes continuing millions of millions of ages, until after multitudinous changes the chapter of accidents has so combined them, and so distributed them in plants and animals, that after coming to form portions of my food they are here present before you. Passing from the mere illustration of the thought, is not the thought itself striking and suggestive, that not only the earth on which we move, but everything we see or touch, and every particle in body and brain, has sped during countless ages through the immensity of space?

The great mass of glowing gas which formed our earth in the earliest stage of its history was undergoing two noteworthy processes,—first, the process of cooling by which the mass was eventually to become at least partially solid, and secondly a process of growth due to the gathering in of meteoric and cometic matter. As respects the latter process, which will not hereafter occupy our attention, I must remark that many astronomers appear to me to give far less consideration to the inferences certainly deducible from recent discoveries than the importance of these discoveries would fairly warrant. It is now absolutely certain that hour by hour, day by day, and year by year, the earth is gathering in matter from without. On the most moderate assumption as to the average weight of meteors and shooting stars, the earth must increase each year in mass by many thousands of tons. And when we consider the enormous, one may almost say the awful time-intervals which have elapsed since the earth was in a gaseous condition, we cannot but perceive that the process of accretion now going on indicates the existence of only the merest residue of matter (ungathered) compared with that which at the beginning of those time-intervals was freely moving around the central aggregation. The process of accretion which now does not sensibly increase the earth's mass was then a process of actual growth. Jupiter and Saturn might then no longer be gathering in matter appreciably increasing their mass, although the quantity of matter gathered in by them must have been far larger than all that the other forming earth could gather in equal times. For those planets were then as now so massive that any possible increment from without was as nothing compared with the mass they had already attained. We have to throw back into yet more awful time-depths the birth and growth of those giant orbs. And even those depths of time are as nothing compared with the intervals which have elapsed since the sun himself began to be. Yet it is with time-intervals measurable by hundreds of millions of years that we have to deal in considering only our earth's history,—nay, two or three hundred millions of years only carry us back to a period when the earth was in a stage of development long sequent to the gaseous condition we are now considering. That the supply of meteoric and cometic matter not gathered in was then enormously greater than that which still exists within the solar domain, appears to me not a mere fanciful speculation, nor even a theoretical consideration, but as nearly a certainty as anything not admitting of mathematical demonstration can possibly be. That the rate of in-gathering at that time enormously exceeded the present rate, may be regarded as certain. That the increase resulting from such in-gathering during the hundreds of millions of years that it has been in operation since the period when the earth first existed as a gaseous mass, must have resulted in adding a quantity of matter forming no inconsiderable aliquot part of the earth's present mass, seems to me a reasonable inference, although it is certain that the present rate of growth continued even for hundreds of millions of years would not appreciably affect the earth's mass.* And it is a thought worthy of consideration, in selecting between Laplace's theory of contraction and the theory of accretion, that accretion being a process necessarily exhaustive, we are able to

* It is, perhaps, hardly necessary to explain that I refer here not to absolute but to relative increase. The absolute increase of mass would amount to many millions of tons, but the earth would not be increased by the billionth part of her present mass.

trace it back through stages of gradually increasing activity without limit until we reach that stage when the whole of the matter now forming our solar system was as yet unformed. Contraction may alternate with expansion, according to the changing condition of a forming system; but accretion is a process which can only act in one direction; and as accretion is certainly going on now, however slowly, we have but to trace back the process to be led inevitably, in my judgment, to regard our system as having its origin in processes of accretion,—though it seems equally clear that each individual orb of the system, if not each subordinate scheme within it, has also undergone a process of contraction from a former nebulous condition.

In this early gaseous stage our earth was preparing as it were to become a *sun*. As yet her gaseous globe probably extended beyond the smaller aggregation out of which the moon was one day to be formed. This may be inferred, I think, from the law of the moon's rotation. It is true that a moon independently created, and started on the moon's present course, with a rotation-period nearly equalling its period of revolution, would gradually have acquired a rotation-period exactly equalling the mean period of revolution. But there is no reason in nature why there should have been any such near approach; whereas, if we suppose the moon's gaseous globe to have been originally entangled within the outskirts of the earth's, we see that the peculiar relation in question would have prevailed from the beginning of the moon's existence as a separate body. The laws of dynamics show us, moreover, that although the conditions under which the moon moved and rotated must have undergone considerable changes since her first formation, yet that since those changes took place very slowly, the rotation of the moon would be gradually modified, *pari passu*, so that the peculiar relation between the moon's rotation and revolution would continue unimpaired.*

In her next stage, our earth is presented to us as a sun. It may be that at that time the moon was the abode of life, our earth affording the supplies of light and heat necessary for the wants of creatures living on the moon. But whether this were so or not, it may be safely assumed that when the earth's contracting gaseous globe first began to have liquid or solid matter in its constitution, the earth must have been a sun so far as the emission of heat and light were concerned. I must warn you, however, against an undue regard for analogy which has led some astronomers to say that all the members of the solar system have passed or will pass through exactly similar stages. That our earth once gave out light and heat, as the sun does now, may be admitted as probable; and we may believe that later the earth presented the characteristics which we now recognize in Jupiter; while hereafter

---

* On the theory of evolution some such view of the origin of the moon's rotation *must* be adopted, unless the matter be regarded as the result of a strange chance. If we believe, on the contrary, that the arrangement was specially ordained by the Creator, we are left to wonder what useful purpose a relation so peculiar and so artificial can have been intended to subserve.

it may pass through a stage comparable with that through which our moon is now passing. But we must remember that the original quantity of matter in any orb passing through such stages must very importantly modify the actual condition of the orb in each of those stages, as well, of course, as the duration of each stage; and it may even be that no two orbs in the universe were ever in the same, or very nearly the same condition, and that no change undergone by one has corresponded closely with any change undergone by another.

We know so little respecting the sun's actual condition, that even if we could be assured that in any past stages of her history the earth was nearly in the same state, we should nevertheless remain in almost complete ignorance as to the processes to which the earth's orb was at that time subject. In particular we have no means of forming an opinion as to the manner in which the elementary constituents of the earth's globe were situated when she was in the sun-like stage. We may adopt some general theory of the sun's present condition; for example, we may accept the ingenious reasoning by which Professor Young, of Darmouth, N.H., has supported his theory that the sun is a gigantic bubble;* but we should be far from having

* "The eruptions which are all the time" (*Anglice*, 'always') "occurring on the sun's surface," says Professor Young, "almost compel the supposition that there is a crust of some kind which restrains the imprisoned gases, and through which they force their way with great violence. This crust may consist of a more or less continuous sheet of rain,—not of water, of course, but of materials whose vapours are shown by means of the spectroscope to exist in the solar atmosphere, and whose condensations and combinations are supposed to furnish the

any exact idea of the processes actually taking place within the solar globe, even if we were absolutely certain that that or some other general theory were the true one.

Assuming that our earth, when in the sun-like stage, was a gaseous mass within a liquid non-permanent shell, we can see that as the process of cooling went on the showers forming the shell would attain a greater and greater depth, the shell thus becoming thicker, the space within the shell becoming less, the whole earth contracting until it became entirely liquid; or rather these changes would progress until no considerable portion of the earth would be gaseous, for doubtless long before this stage was reached large portions of the earth would have become solid. As to the position which the solid parts of the earth's globe would assume when the first processes of solidification took place, we must not fall into the mistake of judging from the formation of a crust of ice on freezing water that

solar heat. The continuous outflow of the solar heat is equivalent to the supply that would be developed by the condensation from steam to vapour of a layer about five feet thick over the whole surface of the sun per minute. As this tremendous rain descends, the velocity of the falling drops would be increased by the resistance of the dense gases underneath, the drops would increase until continuous sheets would be formed; and the sheets would unite and form a sort of bottomless ocean, resting upon the compressed vapours beneath and pierced by innumerable ascending jets and bubbles. It would have nearly a constant depth in thickness, because it would re-evaporate at the bottom nearly as fast as it would grow by the descending rains above, though probably the thickness of this sheet would continually increase at some slow rate, and its whole diameter diminish. In other words, the sun, according to this view, is a gigantic bubble, whose walls are gradually thickening and its diameter diminishing at a rate determined by its loss of heat. It differs, however, from ordinary bubbles in the fact that its skin is constantly penetrated by blasts and jets from within."

these solid parts would form a crust upon the earth. Water presents an exception to other substances, in being denser in the liquid form than as a solid. Some metals and alloys are like water in this respect; but with most earthy substances, " and notably," says Dr Sterry Hunt, " the various minerals and earthy compounds like those which may be supposed to have made up the mass of the molten globe, the case is entirely different. The numerous and detailed experiments of St Clair Deville, and those of Delesse, besides the earlier ones of Bischof, unite in showing that the density of fused rocks is much less than that of the crystalline products resulting from their slow cooling, these being, according to Deville, from one-seventh to one-sixteenth heavier than the fused mass, so that if formed at the surface they would, in obedience to the laws of gravity, tend to sink as soon as formed." *

Nevertheless, inasmuch as solidification would occur at the surface, where the radiation of heat would take place most rapidly, and as the descending solid matter would be gradually liquified, it seems certain that for a long time the solid portions of the earth, though not forming a solid crust, would occupy the exterior parts of the earth's globe. After a time, the whole globe would have so far cooled that a process of aggregation of solid matter around the centre of the earth would take place. The matter so aggregated consisted probably of metallic and metalloidal compounds denser than the material forming the crust of

* It is as yet doubtful, how far the recent experiments of Mallet affect this reasoning.

the earth. Between the solid centre and the solidifying crust, there would be a shell of uncongealed matter, gradually diminishing in amount, but a portion probably retaining its liquid condition even to the present time, whether existing in isolated reservoirs, or whether, as Scrope opines, it forms still a continuous sheet surrounding the solid nucleus. One strange fact of terrestrial magnetism may be mentioned in partial confirmation of the theory that the interior of the earth is of this nature,—a great solid mass, separated from the solid crust by a viscous plastic ocean: the magnetic poles of the earth are changing in position in a manner which seems only explicable on the supposition that there is an interior solid globe rotating under the outer shell, but at a slightly different rate, gaining or losing one complete rotation in the course of about 650 years.

Be this as it may, we find in this theory an explanation of the irregularities of the earth's surface. The solid crust, contracting at first more rapidly than the partially liquid mass within, portions of this liquid matter would force their way through and form glowing oceans outside the crust. Geology tells us of regions which, unless so formed, must have been produced in the much more startling manner conceived by Meyer, who attributed them to great meteoric downfalls.* At a later stage, when the crust,

* There is very little new under the sun. In dealing with the multitudinous lunar craters, which were certainly formed in ages when unattached meteors were enormously greater in number and size than at present, I mentioned as a consideration not to be overlooked the probability that some of the meteoric matter falling on the moon

having hitherto cooled more rapidly than the interior, began to have a slower rate of cooling, the retreating nucleus left the crust to contract upon it, corrugating in the process, and so forming the first mountain ranges upon the spheroidal earth, which preceding processes had left partially deformed and therefore ready to become in due time divided into oceans and continents.

At this stage the earth must have been surrounded by an atmosphere much denser than that now existing, and more complex in constitution. We may probably form the most trustworthy opinion of the nature of the earth's atmosphere and the probable condition of the earth's surface at this early epoch by following the method of

when she was plastic with intensity of heat might be expected to leave traces which we could discern; and although none of the larger lunar craters could be so formed, yet some of the smaller craters in these lunar regions where craters overlap like the rings left by raindrops which have fallen on a plastic surface, might be due to meteoric downfall. I find that Meyer had far earlier advanced a similar idea in explanation of those extensive regions of our earth which present signs of having been in a state of igneous fluidity. Again, two or three years ago, Sir W. Thomson startled us all by suggesting the possibility that vegetable life might have been introduced upon our earth by the downfall of fragments of old worlds. Several years before, Dr. Sterry Hunt had pointed to evidence which tends to show that large meteoric globes had fallen on the earth, and he shewed further that some meteors contain hydrocarbons and certain metallic compounds indicating processes of vegetation. Dr. Hunt tells me that, in his opinion, some of the meteors whose fragments have fallen on the earth in historic times were once covered with vegetation, since otherwise, according to our present chemical experience, the actual condition of these meteoric fragments would be inexplicable. He does not regard them as fragments of a considerable orb comparable even with the least of the planets, but still, whatever their dimensions may have been, he considers that vegetable life must have formerly existed upon them.

reasoning employed by Dr. Sterry Hunt. It will be remembered that he conceives an intense heat applied to the earth as at present existing, and infers the chemical results. It is evident that such a process would result in the oxidation of every form of carbonaceous matter; all carbonates, chlorides, and sulphates would be converted into silicates,—carbon, chlorine, and sulphur being separated in the form of acid gases. These gases, with nitrogen, an excess of oxygen, and enormous quantities of aqueous vapour, would form an atmosphere of great density. In such an atmosphere condensation would only take place at a temperature far above the present boiling point; and the lower level of the slowly cooling crust would be drenched with a heated solution of hydrochloric acid, whose decomposing action, aided by its high temperature, would be exceedingly rapid. The primitive igneous rock on which these heavy showers fell, probably resembled in composition certain furnace-slags or basic volcanic glasses. Chlorides of the various bases would be formed, and silica would be separated under the decomposing action of the heated showers until the affinities of the hydrochloric acid were satisfied. Later, sulphuric acid would be formed in large quantities by the combination of oxygen with the sulphurous acid of the primeval atmosphere. After the compounds of sulphur and chlorine had been separated from the air, carbonic acid would still continue to be an important constituent of the atmosphere. This constituent would gradually be diminished in quantity, during the conversion of the complex aluminous silicates into hydrated silicate of alumina, or clay, while the separated lime, magnesia, and alkalies would be changed into bicarbonates, and carried down to the sea in a state of solution.

Thus far the earth was without life, at least no forms of life, vegetable or animal, with which we are familiar, could have existed while the processes hitherto described were taking place. The earth during the long series of ages required for these changes, was in a condition comparable with the condition through which Jupiter and Saturn are apparently at present passing. A dense atmosphere concealed the surface of the earth, even as the true surface of Jupiter is now concealed. Enormous cloud-masses were continually forming and continually pouring heavy showers on the intensely heated surface of the planet, throughout the whole of the enormous period which elapsed between the time when first the earth had a surface, and the time when the atmosphere began to resemble in constitution the air we breathe. Even when vegetable life, such as we are familiar with, was first possible, the earth was still intensely heated, and the quantity of aqueous vapour and cloud always present in the air must have been far greater than at present.

It has been in vain, thus far, that men have attempted to lift the veil which conceals the beginning of life upon the earth. It would not befit me to express an opinion on the controversy whether the possibility of spontaneous generation has, or has not, been experimentally verified.

That is a question on which experts alone can give an opinion worth listening to; and all that can here be noted is that experts are not agreed upon the subject. As a mere speculation it may be suggested that, somewhat as the elements when freshly released from chemical combination show for a short time an unusual readiness to enter into new combinations, so it may be possible that, when the earth was fresh from the baptism of liquid fire to which her primeval surface had for ages been exposed, certain of the substances existing on her surface were for the time in a condition fitting them to pass to a higher order of existence, and that then the lower forms of life sprang spontaneously into existence on the earth's still throbbing bosom. In any case, we need not feel hampered by religious scruples in considering the possibility of the spontaneous generation of life upon the earth. It would be straining at a gnat and swallowing a camel, if we found a difficulty of that sort *here*, after admitting, as we are compelled by clearest evidence to admit, the evolution of the earth itself and of the system to which the earth belongs, by purely natural processes. The student of science should view these matters apart from their supposed association with religious questions, apart in particular from interpretations which have been placed upon the Bible records. We may be perfectly satisfied that the works of God will teach us aright if rightly studied. Repeatedly it has been shown that ideas respecting creation which had come to be regarded as sacred because they were ancient, were altogether erroneous, and it may well be so in this matter of the creation of life.*

Whatever opinion we form on these points, it seems probable that vegetable life existed on the earth before animal life, and also that primeval vegetation was far more luxuriant than the vegetation of our own time. Vast forests were formed, of which our coal-fields, enormous as is their extent, represent merely a small portion preserved in their present form through a fortuitous combination of exceptional conditions. By far the greater portion of those forest masses underwent processes of vegetable decay effectually removing all traces of their existence. What escaped, however, suffices to show the amazing luxuriance with which vegetation formerly throve over the whole earth.

In assuming the probability that vegetable life preceded animal life, I may appear to be opposing myself to an accepted palæontological doctrine, according to which animal and vegetable life began together upon the earth. But I would remind you that the actual teaching of the ablest, and therefore the most cautious, palæontologists on

* It is not for me to undertake to reconcile the Bible account of creation with the results which science is bringing gradually more clearly before us. It seems to me unfortunate, in fact, that such reconciliation should be thought necessary. But it must be conceded, I suppose, by all, that it is not more difficult to reconcile modern biological theories of evolution with the Bible record, than it is to reconcile with that record theory of the evolution of the solar system. Yet strangely enough many oppose the biological theories (not without anger), who readily admit that some form or other of the nebular hypothesis of the solar system must be adopted in order to explain the peculiarities of structure presented by that system.

this point, amounts merely to this, that if the geological record as at present known be assumed to be coeval with the commencement of life upon the globe, then animals and plants began their existence together. In a similar way the teachings of geology and palæontology as to the nature of the earliest known forms of life and as to the succession of faunæ and floræ, depend on an admittedly imperfect record. Apart, however, from this consideration, I do not think it would serve any useful purpose if I were to attempt, I will not say to discuss, for that is out of the question, but to speak of the geological evidence respecting that portion of the past history of our earth which belongs to the interval between the introduction of life upon the surface and the present time. In particular, my opinion on the interesting question, whether *all* the forms of life upon the earth, including the various races of man, came into being by processes of evolution, could have no weight whatever. I may remark that, even apart from the evidence which the most eminent biologists have brought to bear on this question, it seems to me illogical to accept evolution as sufficient to explain the history of our earth during millions of years prior to the existence of life, and to deny its sufficiency to explain the development of life (if one may so speak), upon the earth. It seems even more illogical to admit its operation up to any given stage in the development of life, and there to draw a hard and fast line beyond which its action cannot be supposed to have extended.* Nor can I understand why it should be

---

* Since I thus spoke, a new and as it seems to me an even more illogical limit has been suggested for the operation of the process of

considered a comforting thought, that at this or that epoch in the history of the complex machine of life, some imperfection in the machinery compelled the intervention of God,—thus presented to our contemplation as Almighty, but very far from being All-wise.

There is, however, one aspect in which the existence of life has to be considered as intimately associated with the future history of our earth. We perceive that the abundance of primeval vegetation during long ages, aided by other processes tending gradually to reduce the amount of carbonic acid gas in the air, must have led to a gradual change in the constitution of the atmosphere. At a later epoch, when animal life and vegetable life were more equally proportioned, a state of things existed which, so far as can be judged, might have lasted many times as long as it has already lasted had not man appeared upon the scene. But it seems to me impossible to consider what is actually taking place on the earth at present, without perceiving that within periods, short indeed by comparison with geological eras, and still shorter compared with the intervals to which the astronomical history of our earth has introduced us, the condition of the earth as an abode of life will be seriously modified by the ways and works of man. It is only in the savage state that man

evolution as affecting the development of life, and this by an advocate of the general doctrine of evolution. I refer to the opinion advanced by Mr. J. Fiske, of Harvard College (U.S.), " that no race of organisms can in future be produced through the agency of natural selection and direct adaptation, which shall be zoologically distinct from, and superior to, the human race."

is content to live upon the produce of the earth, taking his share, as it were, of what the earth (under the fruitful heat of the sun, which is her life) brings forth,—day by day, month by month, year by year, and century by century. But civilized man is not content to take his share of the earth's *income*, he uses the garnered wealth which is the earth's *capital*—and this at a rate which is not only ever increasing, but is increasing at an increasing rate. The rapid consumption of coal is but a single instance of his wasteful expenditure of the stores which during countless ages have been gathered together, seemingly for the use of man. In this country (America), I need not dwell upon the fact that, in many other ways, man is consuming, if not wasting, supplies of earth-wealth which cannot be replaced. It is not merely what is found within the earth, but the store of wealth which clothes the earth's surface, which is thus being exhausted. Your mighty forests seem capable of supplying all the timber that the whole race of man could need for ages; yet a very moderate computation of the rate at which they are being cut down, and will presumably continue to be, by a population increasing rapidly in numbers and in the destructive capabilities which characterize modern civilization, would show that America will be denuded of its forest-wealth in about the same period which we in England have calculated as probably limiting the effective duration of our stores of coal. That period—a thousand or twelve hundred years—may seem long compared with the life of individual men, long even compared with the duration of any nation in the height of power; but though men and nations pass away the human race continues, and a thousand years are as less than a day in the history of that race. Looking forward to that future day, seemingly so remote, but (on the scale upon which we are at present tracing our earth's history) in reality the *to-morrow* of our earth, we see that either a change in their mode of civilization will be forced on the human race, or else it will then have become possible, as your Ericsson has already suggested, to make the sun's daily heat the mainspring of the machinery of civilization.

But turning from those portions of the past and future of our earth which, by comparison with the astronomical eras of her history, may be regarded as present, let us consider, so far as known facts permit, the probable future of the earth after astronomical eras comparable with those which were presented to us when we consider her past history.

One of the chief points in the progression of the earth towards her present condition was the gradual passing away of the heat with which formerly her whole globe was instinct. We have now to consider whether this process of cooling is still going on, and how far it is likely to extend. In this inquiry we must not be misled by the probable fact, for such it seems, that during hundreds of thousands of years the general warmth of the surface of the earth has not appreciably diminished. In the first place, hundreds of thousands of years are the seconds of the time-measures we have now to deal with; and next, it is known that the loss of temperature which our earth is at present under-going chiefly affects the interior parts of her globe. The inquiries of Mallet and others show that the present vulcanian energies of the earth are due in the main to the gradual withdrawal of the earth's nuclear parts from the surface crust, because of the relatively more rapid loss of heat by the former. The surface crust is thus left to contract under the action of gravity, and vulcanian phenomena—that is, volcanoes and earthquakes,—represent the mechanical equivalent of this contraction. Here is a process which cannot continue for ever, simply because it is in its very nature exhaustive of the energy to which it is due. It shows us that the earth's nuclear regions are parting with their heat, and as they cannot part with their heat without warming the surface-crust, which nevertheless grows no warmer, we perceive that the surface-heat is maintained from a source which is being gradually exhausted. The fitness of the earth to be the abode of life will not only be affected directly in this way, but will be indirectly affected by the loss of that vulcanian energy which appears to be one of its necessary conditions. At present, the surface of the earth is like the flesh clothing the living body; it does not wear out because (through the life which is within it) it undergoes continual change. But even as the body itself is consumed by natural processes so soon as life has passed from it, so, when the internal heat of the earth, which is its life, shall have passed away, her surface will "grow old as doth a garment;" and with this inherent terrestrial vitality will pass away by slow degrees the life which is upon the earth.

In dealing with the past history of our earth, we recognized a time when she was a sun, rejoicing as a giant in the strength of youth; and later we considered a time when her condition resembled that of the planets Jupiter and Saturn, whose dense atmospheres seem to be still loaded with the waters which are to form the future oceans of those noble orbs. In considering our earth's future, we may recognize in the moon's actual condition a stage through which the earth will hereafter have to pass. When the earth's inherent heat has passed away and long ages have elapsed since she had been the abode of life, we may believe that her desert continents and frost-bound oceans will in some degree resemble the arid wastes which the astronomer recognizes in the lunar surface. And yet it is not to be supposed that the appearance of the earth will ever be closely similar to that presented by the moon. The earth may part, as completely as the moon has, with her internal heat; the rotation of the earth may in hundreds of millions of years be slowed down by tidal action into agreement with the period in which the moon completes her monthly orbit; and every form of animal and vegetable life may perish from off the face of the earth: yet ineffaceable traces of the long ages during which her surface was clothed with life and instinct with inherent vitality, will distinguish her from the moon, where the era of life was incomparably shorter. Even if the speculations of Stanislas Meunier be just, according to which the oceans will gradually be withdrawn beneath the surface crust and even the atmosphere almost wholly disappear, there would for ever remain the signs of changes brought about by rainfall and snowfall, by wind and storm, by river and glacier, by ocean waves and ocean currents, by the presence of vegetable life and of animal life during hundreds of millions of years, and even more potently by the fiery deluge poured continually on the primeval surface of our globe. By all these causes the surface of the earth has been so wrought upon as no longer to resemble the primary igneous rock which we seem to recognize in the scarred surface of our satellite.

Dare we look onwards to yet later stages in the history of our earth? Truly it is like looking beyond death; for now imagination presents our earth to us as an inert mass, not only lifeless as at the beginning, but no longer possessing that potentiality of life which existed in her substance before life appeared upon her surface. We trace her circling year after year around the sun, serving no useful purpose according to our conceptions. The energy represented by her motions of rotation and revolution seems to be as completely wasted as are those parts (the whole save only one 230,000,000th portion) of the sun's light and heat, which, falling on no planet, seem to be poured uselessly into desert space. Long as has been, and doubtless will be, the duration of life upon the earth, it seems less than a second of time compared with those two awful time-intervals—one past, when as yet life had not begun, the other still to come, when all life shall have passed away.

But we are thus led to contemplate time-intervals of a yet higher order—to consider the eras belonging to the life-time of the solar system itself. Long after the earth shall have ceased to be the abode of life other and nobler orbs will become in their time fit to support millions of forms as well of animal as of vegetable existence; and the later each planet is in thus "putting on life," the longer will be the duration of the life-supporting era of its own existence. Even those time-intervals will pass, however, until every orb in turn has been the scene of busy life, and has then, each after its due life-season, become inert and dead. One orb alone will then remain, on which life will be possible,—the sun, the source whence life had been sustained in all those worlds. And then, after the lapse, perchance, of a lifeless interval, compared with which all the past eras of the solar system were utterly insignificant, the time will arrive when the sun will be a fit abode for living creatures. Thereafter, during ages infinite to our conceptions, the great central orb will be (as now, though in another sense) the life of the solar system. We may even look onwards to still more distant changes, seeing that the solar system is itself moving on an orbit, though the centre round which it travels is so distant that as yet it remains unknown.. We see in imagination change after change, cycle after cycle, till

> Drawn on paths of never-ending duty,
> The worlds—eternity begun—
> Rest, absorbed in ever glorious beauty
> On the Heart of the All-Central Sun.

But in reality it is only because our conceptions are finite that we thus look forward to an end even as we seek to trace events back to a beginning. The notion is inconceivable to us that absolutely endless series of change may take place in the future and have taken place in the past; equally inconceivable is the notion that series on series of material combinations, passing onwards to ever higher orders,—from planets to suns, from suns to sun-systems, from sun-systems to galaxies, from galaxies to systems of galaxies, from these to higher and higher orders, absolutely without end,—may surround us on every hand. And yet, as I set out by saying, these things are not more inconceivable than infinity of time and infinity of space, while the idea that time and space are finite is not merely inconceivable but opposed directly to what the mind conceives of space and time. It has been said that progression necessarily implies a beginning and an end; but this is not so where the progression relates to absolute space or time. No one can indeed doubt that progression in space is of its very nature limitless. But this is equally true, though not less inconceivable, of time. Progression implies only relative beginning and relative ending; but that there should be an absolute beginning or an absolute end is not merely inconceivable, like absolute eternity, but is inconsistent with the necessary conditions of the progression of time as presented to us by our conceptions. Those who can may find relief in believing in absolutely void space and absolutely unoccupied time before some very remote but not infinitely remote epoch, which may in such belief be called the beginning of all things; but the void time before *that* beginning can have had no beginning, unless it were preceded by time not unoccupied by events, which is inconsistent with the supposition. We find no absolute beginning if we look backwards; and looking forwards we not only find an absolute end inconceivable by reason, but revealed religion—as ordinarily interpreted—teaches—that on *that* side lies an eternity not of void but of occupied time. The time-intervals, then, which have presented themselves to our contemplation in dealing with the past and future of our earth, being in their nature finite, however vast, are less than the shortest instant in comparison with absolute time, which—endless itself—is measured by endless cycles of change. And in like manner, the space seemingly infinite from which our solar system has drawn its materials—in other words, the universe as partially revealed to us in the study of the star-depths—is but the merest point by comparison with absolute space. The end, seemingly so remote, to which our earth is tending, the end infinitely more remote to which the solar system is tending, the end of our galaxy, the end of systems of such galaxies as ours—all these endings (each one of which presents itself in turn to our conceptions as the end of the universe itself) are but the beginnings of eras comparable with themselves, even as the beginnings to which we severally trace back the history of our planet, of the planetary system, and of galaxies of such systems, are but the endings of prior conditions which have followed each other in infinite succession. The wave of life which is now passing over our earth is but a ripple in the sea of life within the solar system; this sea of life is itself but as a wavelet on the ocean of eternal life throughout the universe. Inconceivable, doubtless, are these infinities of time and space, of matter, of motion, and of life. Inconceivable that the whole universe can be for all time the scene of the operation of infinite personal power, omnipresent, all-knowing. Utterly incomprehensible how Infinite Purpose can be associated with endless material evolution. But it is no new thought, no modern discovery, that we are thus utterly powerless to conceive or comprehend the idea of an Infinite Being, Almighty, All-knowing, Omnipresent, and Eternal, of whose inscrutable purpose the material universe is the unexplained manifestation. Science is in presence of the old, old mystery; the old, old questions are asked of her,—"Canst thou by searching find out God? canst thou find out the Almighty unto perfection? It is as high as heaven; what canst thou do? deeper than hell; what canst thou know?" And science answers these questions, as they were answered of old,—"As touching the Almighty, we cannot find Him out."

OF SEEMING WASTES IN NATURE.

IT was formerly the custom to regard the study of science as calculated to present to us *in a way which all could understand*, the wisdom and benevolence of that God in whom we believe. So thoroughly was this accepted, that we find many students of science adopting, almost as a scientific principle—at any rate, as an incontrovertible axiom—this supposed fact. If a choice lay between two explanations of any observed relations, and one explanation seemed to accord well, while the other seemed to accord ill, with conceptions commonly entertained respecting the ways of God, the former explanation was accepted, even though the balance of evidence might be in favour of the latter.

This was true of all departments of science; but perhaps the application of the principle was more remarkable in the case of astronomy than in that of any other subject. It was first taken for granted that the celestial orbs were intended for the support of life; and then that, to this end, they must all be at all times inhabited. We find even the observant Herschel so adapting observed facts respecting the constitution of the sun to the idea that the sun's great mass was intended to be the abode of life, as to lose sight of evidence which, even in his day, was all but overwhelming against the theory of the sun's habitability. Brewster, in like manner, was misled by similar considerations in such sort as to overlook circumstances which he would scarcely otherwise have omitted to notice. For example, regarding the noble orb of Jupiter, the mighty sweep of its orbit, and the symmetrical scheme of bodies circling round the planet, Brewster inferred that Jupiter was certainly intended to be the abode of life; and forthwith, in his zeal to show the fitness of the planet for the purpose, he neglected to consider the circumstances unfavourable to the theory, the reduced supply of heat from the sun at Jupiter's great distance, the small density of the planet, the deep atmosphere enveloping it, and the signs of disturbances indicating an intense heat in the planet's mass. Nay more: still with the excellent purpose of indicating the beneficent supervision exerted by the Almighty to provide for the giant planet of the solar system, Brewster dwelt upon the arrangement made to supply Jupiter with reflected light from the four satellites which circle around him, failing to notice that all these moons, if full at the same time (which they can never be), would not supply Jupiter with one sixteenth part of the light which we receive from our single moon when she is full.* And many other similar cases might be cited from the pages of Brewster, Chalmers, Dick, and others who have advocated the fascinating theory that all the orbs of heaven exist either as the abodes of life, or to support life in other worlds.

* 'Expanse of Heaven,' pp. 86, *et seq.*

Now, there can be no question that it is a just and excellent view of the wonders which the study of science brings continually before us, to regard them all as symbols of the might and wisdom of God. Nor can there be any objection to the consideration of any special object as illustrating the benevolence of the Creator towards His creatures, so only that the object be judiciously selected, and the evidence of the useful purposes subserved by it be clear and unmistakable. But it appears to me that great mischief may be done, that in fact great mischief has often been done, by the too frequent attempt to refer all things to some special design in the interests of such and such creatures. The reader of works in which such attempts are made is apt to regard these special indications of divine economy (so to speak) as forming a necessary part of the evidence on which he is to base his belief in the wisdom and benevolence of God, and accordingly to lose faith to some degree, if he come to learn that the special purpose supposed to be fulfilled is not in reality fulfilled, that the seeming display of care for the wants of certain creatures must be otherwise interpreted.

It appears to me, therefore, most desirable that in studying the wonders of nature, we should view facts as they are—not in an artificial light, however excellent the source of that light may be. We may believe, with all confidence, that could we but understand the whole of what we find around us, the wisdom with which each part has been designed would be manifest; but we must not fall into the mistake of supposing that we can so clearly understand all as to be able to recognise the purpose of this or that arrangement, the wisdom of this or that provision. Nor, if any results revealed by scientific research appear to us to accord ill with our conceptions of the economy of nature, should we be troubled, on the one hand, as respects our faith in God's benevolence, or doubt, on the other, the manifest teachings of science. In a word, our faith must not be hampered by scientific doubts, our science must not be hampered by religious scruples.

It is very necessary in this age of great scientific discoveries to bear this rule in mind. Again and again it has been proved, as science has advanced, that the interpretation of observed facts by those who viewed science specially with reference to religious teachings, had been erroneous, and again and again the mischief thus temporarily wrought has been remedied after a longer or shorter interval of suspense. But now that science is making more rapid strides than of yore, the mischief produced by over-hasty attempts to interpret science in a manner favourable to preconceived ideas is likely to be wider and more enduring. I conceive, then, that nothing can be clearer than the inference to which past experience should lead us. Since formerly mistakes *have* been made, and mischief, more or less extensive, *has* been wrought by the practice to which I refer, while little good has ever resulted, even temporarily, from it, the time has arrived for adopting a better course. We need not suppose for a moment that science is irreconcilable,—I will not say with religion, but with ideas—even such as we might conceive—of the wisdom and benevolence of God ; we need not doubt that, if we could understand the whole scheme of the Almighty, it would appear most beautiful, and all its parts perfectly adapted to His purposes; the believer may still say to the unbeliever—

> 'All nature is but art unknown to thee ;
> All chance, direction, which thou canst not see ;
> All discord harmony not understood ;
> All partial evil universal good.'

But we must remember that the believer also cannot expect to be able to interpret all that science reveals. And recognizing this, we should, as I think, study science with singleness of purpose, not seeking on the one hand for evidence of design whereby to discomfit those from whom we differ, nor fearing, on the other hand, that our faith will be shaken by discoveries not according altogether with the ideas we had formed as to the Almighty's mode of dealing with his universe.

Such considerations as these are specially to be borne in mind in dealing with the apparent waste of power and material frequently observable in Nature's operations. It is not desirable, on the one hand, to close our eyes to these seeming instances of waste, while it is equally undesirable to adopt the opinion that there is necessarily a real waste; the proper course, then, would appear clearly to be, that, while recognising the seemingly exuberant display of energy in Nature, we should be content to believe, though at present we may be quite unable to prove, that the waste is apparent only, not real, and to admit that we see too small a part of the scheme of the Creator to pronounce an opinion on the economy or wisdom of the observed arrangements.

Although astronomy, bringing us as it does in presence of the infinities of space, and indicating the operations of an infinity of force acting during infinite time, is of all others the science which seems to present to us the most striking instances of waste in nature, it would yet be easy to cite many instances of seeming waste without leaving the teachings of our earth. How many seeds are scattered over the face of the earth to no visible purpose, for each one that falls on good ground and grows to perfection? How many creatures are brought to life that perish before they reach maturity? This, true of all races of animals, is true of man. True of the individual man, it is also true of nations, of races of men. History shows us, and we see in our own day, whole tribes of men disappearing without having reached that degree of civilization which we may regard as the measure of maturity in races and nations.

If we look back at the history of our earth before man appeared, we find even more abundant evidence of seeming waste, and, in particular, if we adopt that favourite view of many, according to which the recognition of the Almighty's power in the heavens is regarded as one of the chief ends for which the celestial orbs were made, how strange seems the thought that for ages on ages all the wonders of the heavens were displayed with none on the earth to recognise their meaning. The sun showed his

Of Seeming Wastes in Nature.

glories in the skies day after day, the moon shed her silver light on the ocean, the planets traversed their devious ways amongst the stars, and the constellations shone in all their splendour, while not a creature existed on the earth which could appreciate the glorious display or reason respecting its significance.

Passing still farther back we reach a time when the whole mass of the earth appears to us as a mere waste. It is scarcely open to question that, for millions of years before life existed on the earth, the whole of the terrestial globe was in a state of intense heat, was the scene of processes of tremendous activity, but was utterly unfit to be the abode of any kind of life.

Nor is it in the past only, of which records remain to us, which science can interpret, but in the future also, which science reveals to us scarcely less clearly through processes of inference, that this seeming waste is recognised. When we look forward to the future of this earth on which we live, we find, far off it may be, but still discernible, a time when all life will have perished from off the earth's face. Then will she circle around the central sun, even as our moon circles, a dead though massive globe, an orb bearing only the records and the memories of former life, but, to our conceptions, a useless desert scene.

So might we study the lessons presented by our earth, her present condition, her past history, her future fate, still finding fresh evidence of the seeming waste of nature's powers, and of that which we call time, as well as of the material substance in and through which nature works, throughout all time. Hereafter I propose to discuss such considerations, and to apply them to another purpose. But I wish now to turn from the earth to consider how the heavens present to us instances, altogether more striking, of apparent waste in nature.

Take, first, the sun—that orb whence all the supplies of force and energy known to us on earth may truly be said to be derived. What can seem clearer, at a first view, than that the sun is set at the centre of the solar system to supply light and heat to the worlds constituting that system? So viewing him, and remembering the wonderful processes taking place within his globe, and the marvellous manner in which the fires of the great central furnace are sustained, we justly regard the sun as a fitting subject for our admiring contemplation. But yet, so soon as we inquire into the adaptation of the sun's powers to the work which we have regarded as specially assigned to him, we recognise a mystery of mysteries in the seeming waste of his gigantic energies. Our earth receives less than the 2000 millionth part of the heat and light emitted by the sun; all the planets together receive less than the 230 millionth part; the rest is seemingly scattered uselessly through the interstellar depths. To other worlds, circling around other suns, our sun may indeed appear as a star; but how minute the quantity of light and heat so received from him compared with the enormous quantity apparently wasted. The portion which seems squandered is scarcely affected at all by such small uses; and that portion is more than 230 millions of times as great as the portion used to warn and to illuminate the solar system. And then consider what is the actual amount of energy thus seemingly wasted. I have computed (adopting Sir J. Herschel's estimate of the amount of heat poured by the sun upon each square mile of the earth's surface) that the sun emits in each second as much heat as would result from the burning of 11,600,000,000,000,000 tons of coal, and of this enormous amount of energy the portion utilized (that is, the heat received by the various members of the solar system) corresponds only to that due to the consumption of about 50 millions of tons—only fifty millions out of 11,600 millions of millions.

And now, remembering that what is true of the sun is true of his fellow-suns, the stars, that all the thousands of stars we see, all the millions revealed by the telescope, as well as many myriads of times as many more that lie beyond the range of our most powerful telescopes, are suns similarly pouring heat and light into space, how enormous, according to our conceptions, is the waste of energy. The force wasted is, in fact, very nearly the whole of the inconceivable amount expended.

How, then, are we to view the startling fact thus brought before us? Must we admit that so much of the Creator's work is vain in truth as in appearance? or, on the other hand, must we reject the evidence of science? As it seems to me, we need do neither one nor the other. We have before us a great mystery; but it is not a new thing to find the ways of God unsearchable by man. Our faith in the wisdom of God need not be shaken unless we assume that our science teaches us the whole of that which is. But inasmuch as science itself has taught us over and over again how little we really know, how little we can know, I think that we may very well believe in this instance that the seeming mystery arises from the imperfectness of our knowledge. If we could see the whole plan of the Creator, instead of the minutest portion; if we could scan the whole of space, instead of the merest corner; if all time were before us, instead of a span, we might pronounce judgment. As it is, what, after all, has science taught us but what we had already learned? 'The judgments of God are unsearchable, and His ways past finding out.'

A NEW THEORY OF LIFE IN OTHER WORLDS.

Two opposite views have been entertained respecting life in other worlds. One is the theory which Brewster somewhat strangely described as the creed of the philosopher and the hope of the Christian, that nearly all the orbs which people space are the abode of life. Brewster, Chalmers, Dick, and a host of other writers, have adopted and enforced this view, Brewster going so far as to maintain the probability that life may exist upon the moon, dead though her surface seems, or beneath the glowing photosphere of the sun. But even where so extreme an opinion has not been entertained, the believers in the theory of a plurality of worlds have maintained that all the celestial orbs have been created to be, and are at this present time, the abodes of life, or else minister to the wants of creatures living in other orbs. It is worthy of notice that this view has been entertained even by astronomers, who, like the Herschels, have devoted their lives to the scientific study of the heavens. So completely has the theory been identified, as it were, with modern astronomy, that we find the astronomer passing from a statement respecting some observed fact about a planet, to the consideration of the bearing of the fact on the requirements of living creatures on the planet's surface, without expressing any doubt whatever as to the existence of such creatures. For example, Sir John Herschel, writing about the rings of Saturn, after discussing Lardner's supposed demonstration that the eclipses caused by the rings would last but for a short time;* says, 'This will not prevent, however, some considerable regions of Saturn from suffering very long total interception of the solar beams, affording to our ideas but an inhospitable asylum to animated beings, ill compensated by the feeble light of the satellites; but we shall do wrong to judge of the fitness or unfitness of their condition from what we see around us, when perhaps the very combinations which convey to our minds only images of horror may be, in reality, theatres of the most striking and glorious displays of beneficent contrivance.' And many other such cases might be cited.

Before passing to the opposite view of life in other worlds, a view commonly associated with the name of the late Dr. Whewell, I shall venture to quote a few passages from his Bridgewater Treatise on Astronomy and General Physics, in which he writes very much like a supporter of the theory he subsequently opposed in his 'Plurality

---

* This is disproved, and the justice of Herschel's views demonstrated in chapter vii. of my treatise on Saturn, in which work I give a table of the climatic relations in Saturn (for I also once adopted the theory criticized above) the time and place of sunrise and sunset in Saturnian latitudes in Saturnian Spring, Summer, Autumn, and Winter, and so on. Labour wasted, I fear, except as practice in Geometrical Astronomy.

of Worlds.' Thus, speaking of the satellites in the solar system, he says,—'There is one fact which immediately arrests our attention; the number of these attendant bodies appears to increase as we proceed to planets farther and farther from the sun. Such, at least, is the general rule. Mercury and Venus, the planets near the sun, have no attendants; the earth has but one. Mars, indeed, who is still further removed, has none, nor have the minor planets, so that the rule is only approximately verified. But Jupiter, who is at five times the earth's distance, has four satellites; and Saturn, who is again at a distance nearly twice as great, has seven' (now eight) 'besides that most extraordinary phenomenon, his ring, which for purposes of illumination is equivalent to many thousand satellites. Of Uranus it is difficult to speak, for his great distance renders it almost impossible to observe the smaller circumstances of his condition. It does not appear at all probable that he has a ring like Saturn; but he has at least four satellites which are visible to us, at the enormous distance of 900 millions of miles, and I believe that the astronomer will hardly deny that he may possibly have thousands of smaller ones circulating about him. But leaving conjecture, and taking only the ascertained cases of Venus, the Earth, Jupiter, and Saturn, we conceive that a person of common understanding will be strongly impressed with the persuasion that the satellites are placed in the system *with a view to compensate for the diminished light of the sun at greater distances.*' Then he presently adds, after considering the exceptional case of

Mars,—' No one familiar with such contemplations will, by one anomaly, be driven from the persuasion that the end which *the arrangements of the satellites seem suited to answer is really one of the ends of their creation.*' Here is the theory of life in other worlds definitely adopted, and moreover presented in company with the extremest form of the teleological argument, and that, too, by Whewell, whose name afterwards became associated with the extremest development of the doctrine of the paucity of worlds!

The Whewellite theory is tolerably well known, though certainly it is not held in very great favour. For my own part, I used, at one time, to think that Whewell only advanced it in jest; but now (perhaps because my own researches and study have led me to regard the Brewsterian theory as untenable) I recognise in Whewell's later views the result of longer and more careful study than he had given to the subject, when (nearly a quarter of a century earlier) he wrote his Bridgewater Treatise.

Whatever opinion we form as to the theory advanced in the 'Plurality of Worlds,' we must admit that Whewell did good service to science in breaking the chains of old-fashioned ideas, and inaugurating freedom of discussion. The stock writers on astronomy had been repeating so often the imperfect analogies on which astronomers had earlier insisted, that the suggestions based on such analogies had come to be regarded as so many scientific facts. The Earth is a planet, and Mars is a planet, therefore what we know about the Earth may be inferred respecting Mars, no account being taken of the known difference in the condition of the two planets: accordingly, not only are the white spots at the Martian poles to be regarded as snow-covered regions, and the blue markings on his surface as seas, but we are to infer a similarity of climatic conditions and other habitudes, without entering into any close consideration of the probable extent of the planet's atmosphere, the heat received from the Sun by Mars, and a variety of other relations respecting which we are at least as well informed as we are respecting the analogies in question. Jupiter, again, is a planet, and though he is so much larger than the Earth that we might be disposed at the outset to regard him as a body of another order, we must be so guided by analogies (which, after all, may be imaginary) as to consider that his size only renders him so much the nobler an abode for such life as we are familiar with: and instead of being struck by the fact that Jupiter, unlike Mars, shows no polar snow-caps, we are to direct our attention to his belts, and to regard them as cloud-belts analogous to the tropical cloud-zone of the Earth. Nor are we to enquire too closely whether the aspect of his equatorial belt, to say nothing of his other belts, corresponds in any degree with that which the cloud-zone of our Earth would present to observers on another planet:—Let it suffice to note a few analogies, as thus—" The Earth is a planet, Jupiter is a planet; the Earth rotates and therefore has a day, Jupiter rotates and has a day; the Earth has a year, Jupiter has a year; the Earth has clouds, Jupiter has clouds; the Earth has a moon, Jupiter has four moons: this done, every other consideration may be conveniently overlooked, and we may proceed to descant on the wonderful extent and dignity of this distant world, with as little question of its being inhabited as though we had seen with our own eyes the creatures which exist upon the planet's surface. So with Saturn, and the rest."

Whewell broke through all these old-fashioned methods. He dealt with the several planets on the true scientific principle long since enunciated by Descartes, taking nothing for granted that had not been proved. He showed how unlike the conditions prevailing in the other planets must be to those existing on the Earth, and without pretending to demonstrate absolutely that none of the higher forms of life can exist on certain planets, he showed that at any rate the probabilities are in favour of that hypothesis. Passing on to the stars, he did good service by showing how much had been taken for granted by astronomers in their assumptions respecting those orbs; nor is the value of his work, in this field, by any means diminished, by the circumstance that during recent years evidence which was wanting when Whewell wrote has been obtained, and the stars have been shown demonstratively to be suns. And lastly, he dealt in an independent, and therefore instructive manner, with the star-cloudlets or nebulæ, giving many strong reasons for doubting the views which were at that time repeated in every text-book of astronomy.

The conclusions to which Whewell was led were (1) that no sufficient reason exists for believing in other worlds than ours; and (2) if the other planets are inhabited, it can only be, in all probability, by creatures belonging to the lowest orders of animated existence. He somewhat softened the harshness of these inferences by pointing out that our conceptions of the glories of God's kingdom need not be enfeebled by our doubts as to the existence of life in the planets of our own system, or of systems circling around other suns. "However destitute," he wrote, "planets, moon, and rings may be of inhabitants, they are at least vast scenes of God's presence, and of the activity with which He carries into effect everywhere the laws of nature; and the glory of creation arises from its being, not only the product, but the constant field of God's activity and thought, wisdom, and power." And, in passing, I may note that Sir David Brewster, when commenting somewhat angrily and contemptuously on this remark, failed really to grasp Whewell's meaning. Brewster was at great pains to shew how large a portion of the glories of the heavens is invisible and useless to man; but Whewell was manifestly not referring to the glories of God as revealed to man, but as they exist in themselves. It must be admitted, indeed, even by those who prefer Brewster's theory, that he maintained it with much more warmth than was necessary in such a discussion. In presence of Whewell's philosophic, calm, and dispassionate force of reasoning, there was something almost ludicrous in the impassioned outbursts of the great physicist who took the doctrine of life in other worlds under his protection. "Where," says he, "is the grandeur, where the utility, where the beauty, where the poetry, of the two almost invisible stars which usurp the celestial names of Uranus and Neptune, and which have been seen by none but a very few even of the cultivators of astronomy? The seaman in the trackless ocean never seeks their guidance; to him they have not even the value of the pole star; they contribute nothing to the arts of terrestrial life: they neither light the traveller on his journey, nor mark by their feeble ray the happy hours which are consecrated to friendship and to love." All this is very pretty writing, but it is very little to the purpose, and while it has no bearing whatever on what Whewell had urged, it is a very long way from establishing what Brewster desired to prove, viz., that 'Uranus and Neptune must have been created for other and nobler ends; to be the abodes of life and intelligence, the colossal temples where their Creator is recognised and worshipped; the remotest watch-towers of our system, from which His works may be better studied, and His distant glories more readily descried.'

Here, however, are two theories—opposed to each other, and not admitting of being reconciled. If we are to make a selection between them, to which shall we turn in preference? The balance of evidence is on the whole in favour of Whewell's, (so at least the matter presents itself to me after careful and long-continued study); but certainly Brewster's is the theory which commends itself most favourably to the mind which would believe that God "hath done all things well," and that nothing that He has made was made in vain. Even those who, like myself, are indisposed to admit that the ways and works of God are to be judged by our conceptions of the fitness of things, (though we may be altogether certain that all things are made in wisdom and fitness), would prefer to accept the Brewsterian theory, if decision were to be made between the two. For, what amount of evidence could reconcile us to the belief (even though it forced this belief upon us) that our Earth alone of all the countless orbs which people space, is the abode of reasoning creatures, capable of recognising the glories of the universe, and of lauding the Creator of those wonders and of their own selves? Nevertheless we must be guided in these matters by evidence, not by sentiment—by facts, not by our feelings. It is well, therefore, to note that the decision does not lie between the two theories which have just been dealt with. Another theory, holding a position intermediate between those two, and combining in my judgment the evidence which favours one theory with the fitness characterising the other, remains yet to be presented. The last essay was intended to prepare the way for this theory.

I propose to take, as the basis of the new theory of life in other worlds, the analogy which has commonly been regarded as affording the strongest evidence in favour of the Brewsterian theory,—only I shall take a more extended view of the subject than has been customary.

Before introducing that Brewsterian argument, I may remark that the mere fact that our Earth is an inhabited world is not in itself sufficient even to render probable the theory that there is life in other worlds than ours. An equally strong argument might be derived against that theory from the study of our Moon,—the only other planet of which we have obtained reliable information,—for few can suppose that the Moon is fit to be the abode of life. Since then of the two planets we can examine, one—the Earth—is inhabited, while the other—the Moon—is probably not inhabited, the only evidence we have is almost equally divided between the Whewellite and Brewsterian theories, whatever balance remains in favour of the latter being too slight to afford any sufficient basis for a conclusion.

But while this reasoning is just, as applied to the mere fact that the Earth is inhabited, it is by no means capable of overthrowing the evidence which is derived from the *manner* in which life exists on the Earth. When we consider the various conditions under which life is found to prevail, that no difference of climatic relations or of elevation, of land or of air or of water, of soil in land, of freshness or saltness in water, of density in air, appears (so far as our researches have extended) to render life impossible, we are compelled to infer that the power of supporting life is a quality which has an exceedingly wide range in nature. I refrain, it will be noticed, from using here the usual expression, and saying, as of yore, that 'the great end and aim of all the workings of nature is to afford scope and room for the support of life,' because this mode of speaking may be misunderstood. We can see what nature actually does, and we may infer, if we so please, that such or such is the end and aim of the God of nature; nevertheless we must remember that the evidence we have belongs to the former relation not to the latter. I am careful to dwell on this point because the longer I study such matters the more clearly do I recognise the necessity of most studiously limiting our statements to that which the evidence before us really establishes.

Passing beyond the evidence which the Earth at present affords, we find that during many ages the Earth has presented a similar scene. 'Geology,' I wrote four years ago, 'teaches us of days when this Earth was peopled with strange creatures such as now are not found upon its surface. We turn our thoughts to the epochs when these monsters throve and multiplied, and picture to ourselves the appearance which our Earth then presented. Strange forms of vegetation clothe the scene which the mind's eye dwells upon. The air is heavily laden with moisture to nourish the abundant flora; hideous reptiles crawl over their slimy domain, battling with each other, or with the denizens of the forest; huge bat-like creatures sweep through the dusky twilight which constituted the primæval day; weird monsters pursue their prey amid the depths of ocean: and we forget, as we dwell upon the strange forms which existed in those long past ages, that the scene now presented by the Earth is no less wonderful, and that the records of our time may, perhaps, seem one day as perplexing as we now find those of the geological eras.' In the past, then, as in the present, this Earth was inhabited by countless millions of living creatures, and during the enormous period which has elapsed since life first appeared on the surface of the Earth, myriads if not millions, of orders of living creatures have appeared, have lived the life appointed to their order, and have vanished, or exist only under modified forms. As each individual has had its period of life, so also has each race, and we may say with the poet (noting always that the personification of nature is but a poetical idea, and does not present any real substantive truth),—

> Are God and Nature then at strife,
> That Nature lends such evil dreams?
> So careful of the type she seems.
> So careless of the single life.
>
> . . . . . .
>
> 'So careful of the type?' but no,
> From scarped cliff and quarried stone
> She cries, 'A thousand types are gone;
> I care for nothing, all shall go.'

Abundant life, in ever-varying forms, and under all-various conditions, continuing age after age during hundreds of thousands of years, such is what our Earth presents to us when we turn our thoughts to its past history. And looking forward, a similar scene is presented to our contemplation. For many a long century, probably for hundreds of thousands of years, life will continue on the Earth, unless some catastrophe (the occurrence of which we have as yet no reason to anticipate) should destroy life suddenly from off her surface.

So viewing this Earth, we seem to find forced upon us the belief that the support of life is the object for which the Earth was created, and thus we-are led to regard the other orbs which, like her, circle around a central Sun, as intended to be the abode of life. The only object which, so far as we can see, the Earth has fulfilled during an indefinitely long period has been to present a field, so to speak, for the support of life, nor can we recognise any other purpose which she will fulfil in the future. If we admit this, and if we also believe that God made nothing without some purpose, of course we have no choice but to admit that the purpose with which the Earth was made was the support of life. And reasoning from analogy, we infer that the other planets, as well those of our own system as those which we believe to exist, 'wheeling in perpetual round,' as attendants upon other Suns, were similarly created to be the abode of life.*

* I shall venture to quote here the once celebrated argument advanced by Dr. Bentley in favour of the plurality of worlds:— "Considering," he says, "that the soul of one virtuous and religious man is of greater worth and excellency than the Sun and all his planets, and all the stars in the heavens, their usefulness to man might be the sole end of their creation if it could be proved that they were as beneficial to us as the pole star formerly was for navigation, or as the Moon is for producing the tides and lighting us on winter nights. But we dare not undertake to show what advantage is brought to us by those innumerable stars in the galaxy of other parts of the firmament, not discernible by naked eyes, and yet each many thousand times bigger than the whole body of the Earth. If you say they beget in us a great idea and veneration of the mighty author and governor of such stupendous bodies, and excite and devote our minds to His adoration and praise, you say very truly and well. But would it not raise in us a higher apprehension of the infinite majesty and boundless beneficence of God, to suppose that those remote and vast bodies were formed, not merely upon our account, to be peeped at through an optic glass, but for different ends and nobler purposes? And yet who will deny that there are great multitudes of lucid stars even beyond the

But, before we infer from the strength of this reasoning that the other planets are inhabited worlds, let us look somewhat more closely into the circumstances, or rather, instead of examining only a portion of the evidence, let us take a wider survey and examine all the evidence we possess. It may appear, at a first view, that already we are dealing with periods which, to our conceptions, are practically infinite. How long, compared with the brief span of human life, are the eras with which history deals! how enormous, even by comparison with these eras, appears the range of time (tens of thousands, if not hundreds of thousands of years), since man first appeared upon this earth! and, according to the teachings of geology, we have to deal with a yet higher order of time in passing to the beginning of life upon our globe. From one million of years to ten millions! It is between such limits, say the most experienced geologists, that the choice lies. Surely we may be content with periods such as these, periods as

reach of the best telescopes; and that every visible star may have opaque planets revolving about them which we cannot discover? Now if they were not created for our sakes it is certain and evident that they were not made for their own; for matter has no life or perception, is not conscious of its own existence, nor capable of happiness, nor gives the sacrifice of praise and worship to the author of its being. It remains, therefore, that all bodies were formed for the sake of intelligent minds; and as the Earth was principally designed for the being and service and contemplation of men, why may not all other planets be created for the like uses, each for their own inhabitants which have life and understanding?' The objection to Dr. Bentley's argument resides, not in the belief which he expresses in the Wisdom and Beneficence of the Creator, but in the confidence with which he assumes that the Creator had such and such purposes,—and not perhaps others such as we not only cannot discover, but cannot even conceive.

utterly beyond our powers of conception as the duration of the pyramids would be to creatures like the ephemeron, did such creatures possess the power of reason!

And yet, why should we stop at the beginning of life upon this Earth? We have passed to higher and higher orders of time-intervals, but the series has no limit that we know of, while it possesses terms, recognisable by us, of higher order than those we have been dealing with. We know that in the far-off times before life appeared,

> The solid Earth whereon we tread
> In tracts of fluent heat began,
> And grew to seeming-random forms,
> The seeming prey of cyclic storms.

Let us look back at that part of the Earth's history, and see whether the long periods which we have contemplated may not be matched and more than matched by the æons which preceded them. When we thus

> Contémplate all this work of Time
> The giant labouring in his youth,

we see how far we have been from recognising the true breadth of the mighty waves on one of which the life upon this Earth has been borne, we see that as yet we have not

> Come on that which is, and caught
> The deep pulsations of the world,—
> Æonian music measuring out
> The steps of time.

Taking as the extremest span of the past existence of life upon the Earth ten millions of years, we learn from the researches of physicists that the age preceding that of life (the age during which the world was a mass of molten rock), lasted more than thirty-five times as long, since Bischoff has shown that the Earth would require 350 millions of years to cool down from a temperature of 2,000° Centigrade to 200°. But far back beyond the commencement of that vast era, our Earth existed as a nebulous mass, nor can we form even a conjecture as yet respecting the length of time during which that earlier stage of the Earth's existence continued.

So much for the past. Of the future we know less. But still we recognise, not indistinctly, a time when all life will have ceased upon the Earth. Whether by the process of refrigeration which is going on, or by the gradual exhaustion of the forces which at present reside in the Earth, or by the change in the length of the day which we know to be slowly taking place, a time must come when the condition of our earth will no longer be suited for the support of life. Or it may be that Stanilas Meunier is right in his theory that as a planet grows older, the oceans, and even the atmosphere, are gradually withdrawn into the interior of the planet's globe, where space is formed for them by the cooling and contracting of the solid frame of the planet. But apart from all such considerations, we know that a process of exhaustion is taking place, even in the Sun himself, whence all that exists upon the Earth derives its life and daily nourishment. So that indirectly by the dying out of the source of life, if not directly by the dying out of life, this Earth must one day become as bleak and desolate a scene as we believe the Moon to be at this present time.

It is easy to recognise the bearing of these considerations upon the question of life in other worlds. We had been led by the contemplation of the long continuance of life upon this Earth, to regard the support of life as in a sense the object of planetary existence, and therefore to view the other planets as the abode of life. But we now see that the time during which life has existed on the earth, has been a mere wavelet in the sea of our Earth's lifetime, this sea itself being but a minute portion of the infinite ocean of time, while, as Tyndall has well remarked, in that infinite ocean, the history of man (the sole creature known to us that can appreciate the wonders of creation) is but the merest ripple. We learn, then, from the Earth's history, a lesson the very reverse of that which before we had seemed so clearly to read there. It is not the chief, but only a minute portion of the Earth's existence which has been characterised by the existence of life upon our globe; and if we adopted the teaching now brought before us, as readily as before we learned that other lesson, we should say, 'It is not the chief, but only an utterly subordinate part of nature's purpose, to provide for the existence and support of life.'

We have been led by the study of the probable past history of the earth, and by the consideration of her probable future fortunes, to the conclusion, that although life has existed on her surface for an enormously long period, and will continue for a corresponding period in the future, yet the whole duration of life must be regarded but as a wave on the vast ocean of time, while the duration of the life of creatures capable of reasoning upon the wonders which surround them, is but as a ripple upon the surface of such a wave. It matters little then whether we take life itself, without distinction of kind or order, or whether we take only the life of man, we still find a disproportion which must be regarded as practically infinite, between the duration of such life, and the duration of the preceding and following periods when there has been and will be no such life upon the earth.

But yet, in passing, I cannot but point to the fact that in considering the usual arguments for life in other worlds, I might limit myself to the existence of rational beings. It would be difficult to show that mere life, without the power which man possesses of appreciating the wonders of the universe, is a more fitting final purpose in creation than the existence of lifeless but moving masses like the suns and their attendant planets. The insect or the fish, the bird or the mammal, the minutest microscopic animalcule or the mightiest cetacean, may afford suggestive indications of what we describe as beneficent contrivance; yet it is hard to see in what essential respect a universe of worlds beyond our own, inhabited only by such animals, would accord better with those ideas which the believers in the plurality of worlds entertain respecting the purpose of the Almighty, than a universe with none but vegetable life, or a universe with no life at all, yet replete with wonderful and wonderfully moving masses of matter. It is rational life alone to which the arguments of our Brewsters and Chalmers really relate. Nor would it be difficult to raise here another perplexing consideration, by inquiring what degree of cultivation of the intellect in human races accords with the 'argument from admiration' which the followers of Brewster delight to employ. The savage engaged in the mere effort to support life or to combat his foes, knows nothing of the glories whereof science tells us. The wonders of nature, so far as they affect him at all, tend to give ignoble and debasing ideas of the being or beings to whose power he attributes the occurrence of natural phenomena. Nor as we advance in the scale of civilization, do we quickly arrive at the stage where the admiration of nature begins to be an ordinary exercise even of a few minds. Still less do we arrive quickly, even in reviewing the progress of the most civilized races, at the stage when the generality of men give much of their thoughts to the natural wonders which surround them. Is it saying too much to assert that this stage has never yet been attained by any nation, even the most advanced and the most cultured? If we limit ourselves, however, to the existence merely of some few nations, amongst whom the study of nature has been more or less in vogue, how brief in the history of this earth has been the period when such nations have existed! how brief the continuance of those among such nations which belong to the past, and whose whole history is thus known to us! how few even in such nations the men who have been so deeply impressed with the wonders of nature, as to be led to the utterance of their thoughts! If the life of man is but as a ripple where life itself is as a wave on the ocean of time, surely the life of man as the student and admirer of nature, is but as the tiniest of wave-crests upon the ripple of human life.

How, then, does all this bear upon the question of life in other worlds? The answer will be manifest if we apply to these considerations the same argument which Brewster and Chalmers have applied to the evidence which indicates the enormous duration of life upon the earth. Since this enormous duration, taking life even in its most general aspect, has been shown to be as a mere nothing by comparison with the practically infinite duration of the earth without life, the argument as respects life in any other world (at least, in any world of which antecedently we know nothing) must be directly reversed. It is far more probable that that world is now passing through a part of the stage preceding the appearance of life, or of the stage following the appearance of life, than that this particular epoch belongs to the period when that particular world is inhabited. If, indeed, we had some special reason for believing that this epoch to which terrestrial life belongs has some special importance as respects the whole universe, we might feel unwilling to consider the question of life in any other world independently of preconceptions derived from our experience in this world. But I apprehend that we have no reason whatever for so believing. It appears to me that such a belief—that is, the belief that life in this earth corresponds with a period special for the universe itself—is as monstrous as the old belief that our earth is the centre of the universe. It is, in fact, a belief which bears precisely the same relation to time that the last-mentioned belief bears to space. According to one belief, the minute space occupied by our earth was regarded as the central and most important part of all space, and the only part which the Creator had specially in His plans, so to speak, in creating the universe; according to the other, the minute time occupied by the existence of life on the earth is the central and most important part of all time, and the only part during which the Creator intended that living creatures should exist anywhere. Both ideas are equally untenable, though one only has been formally discarded.

This present time, then, is a random selection, so to speak, regarded with reference to the existence of life in any other world, and being a random selection, it is much more likely to belong to the period when there is no life there. Let me illustrate my meaning by an example. Suppose I know that a friend of mine, living at a distance, will be at home for six minutes exactly, some time between noon and ten on any given day, but that I have no means of forming any opinion as to when the six minutes will be. Then, if at any given moment, say at three, I ask myself the question, 'Is my friend at home?' although I cannot know, I can form an opinion as to the probability of his being so. There are six hundred minutes between noon and ten and he is to be at home only six minutes, or the one-hundredth part of the time,—accordingly, the chance that he is at home is one in a hundred, or speaking in a general way it is much more likely that he is not at home than that he is. And so precisely with any given planet, apart from any evidence we may have as to its condition,—what we know about life on our earth teaches us that the probability is exceedingly minute that that planet is inhabited. The argument is the favourite argument from analogy. Thus: life on our earth lasts but a very short time compared with the duration of the earth's existence; therefore life in any given planet lasts but a very short time compared with the planet's existence; accordingly, the probability that that planet is inhabited at this present moment of time is exceedingly small, being, infact, as the number of years of life to the number of years without life, or as one chance in many hundreds at the least.

This applies to the planets of our solar system only in so far as we are ignorant of their condition. We may know enough about some of them to infer either a much higher probability that life exists, or almost certainly that life cannot exist. Thus we may view the condition of Venus or Mars as perchance not differing so greatly from that of our earth as to preclude the probability that many forms of life may exist on those planets. Or on the other hand, we may believe from what we know about Jupiter and Saturn that both these planets are still passing through the fiery stages which belong to the youth of planet life; while in our moon we may see a world long since decrepit, and now utterly unfit to support any forms of animated existence. But even in the case of our solar system, though the evidence in some cases against the possibility of life is exceedingly strong, we do not meet with a single instance in which evidence of the contrary kind is forcible, still less decisive. So that in the solar system the evidence is almost as clear in favour of the conclusion above indicated as where we reason about worlds of whose actual condition we know nothing. As respects such worlds,—that is, as respects the members of those systems of worlds which circle, as we believe (from analogy), around other suns than ours,—the probability that any particular world is inhabited at this present time is exceedingly small.

But let us next consider what is the probability that there is life on *some member or other* of a scheme of worlds circling around any given sun. Here, again, the argument is from analogy, being derived from what we have learned or consider probable in the case of our own system. And I think we may adopt as probable some such view as I shall now present. Each planet, according to its dimensions, has a certain length of planetary life, the youth and age of which include the following eras:—a sunlike state; a state like that of Jupiter or Saturn, when much heat but little light is evolved; a condition like that of our earth; and lastly, the stage through which our moon is passing, which may be regarded as planetary decrepitude. In each case of world-existences the various stages may be longer or shorter, as the whole existence is longer or shorter, so that speaking generally the period of habitability bears the same proportion in each world to the whole period of its existence; or perhaps there is no such uniform proportion, while, nevertheless, there exists in all cases that enormous excess of the period when no life is possible over the period of habitability. In either case, it is manifest that regarding the system as a whole, now one, now another planet (or more generally, now one, now another member of the system) would be the abode of life, the smaller and shorter-lived having their turn first, then larger and larger members, until life has existed on the mightiest of the planets, and even at length upon the central sun himself. We need not concern ourselves specially with the peculiarities affecting the succession of life in the case of subordinate systems, or of the members of the asteroidal family, or in other cases where we have little real knowledge to guide us: the general conclusion remains the same, that life would appear successively in planet after planet, step by step from the smaller to the larger, until the approach of the last scene of all, when life would have passed from all the planets, and our sun would alone remain to be in due time inhabited, and then in turn to pass (by time-intervals to us practically infinite) to decrepitude and death.

During all this progression, the intervals without life would in all probability be far longer than those when one or other planet was inhabited. In fact, the enormous excess of the lifeless periods for our earth over the period of habitability, renders the conclusion all but certain that the lifeless gaps in the history of the solar system must last very much longer than the periods of life (in this or that planet) with which they would alternate.

If we apply this conclusion to the case of any given star or sun with its scheme of dependent worlds, we see that even for a *solar system* so selected at random the probability of the existence of life is small. It is, of course, greater than for a single world taken at random ;—just as if I had ten friends who were to be at home each for six minutes between noon and ten, the chance would be greater that *some* one of the number would be at home at a given moment of that interval than would be the chance that a *given* one of the number would be then at home ; while yet even taking all the ten it would still be more likely than not that at that moment not one would be at home.

Thus when we look at any star, we may without improbability infer that *at the moment* that star is not supporting life in any one of those worlds which probably circle round it.

Have we then been led to the Whewellite theory that our earth is the sole abode of life? Far from it. For not only have we adopted a method of reasoning which teaches us to regard every planet in existence, every moon, every sun, every orb in fact in space, as having *its period* as the abode of life, but the very argument from probability which leads us to regard any given sun as not the centre of a scheme in which at this moment there is life, forces upon us the conclusion that among the millions on millions, nay, the millions of millions of suns which people space, millions have orbs circling round them which are at this present time the abode of living creatures. If the chance is one in a thousand in the case of each particular star, then in the whole number (practically infinite) of stars, one in a thousand has life in the system which it rules over: and what is this but saying that millions of stars are life-supporting orbs? There is then an infinity of life around us, although we recognise infinity of time as well as infinity of space as an attribute of the existence of life in the universe. And remembering that as life in each individual is finite, in each planet finite, in each solar system finite, and in each system of stars finite, so (to speak of no higher orders) the infinity of life itself demonstrates the infinity of barrenness, the infinity of habitable worlds implies the infinity of worlds not as yet habitable, or which have long since passed their period of inhabitability. Yet is there no waste, whether of time, of space, of matter, or of force; for waste implies a tending towards a limit, and therefore of these infinities, which are without limits, there can be no waste.

A MISSING COMET.

MANY persons were alarmed in August 1872 lest it should be true (as reported) that Plantamour, the Swiss astronomer, had predicted the earth's destruction by a comet on the twelfth of that month. When once a prediction of this sort has been announced, it is almost impossible to remove the impression produced by it. The reputed author of the prediction may deny flatly that he had ever announced even the approach of a comet; every astronomer of repute may add his testimony to the effect that no comet is due at the time indicated for the earth's destruction; the way in which the mistake arose may be explained, and every effort made to spread the explanation as widely as possible: yet the impression will nevertheless remain that there must have been some ground for the prediction, or—if it be insisted that no prediction was made—then there must have been some ground for the story of the prediction. Confidence is not completely restored until the day and hour announced for the earth's destruction have passed without mishap.*

---

* Being at Sheffield in October 1872, I was told an excellent story about the comet. The story has the advantage over most others of the kind, of being strictly true :—In a certain house, in Sheffield, Monday, August 12, had been appointed a great washing-day. On the morning

A striking illustration of the proneness of men to believe in astronomical predictions of the earth's destruction, was afforded by a circumstance in the history of a comet, which has since given trouble to astronomers in another way. The "missing comet," about which I now propose to speak, has been in its day a source of terror to the nations.

About forty years ago, it was widely announced that astronomers were on the watch for a comet whose path approaches very closely to the earth's—in fact, within the astronomically minute distance of 20,000 miles, or thereabouts. Immediately the news spread that the earth was to be destroyed. A comet must be small indeed which has not a head more than forty or fifty thousand miles in diameter—so that the coming comet might be expected to extend far beyond the 20,000 miles separating its track from the earth's. The terrible head of the comet would therefore envelop the earth, and either the earth would be dissolved with fervent heat, or else, perhaps, drowned by a second flood. Even if the earth escaped either form of destruction, the shock of the collision would destroy every living creature on her surface. Nay,

of the day, the housekeeper asked for an interview with her master on the subject of the comet. She begged to know if it were really true that the world was to be destroyed on that day. Receiving assurances to the contrary, she expressed some degree of satisfaction: "but sir," she said, "though what you say may be very true, might it not be just as well *to put off the washing till to-morrow?*" Whether she thought a washing-day unsuitable for the comet's visit, or that a good cleaning-up would be desirable on the day after the visit, deponent sayeth not.

granting even—though many were too frightened to admit the possibility—that a comet is but a thin luminous vapour, was it not all but certain that this vapour, permeating our atmosphere, would asphyxiate men and animals?

Astronomers were rather surprised at the interpretation put upon their prediction. They were tolerably well assured that the comet would cross the earth's track very nearly at the time indicated; but they had said nothing about the earth's encountering the comet. In fact, they had announced that the comet would at the end of October cross the part of the earth's track which she traverses at the end of November. The fears of a collision were as absurd as would be the fears of passengers by a certain train, who should be in terror of their lives because nother train was to cross their line at a certain point, an hour before they reached that point. But it was useless for astronomers to point out that the intersection of two *paths* did not imply the collision of bodies following those paths.* The alarm having once been sounded, no reasoning would allay the fears of the general public.

* It is rather singular that mistakes should be made in a matter seemingly so obvious,—and not only by the ignorant, but by well educated persons. Thus, in one of Cooper's novels (I forget which at the moment, but have an impression that it is the "Pathfinder,"—it is one of those in which Leatherstockings, *alias* Hawkeye, appears as a young man), a shooting contest is elaborately described, in which the great feat of all depends on precisely such a mistake as was made about the comet of 1832. The young marksman (not yet called Hawkeye) succeeds in all the trials of skill, until only he and a rival in the heroine's affections are left in the contest. Then the great trial is made. Two persons, standing some distance apart, throw each a potato, in

Nay, some, who understood that the earth herself would not come into collision with the comet, were in dread lest the earth's orbit should suffer!

"Even among those," says Guillemin, "who placed confidence in the precision of astronomical calculations there were some who at least feared a derangement of our orbit. Doubtless to them an orbit was something material,—a metallic circle, for example; 'as if,' says Arago, in relating this curious notion, 'the form of the path in which a bomb after leaving a mortar traverses space was dependent on the number and positions of the paths which other bombs had formerly described in the same region.'"

It is rather singular that the very comet which thus inspired an altogether groundless fear, should have supplied the most striking evidence astronomers have ever obtained respecting the insignificance of the effects which may be expected to follow from the collision of a planet with a comet. Biela's comet—or Gambart's as the French astronomers call it—has not merely been broken up under

such a way that the two paths, as seen by the marksman, intersect, and the marksman is to fire so as to hit both potatoes. The favoured lover succeeds, but the future Hawkeye generously misses. Afterwards, however, to show the heroine that he also could have accomplished the impossible feat, he accomplishes another. He invites her attention to two birds high overhead, and travelling on converging paths; and offers to kill the two with a single bullet. The birds obligingly consent to this arrangement, and when their dead bodies fall at the feet of the maiden, she recognises the generosity of the young rifleman. But not a word is said about the self-sacrificing ingenuity of the birds, or about the amazing skill which the potato-throwers must have acquired to render the other feat a possibility.

the very eyes of astronomers, and in a region of space where no masses of any importance can have encountered it, but since that time it has been so far dissipated,—no one knows how,—that the most powerful telescopes have failed to show the comet, even when its calculated place was such that had it retained its former appearance it would have been visible to the naked eye.

The history of Biela's comet has been singularly interesting throughout.

The comet may be said to have been discovered when Biela, in February 1826, first observed it in Aries; for it was then only that the true nature of this comet's path was recognised. It was found that it travels in an orbit of moderate dimensions, carrying it when farthest from the sun to a distance somewhat exceeding that of the planet Jupiter. It belongs, indeed, to a family or group of comets distinguished by the peculiarity that their paths pass very close to that of Jupiter, insomuch that the notion has been suggested, that either these comets have all been forced to take up their present paths through the tremendous attractive influence of the giant planet, or else that every one of them has been expelled from Jupiter's interior at some very remote epoch!

So carefully was Biela's comet observed in 1826, that it was found possible to trace back the comet's course through former revolutions with sufficient accuracy to determine whether the comet had been before observed. When this was done, it was found that the comet had been seen on March 8, 1772, by Montaigne, at Limoges; and later, up to April

3, by Messier, the great comet hunter.* The comet had also been seen (having returned four times in the interval) by Pons, on November 10, 1805. On this occasion it presented a somewhat remarkable appearance, its head having an apparent diameter equal to about a fourth of the moon's. On December 8, the astronomer Olbers saw it without a telescope. From calculations made on that occasion, some astronomers were led to suspect that this comet might be the same which Montaigne had seen in 1772; but the art of calculating cometic orbits had not then been so thoroughly mastered as to enable any mathematician to speak confidently on this point. Indeed, at that time the idea was very generally entertained that comets travel for the most part in orbits having enormous dimensions. Only one instance—Lexell's comet—had hitherto been known to the contrary, and there were excellent reasons for regarding that instance as altogether exceptional.

In 1826, however, the comet was too carefully observed for any doubts to be further entertained. It was shown by several eminent mathematicians that the comet has a

---

* So thoroughly had Messier identified himself with the work of comet-seeking, that all sublunary events seemed insignificant to him by comparison. It is related of him that he was less troubled at his wife's death than at the circumstance that, owing to the interruption to his labours which her illness had occasioned, he failed to discover a comet, a rival comet-seeker gaining that distinction. A friend met the distracted widower a day or two after Mme. Messier's death, and expressed sympathy with him.—" Ah," replied Messier, "it *was* hard—was it not ?—that after all my watching I was obliged to leave my telescope just when the comet came."

period of about six years and nine months. Santini and Damoiseau assigned November 27, 1832, as the date of this comet's return to its point of nearest approach to the sun. Olbers confirmed this result, showing, moreover, that the comet's course would bring it within 20,000 miles of the earth's path. Remarking on this, Sir John Herschel wrote, in 1866, " The orbit of this comet very nearly indeed intersects that of the earth on the place which the earth occupies on or about the 30th of November. If ever the earth is to be swallowed up by a comet, or to swallow up one, it will be on or about that day of the year. In the year 1832 we missed it by a month. The head of the comet enveloped that point of our orbit; but this happened on the 29th of October, so that we escaped that time. Had a meeting taken place, from what we know of comets, it is probable that no harm would have happened, and that nobody would have known anything about it."

It is important to notice how closely the calculations of astronomers agreed with the observed event on this, the first occasion of the comet's return after its orbit had been calculated. If it be remembered that after 1826 the comet was out of sight for nearly six years, during all which time it was more or less exposed to disturbing attractions, it will be admitted that astronomy would have had no reason to be ashamed if the comet had returned· to its point of nearest approach to the sun, within a week, or even a month of the appointed time. But the actual difference between the observed and calculated time was less than twelve hours. To illustrate this by a terrestrial instance, the case is much as though an express train from Edinburgh should arrive in London within a second of the appointed time—a degree of accuracy not invariably attained, though the terrestrial engineer has the power, which the comet has not, of making up for lost time.

It is also to be noticed, that at each return of a comet, its course can be predicted with greater accuracy; since the error noticed at any particular return affords the means of rectifying former calculations, and providing against similar error at future returns. The reader will presently see why this point is insisted upon: it is essential to notice the degree of mastery which astronomers had acquired, even so far back as 1832, over the motions of this particular comet.

In 1839 the comet returned, but was not seen, owing to the position of the sun at the time when the comet was in our neighbourhood. Throughout its passage near us, in fact, the comet was lost to sight in the splendour of the sun's beams.

At the next return the comet was detected very early,— for whereas it passed the point of its orbit nearest to the sun on February 11, 1846, it was recognised, precisely in its calculated place, on November 28, 1845.

And now one of the most singular events recorded in the history of comets took place. In 1846, "all seemed," says Sir John Herschel, "to be going on quietly and comfortably, when, behold! suddenly, on the 13th of January, the comet split into two distinct comets! each with a head and coma and a little nucleus of its own.

There is some little contradiction about the exact date. Lieutenant Maury, of the United States Observatory of Washington, *reported officially on the* 15*th, having seen it double on the* 13*th;* but Professor Wichmann, *who saw it double on the* 15*th, avers that he had a good view of it on the* 14*th,* and remarked nothing particular in its appearance. Be that as it may, the comet from a single became a double one. What domestic troubles caused the secession it is impossible to conjecture; but the two receded farther and farther from each other up to a certain moderate distance, with some degree of mutual communication, and a very odd interchange of light,—one day one head being brighter, and another the other,—till they seem to have agreed finally to part company. The oddest part of the story, however, is yet to come. The year 1852 brought round the time for their re-appearance, and behold! there they both were, at about the same distance from each other, and both visible in one telescope."

The oddest part of the story had not yet come, however, when Herschel wrote the above lines. But, before passing on to relate the fate of this comet, it may be well to correct a few of the statements in the above passage (presented just as it stands in the original, because it is a good specimen of Sir John Herschel's more familiar style of science-writing).

In the first place, the two companion comets had each a tail, as well as a head, coma, and nucleus. Then, as the object was passing out of view in 1846, the two comets seemed to approach each other. The greatest distance between them was attained on or about March 3, 1846, and amounted to about 157,000 miles. On the return of the double comet, in 1852, the distance had by no means remained unchanged, as Herschel states, but had increased to about 1,250,000 miles. It is worthy of notice, in passing, that Plantamour, of Genoa,—the same astronomer to whom the prediction of the world's destruction by a comet on August 12, last, was mistakenly assigned,—calculated the paths of both the components, and the motions of the comets were found to agree very closely with his results during the whole time that the comets continued visible.

In 1858, the comet probably returned; but, as in 1839, the part of the heavens traversed by it was too close to the sun's place to permit the comet to be seen, I say that the comet probably returned; because we know that in 1852 it safely traversed the part of space where it had formerly divided, and passed from the sun's neighbourhood towards the outer parts of its orbit, apparently unscathed. But what happened to the comet during its passage past the sun in 1859 is not known. It will presently be seen that in all probability the comet was then destroyed or dissipated in some way. In fact, it is manifest that the same reason which leads us to believe that the comet returned in 1859, would lead us to believe, that if it had passed away again uninjured, it would have been seen at the next return, or in 1866. But 1866 came; the path of the comet was assigned; astronomers looked forward with interest to its reappearance, eager to see how far the two component comets had separated from each other;—*and no comet appeared!* Telescopes of great power, and of exquisite defining qualities, swept the whole track on which the comet was to have travelled; nor were the neighbouring regions of the heavens left unexplored; but not a trace of the comet could anywhere be seen. There was not the slightest room for questioning the accuracy of the calculations by which the path had been predicted. Astronomers were certain that if undestroyed or undissipated the comet would follow the assigned path,—as certain as a station-master would be that a train would enter a station along the line of rails assigned to it, unless some accident or mistake should occur. Now comets do not make mistakes; but, as we now see, they are not free from the risk of accidents. This comet had already met with an accident, being broken by some mischance into two parts under the very eyes of astronomers. Probably in 1859 it met with further misfortunes, visible mayhap to astronomers in Venus or Mercury. At any rate, something had happened to the comet since its retreat in 1852. "It is now," wrote Sir J. Herschel at the time (Feb. 1866), "overdue! Its orbit has been recomputed, and an ephemeris" (that is, an account of its motion from hour to hour) "calculated. Astronomers have been eagerly looking out for its reappearance for the last two months, when, according to all former experience, it ought to have been conspicuously visible—but without success! giving rise to the strangest theories. At all events, it seems to have fairly disappeared, and that without any such excuse as in the case of Lexell's, viz., the preponderant attraction of some great planet. Can it have come into contact or exceedingly close approach to some asteroid as yet undiscovered; or, peradventure, plunged into, and got bewildered among, the ring of meteorolites, which astronomers more than suspect?"

Both these explanations seem at a first view available. Biela's comet had a course carrying it through the outskirts of the zone of minor planets; and there was nothing whatever to prevent the comet from coming into collision with one of these bodies, or else approaching so nearly as to be greatly disturbed, and to travel thereafter on a different orbit. But an objection exists which Sir J. Herschel does not seem to have noticed. When the comet retired in 1852 it consisted of two distinct comets, separated by an intervening space of about 1,250,000 miles. Now it would be a singular chance which should bring one of these comets into collision with a minor planet, or so near as to occasion an important disturbance. But supposing this to happen, then the fellow-comet, not travelling in the wake of the first, but side by side, would certainly have escaped. For it must be remembered, that although 1,250,000 miles is a very small distance indeed by comparison with the dimensions of the solar system, it is an enormous distance compared with the dimensions of the minor planets,—some of which have a surface not much greater than that of an English county. The minor planet occasioning the comet's disturbance would presumably be one of the smallest, since it has not yet been detected, and the newly discovered minor planets are on the average much smaller than those first detected. Now, the earth herself would have no very marked influence on a comet or meteor passing her at a distance of 1,250,000 miles; for it is to be remembered, that the comet as well as the earth would have an enormously rapid motion, and the disturbing power of the earth would therefore only act for a short time. But a minor planet—even the largest of the family,—would not have the twenty-thousandth part of the earth's power* to disturb a passing comet. At a distance of 200,000 miles, a comet would pass such an asteroid without any marked disturbance of its motions.

Of course it is not absolutely impossible that one of the comets of the pair should have been encountered by one minor planet, and the other by another; but the improbability against such a contingency is so great that we need scarcely entertain the idea even as a bare possibility.

We are left then to the supposition that the comet was destroyed or dissipated by meteoric streams. It is at once seen that this theory is at least more consistent with observed facts than the other. The comet had been *seen* to divide into two parts in a portion of the solar system, where certainly no bodies but meteorites can be supposed

---

* It is probable that the largest of the minor planets—Vesta—has a diameter of rather more than 200 miles, or at the outside say 260 miles —the thirtieth part of the earth's diameter. Thus, assuming Vesta to have the same density as the earth (whereas, being smaller, she probably is very much less compressed), we get for her mass (or, which is the same thing, her attractive power) the 27,000th part of the earth's— obtaining the number 27,000 by multiplying 30 twice into itself.

to travel. It seems reasonable to suppose, that on that occasion the head of the comet had come right upon some group of meteors, and so had divided as a stream of water divides against a rock. Assuming this, we find reason for believing that the track of this comet crosses a rich meteor-region. The particular group which had caused the division of the comet would of course pass away, and would not probably come again in the comet's way for many years or even centuries. But another group belonging to the same system might in its turn encounter the comet, and complete the process of dissipation which the former had commenced. On this theory, the distance between the companion comets would introduce no difficulty. For not only is it quite a common circumstance for meteoric systems to have a range of several millions of miles,* but —a much more important consideration—*both* the comets would be bound to return to the scene of the former encounter. It was there that each had been sent off on a new track; but each new track started *from* there, and therefore each new track *must* pass *through* there.

So that it seems far from improbable that, if the comets could have been watched during their return in 1859, they would have been seen to travel onwards towards the place where they had originally separated; as they approached that place, it would have been perceived that they drew nearer together, though they would not reach that point at the same moment; † and then each in turn would have

---

* See the paper on meteors in the "Expanse of Heaven."

† Of course in an article intended like the present for general reading,

appeared to grow more and more diffuse as the encounter with the meteor-group proceeded, until first one and then the other would have vanished altogether from view.

It may be asked, whether any circumstances in the history of comets seem to show that comets really are exposed to dissipation in this way. To this the reply is, that although Biela's is the only comet which has been seen to divide into parts in modern times, or under telescopic scrutiny, yet history records more than one instance of a similar kind,—and that too in the case of distinguished comets, not mere telescopic light-clouds such as Biela's. The following passage from Grant's noble work, "The History of Physical Astronomy," gives nearly all that is known on this point, though some Chinese records might be added did space permit:—"Seneca relates that Ephorus, an ancient Greek author, makes mention of a comet which, before vanishing, was seen to divide itself into two distinct bodies. The Roman philosopher appears to doubt the possibility of such a fact; but Kepler, with characteristic sagacity, has remarked that its actual occurrence was exceedingly probable. The latter astronomer further remarked, that there were some grounds for supposing that two comets, which appeared in the same region of the

---

it is not possible to enter at length into all the considerations which have to be attended to in an exact inquiry into the motions of two comets after separation. It will be sufficient to point out that, unless the collision which caused the separation left the velocity of each exactly equal—a wholly unlikely supposition—they would return to the scene of collision at different epochs. The increased distance between them in 1852 showed that this was actually the case.

heavens in the year 1618 were the fragments of a comet that had experienced a similar dissolution. Hevelius states, that Cysatus perceived in the head of the great comet of 1618 unequivocal symptoms of a breaking up of the body into distinct fragments. The comet, when first seen in the month of November, appeared like a round mass of concentrated light. On the 8th of December it seemed to be divided into several parts. On the 20th of the same month it resembled a multitude of small stars. Hevelius states, that he himself witnessed a similar appearance in the head of the comet of 1661."

It is, of course, always possible that the destruction or dissipation of a comet may be due, not to any collision, but to that action (whatever may be its nature) by which the sun seems, after rousing and disturbing the matter of a comet's head, to repel a part of this matter in such sort as to form a tail, or two or more tails. Indeed, it is worthy of notice that before its division into two comets, Biela's comet had shown two distinct tail-like appendages; and possibly, if the comet could have been constantly watched it would have been found that these two appendages resolved themselves eventually into the two tails of two distinct comets.

Professor Grant adopts this view of the matter. He says, "it is impossible to doubt that the division of Biela's comet arose from the divellent action of the sun, whatever may have been the mode of operation." But I must admit, that I find it quite possible to doubt whether this is indeed the true solution of the difficulty. One can understand how two distinct tails might be expelled or repelled from a single head; but it is not so easy to see how two complete comets could be formed out of one in this way, *nothing apparently remaining.* To make clear the nature of this reasoning, I remind the reader that a comet's tail is either formed out of the head (according to Sir J. Herschel's theory), or else is formed through a certain action exerted by the head (according to Prof. Tyndall's). In the former case, the process never (so far as observation extends) results in completely using up the head; in the latter, very obviously, the head must remain, or the action would cease. In either case, then, the head would remain. So that when two tails were formed they would extend from one and the same head. The head cannot be made double by the same process which produces the double tail. There must be some distinct action on the head to produce such a result. Now the tails, after they are formed, might have the power of drawing away each its own share of the original head; but the supposition seems rather a wild one. On the contrary, the supposition that the comet may have divided upon a meteoric group involves nothing which is not in accordance with known facts, since such meteoric groups exist in countless numbers within the interplanetary spaces.

It is certainly unsafe, however, to dogmatise upon this difficult subject in the present state of our knowledge.

Whatever may have been the cause of this comet's dissipation, it would seem to admit of no possibility of question that the comet has been finally and completely removed from the list of existing comets. Of course, it has not been absolutely destroyed; its fragments exist somewhere: but, as a comet, it has ceased to exist. If it had continued unchanged, it would have been again in view, and on the whole under favourable circumstances, during October in the present year (1872). Prepared to find it much fainter than of yore, or its fragments more widely dispersed, astronomers searched for it with more care than in 1866, not only using more powerful instruments, but extending their search over a wider range. But the comet was not found. At the next return, its path would bring it too near to the sun for astronomers to observe it, even though it retained its original brightness. We may assume that the process of dissipation and dispersion has been all this time in progress. And therefore it is impossible to hope that a trace of the comet will be recognised in 1880,—when it would again have passed into view but for the misfortunes which have befallen it.

This being the case, my readers perhaps will be surprised to hear that in a few days from the appearance of these lines (Nov. 1, 1872), astronomers expect to see certain fragments of *debris* of this very comet. This, however, is actually the case. Since the year 1798, there have appeared from time to time, early in December, certain meteors or falling stars which follow a track closely according with the path of Biela's comet. There is not a perfect agreement; but Dr Weiss, a German astronomer, has shewn that the actual path of the meteors corresponds almost perfectly with that of a comet which appeared in 1818, and which there is now excellent reason for regarding as *itself a fragment of Biela's comet.* Now, between November 25 and December 5, the earth will be passing through the broad tracks of both these comets, or—regarding Biela's as two—through the tracks of these three comets, and so closely behind Biela's pair, that we may fairly expect to see many meteors during that week. Precisely as, in November 1866, there was a splendid display of November meteors, following on the track of Tempel's comet (which had passed early in 1866), so this year there will probably be a display of meteors following the track of Biela's comet, which, though unseen, must have crossed the earth's path about the middle of October. At any rate, the skies should be carefully watched. The shower of meteors (should any occur) will fall in such a direction that shooting-stars might be looked for at any hour of the night. And those belonging to Biela's comet could be very readily distinguished from others, because their tracks would seem to radiate from the constellation Cassiopeia. So that should any of my readers observe, on any night between November 25 and December 5, a shooting-star following such a track, he will have the satisfaction of knowing that in all probability he has seen a fragment or follower of a comet which has divided into two if not three distinct comets, and has followed up that process of dissipation by dissolving altogether away.

It is not easy to form an opinion as to the actual probability that a fine display of meteors will be seen. This particular meteor system has, however, been known to produce somewhat remarkable showers. Thus Brandes, who first recognised the existence of the system, counted no less than four hundred meteors in a few hours, while travelling in a covered carriage on the night of December 7, 1798.

In conclusion, we may draw, I think, from the history of the missing comet the inference that our earth and her fellow-planets have little to fear from collision with comets. The earth passes each year through more than a hundred meteor systems and yet suffers no injury, whereas Biela's comet would seem to have been destroyed during only a few encounters with meteoric groups. It appears evident, then, that it would be the comet, not our earth, which would suffer in any encounter of the sort. Indeed, comets, which once occasioned such dread, seem to be but frail creatures. To quote the words of poor Blanqui, the republican,—who wrote in prison about comets as if he sympathised with them in their trials,—"if comets escape Saturn, it is to fall under the stroke of Jupiter, the policeman of the solar system. On duty in the dark, he scents (*sic*) these hairy nothings (*nihilités chevelues*), before a ray makes them visible, and urges them—distracted—towards perilous passes. There, seized by heat and swollen to monstrosity, they lose their shape, lengthen, disaggregate, and break confusedly through the terrible straits, abandoning the stragglers everywhere, and only managing to regain, with great difficulty, under the protection of cold, their unknown solitudes."

THE LOST COMET AND ITS METEOR-TRAIN.

The meteor-shower which occurred on November 27, 1872, and the circumstances connected with that event, not only attracted a fresh interest to the subject of meteoric astronomy, but afforded important evidence respecting the connection which undoubtedly exists between meteors and comets. I propose in this paper to consider more particularly the events referred to, having already in the last essay but one dealt with the history of meteoric and cometic astronomy.

It has been shown by the labours of Schiaparelli, Adams, Peters, Tempel, and other astronomers, that the meteors of November 13–14 (called the Leonides) travel in the track of Tempel's comet. The meteors of August 10–11, or Perseides, have also been shown to travel in the track of a comet. Other such instances of association have been more or less fully recognised; and now the conclusion has been generally accepted, that in the train or path of comets bodies travel in scattered flights, which, if they fall on the atmosphere of the earth, appear as shooting-stars or meteors.

Until the recent shower, however, the inquiries made in this branch of research had been limited to cases of recognised meteor-systems whose orbits have been found to agree with those of comets. It was a new circumstance in the history of meteoric research when Weiss in Germany, and Alexander Herschel in England, ventured to predict a meteoric display because the earth was about to pass through the orbit of a known comet. It is true that there were some reasons for believing that meteors which had fallen in various years between November 25 and December 7 were attendants upon the comet in question—Biela's or Gambart's. But the evidence was slight, and in some respects unsatisfactory; so that it may be said that in reality the astronomers just named had no other grounds for their anticipations than first the fact that Biela's comet was known to have recently passed the descending node of its orbit (or the place where it passes nearest to the earth's orbit), and secondly their confidence in the theory that meteors and comets are in some way associated. A prediction such as this became therefore in some sense a crucial test of this theory—not indeed that the failure of the prediction would have disproved the theory (because negative evidence counts for little in this matter), but that its fulfilment would supply the only form of positive evidence yet wanting to that theory.

I do not here enter at length on the remarkable circumstances connected with Biela's comet, because they have been elsewhere stated at considerable length,* and are probably known to the majority of those who will read these lines. Let it suffice to say that the comet was one

* See the preceding Essay.

of short period, returning at mean intervals of 6·635 years; that in 1837 it was observed to be divided into two distinct comets; that it returned in 1852, and both the comets were then still in existence; that whether it returned (unchanged in general aspect) in 1858-59 or not, is unknown, because its calculated course was such as to render observation impossible; and lastly that in 1866, and again last year, it was searched for in vain with telescopes of great power.

Now it crossed the earth's path last year nearly twelve weeks before November 27, when the earth herself traversed the place at which the comet crosses her orbit. And since the meteors of November 13-14 have been seen, not merely a few months, but several years after the nodal passage of their comet, it seemed not unreasonable to expect a considerable meteoric display on or about November 27. The exact date was not indeed very accurately determined, and the reason is readily seen. I invite the reader's special attention to the point, because it has been somewhat singularly overlooked even by astronomers of great mathematical attainments. The comet itself had its place of passage readily calculated, and it might seem at first sight that whenever the earth came to that place the display should occur. But manifestly the position of the cometic orbit for November 27, when the earth crossed that orbit's node, would not be identical with the position of that orbit three months or so before, when the comet passed its node. It might then seem that this latter position was what astronomers should calculate, and as a matter of fact this is what was commonly done. We find the position of the node of the orbit for the end of November assigned as the place where the encounter of the earth with the meteoric flight was to take place. But this view is as incorrect as the former. Those particular meteors which were travelling twelve weeks behind the head of the comet, although, speaking generally, they would follow the comet's track, would nevertheless not be found travelling in precisely the same orbit, nor would they cross the earth's orbit precisely where the comet's orbit did at the time. For they would have been subjected to perturbations differing notably in character from those which had affected the comet itself. It must be remembered that the circumstances which separated such meteors by so great a distance from the head have not taken place in a few years, in a few revolutions of the comet, or even in a few centuries. But even if we take only the last half century or so, and consider the history of those meteors during that time, it will be manifest that their perturbations have differed considerably from those which have affected their leader, so to term the comet in whose track they follow. In the course of those years the comet has made seven or eight revolutions, and so have the meteors, while Jupiter, the chief disturber of Biela's comet, has made four or five revolutions. In the course of this period the comet must have been more than once so placed as to be very considerably disturbed by Jupiter, because as a matter of fact the path of the comet passes not very far (near its aphelion) from the path of Jupiter. The same general statement is true, of course, of the meteors twelve weeks behind. Now, whenever it happened that the comet was at its nearest to Jupiter, when passing that critical portion of its orbit, the meteors twelve weeks behind were either not brought so fully under the influence of Jupiter's attraction, or if they were, they were perturbed by him in a different manner. This is manifest if we consider how enormous is the real distance corresponding to the twelve weeks or so by which the meteors are behind the comet. And again, when the meteors chanced to be at their nearest to Jupiter when passing the critical part of their orbit, the comet, twelve weeks in front, was either not brought so fully under Jupiter's influence, or was perturbed in a different way.

Now whenever a perturbation has been produced, it affects the orbit of the perturbed body. Supposing the comet and meteors moving in precisely the same orbit at a particular moment, when Jupiter is pulling the comet in a certain way and the meteors in a different way, then forthwith the comet and meteors travel in different orbits. The difference may be slight, close by the place where such perturbations are produced, but it may nevertheless appreciably affect the positions which will be occupied by the comet and meteors when severally traversing some other and distant part of their orbit (as for instance when they are at their descending node close by the earth's track). And again, although in the long run there are compensatory effects—the comets and the bodies travelling twelve weeks behind being in the course of many years subjected to every variety of perturbative effect in the same respective proportions—yet such cycles of compensation are enormously long in the case of bodies moving in an orbit like that of Biela's comet; and practically it may be said that compensation is never effected.*

So that unless calculations could be made of the perturbations affecting those meteors themselves which are travelling twelve weeks behind the comet, we could not possibly be certain as to the place where the earth would actually encounter the meteor flight, or whether such an encounter would take place at all. The calculation would be one of immense difficulty, even if we knew where and how the meteors had been moving at some particular date;

---

* One may reason thus: Given a body travelling in the orbit of Biela's comet; then the orbit of this body will pass through endless changes. Its eccentricity will wax and wane; its inclination will increase and diminish; its line of apsides will advance and retrograde, advancing on the whole; its line of nodes will advance and retrograde, retrograding on the whole; and countless ages must elapse before its orbit resumes its original figure, for the four kinds of change will not have synchronous periods. Now the same is true of another body, having at the beginning the same orbit but twelve weeks in front or behind. This body will have its orbit passing through endless changes, and will only after countless ages be found travelling in the same orbit as at first. But the period in which this will happen is not the same period in which the former will happen. Each period is enormously long; but after the lapse of either the bodies are not travelling in the same orbit. When one period has elapsed, the other is far from being completed; when the latter is completed, the former is far past. Nor does it follow that the perturbing planets are in the same position as when the changes began. Many thousands of such periods must pass for both bodies before there is a near approach to the original state of things in all respects.

but as we know nothing on either point, it is simply impossible to enter upon the calculation.

It will presently be seen that these considerations bear importantly on the opinion we are to form respecting the events which have recently occurred.

It is in the knowledge of all my readers that on November 27th 1872, the anticipated display of meteors did actually occur. It was a display very remarkable in character. The meteors were even more numerous, in fact they were far more numerous than during the memorable shower of the night between November 13-14, 1866; though the meteors were not so large on the average as those seen on the latter occasion. I select from among many accounts the excellent description given by Professor Grant, because his skill and practice as an observer give great value to his statements. "In their general features," he says, "the meteors did not differ from those of the great display of November 13-14, 1866. They were, however, obviously less brilliant. Their normal colour was white, with a pale train tinged now and then with a very faint greenish hue. The head seldom equalled in brightness a star of the first magnitude. From time to time, however, a meteor of unusual splendour would appear, nearly rivalling Jupiter in brightness. In such cases the train, especially when breaking up, exhibited a reddish tinge. In two instances of large meteors (those of 8h. 13m. and 9h. 33m.) the colour of the train was conspicuously green. In general, however, there was an absence of the brilliant emerald hue which formed so conspicuous a feature of many of the larger meteors of November 1866. The time of visibility of a meteor did not exceed two or three seconds. In two or three instances of bright meteors, however, the *debris* of the train continued visible for about thirty seconds. The arc described varied as usual from zero to forty or fifty degrees. I was unable to detect any pronounced difference in the angular velocity of the meteors as compared with the meteors of November 1866. During the whole time of the occurrence of the shower I directed especial attention to the region of the heavens from which the meteors were issuing, with the view of detecting stationary or nearly stationary meteors, having been convinced, from my experience of the meteoric shower of November 1866, of the facility with which such meteors indicate the position of the radiant-point. Several meteors of this class were seen during the progress of the shower. At 8h. 43m., at 9h. 23m., and at 9h. 35m., absolutely stationary meteors were perceived. They rapidly swelled out, without any vestige of a train, and then suddenly collapsed. They all concurred in placing the radiant-point in a position midway between γ *Andromedæ* and 51 *Andromedæ*, perhaps a little nearer to the former star than to the latter. Assuming the position of the radiant-point to be midway between the two stars just mentioned, it would thus be situated in R.A. 26°, Decl. N. 44°. This conclusion was supported by the observations of nearly stationary meteors in the vicinity of the radiant-point. On the other hand the courses of the

The Lost Comet and its Meteor-Train. 99

more distant meteors when traced back, although in general assigning the same position to the radiant, appeared in many instances to come from a higher region situated in *Cassiopiea*. Of this fact (which is otherwise indicated by the projection of the observations) I do not entertain the slightest doubt, my attention having been directed to it early in the evening. In order to ascertain the time of occurrence of the maximum of the shower, it was necessary to count the number of meteors visible. At first it occurred to me to place two observers, one looking towards the region of the radiant-point, and the other towards the opposite region, but I found that the attempt to carry into effect this arrangement introduced confusion. I therefore directed the observer always to keep the star γ *Andromedæ* as the centre of vision, and to continue counting as many meteors as he could without turning round. The counting of the meteors commenced at 5h. 30m., and was prosecuted without intermission until 11h. 50m.; it consequently embraced an interval of 6h. 20m. The operation was effected by counting the number of meteors visible in each successive interval of five minutes. The meteors counted were thus parcelled out into seventy-six groups, each group extending over five minutes. The number of meteors counted in the first group (5h. 30m. to 5h. 35m.) amounted to 40. The number of meteors in the maximum group (8h. 10m. to 8h. 15m. was 367. The number of meteors in the last group (11h. 45m. to 11h. 50m.) fell to 6. Taking the first seventy-two groups, and forming them into twenty-four groups of fifteen minutes each, we have the following results:—

Quarter of Hour ending h. m.	No. of Meteors Counted	Quarter of Hour ending h. m.	No. of Meteors Counted	Quarter of Hour ending h. m.	No. of Meteors Counted
5 45	150	7 45	881	9 45	233
6 0	174	8 0	930	10 0	246
6 15	292	8 15	1070	10 15	190
6 30	507	8 30	777	10 30	116
6 45	643	8 45	599	10 45	111
7 0	840	9 0	413	11 0	74
7 15	721	9 15	418	11 15	48
7 30	890	9 30	213	11 30	22

"It is clear that the maximum of the shower occurred about 8h. 10m. The aggregate number of meteors counted from 5h. 30m. to 11h. 50m. (by one observer) amounted to 10,579."

To this it may be added that in Italy the shower was even richer, for Signor Denza states that in 6½ hours no less than 33,400 meteors were counted by four observers. "The meteors were very brilliant," he adds, "and were noticed in every part of the sky. The number recorded above is far less than the truth, for we found it frequently impossible to count them. The maximum display took place between 7h. and 9h., and for 21 minutes, between 6h. 35m. and 6h. 56m., *the appearance in the sky was that of a meteoric cloud*. The radiant-point was very clearly indicated near γ *Andromedæ*.

Now in the first place it is to be noticed that there can be no question whatever as to the meteoric display having been produced by bodies which were travelling in the track (speaking generally) of Biela's comet. It is sufficient to compare the position of the radiant-point with that which would have been due to meteors following precisely in the orbit of Biela's comet, as calculated for the last perturbed epoch, 1866. Mr Hind, the superintendent of the "Nautical Almanac," has calculated for the radiant-point due to the comet a place in R. A. 1^h. 41^m., and N. P. D. 48°. We have seen that Professor Grant gives for the observed radiant-point a position in R. A. 26° (or 1^h. 44^m.), and N. P. D. 44°, a singularly close agreement under the circumstances.*

* In passing I would venture to touch on what I cannot but regard as an error in the treatment of this subject by Professor Newton of America, and some other astronomers. They attribute to the indications of the meteoric paths a degree of accuracy which cannot, I conceive, be regarded as to be depended upon. And where, judging from the meteoric motions, the radiant seems to shift in position or to occupy an area rather than to be a mere point, they deduce such and such inferences from one or other circumstance. But it must be remembered that apart from other causes which would tend to spread the radiant region, the meteors must by the action of the atmosphere be very often, if not always, caused to deviate from the direction in which they had been moving before they reached the upper limits of the atmosphere. We cannot assume that because the air is very rare where the meteors first become visible, they therefore encounter an inappreciable resistance. The very fact of a meteor becoming visible shows, on the contrary, that there has been a degree of compression of the atmosphere in front of the meteor, which must necessarily involve a considerable resistance. And it is utterly unlikely that this resistance should take place without to some degree affecting the direction in which the meteor travels. Nor will all meteors be alike affected. For it is to be remembered that of the Meteors seen from any given station some strike the atmosphere in a very different way than others. Some impinge almost squarely upon the upper atmospheric layers, while others fall much more aslant. Then there must often be a difference of

But now comes the most singular part of the whole affair. It occurred to the German astronomer Klinkerfues that if search could be made in the part of the heavens directly opposite to that whence the meteor-shower had appeared to radiate, the cluster of meteoric bodies which had produced the display might be detected. In fact, Klinkerfues appears to have supposed that Biela's comet had itself touched the earth on the evening of November 27, for he telegraphed to Mr Pogson (the Government astronomer at Madras) in the following terms: "*Biela touched earth on 27th; search near Theta Centauri.*" And Pogson understood that it was the comet itself that he was searching for, since he wrote as follows, in describing the results of his search:—"I was on the look out from Comet-rise (16^h.) to Sun-rise the next two mornings, but clouds and rain disappointed me. On the third attempt, however, I had better luck. Just about $17\frac{1}{4}^h$. mean time a brief blue space enabled me to find Biela, and though I could only get four comparisons with an anonymous star, it had moved forward 2.5 s. in four minutes, and that *settled* its being the right object. I recorded it as 'Circular; bright, with a decided nucleus, but no tail, and about 45" in diameter.' This was in strong twilight. Next morning, December 3, I got a much better observation of it; seven comparisons with another anonymous

---

density and of arrangement in the upper strata of our atmosphere. These and other causes which may be pointed out, as well as differences in the size, weight, and density of the individual meteors, must lead to appreciable changes in the direction of motion.

star; two with one of our current Madras Catalogue Stars, and two with 7734 Taylor. This time my notes were: 'Circular, Diameter 75", bright nucleus, a faint but distinct tail, 8' in length and spreading, position angle from nucleus about 280°.' I had no time to spare to look for the other comet, and the next morning the clouds and rain had returned. The positions, the first rough, the second pretty fair, from the two known stars, are:—

	Madras M. T.			R.A.			Apparent N. P. D.		
	h.	m.	s.	h.	m.	s.	°	′	″
Dec. 2.	17	33	21	14	7	27	124	46	
„ 3.	17	25	17	14	22	2·9	125	4	28

It is manifest, however, that whatever the object seen by Pogson may have been, it was not Biela's comet; for the comet was due in that part of its orbit no less than twelve weeks earlier, and any retardation which could have produced so great a delay would have altogether changed the character of the comet's path.

Still it might be supposed that certainly what Pogson saw was on the track of Biela's comet, was in fact the cluster of bodies which produced the meteor-shower of November 27. Even this, however, is so far from being demonstrated that skilful mathematicians consider the object seen by Pogson to have had no connection whatever either with Biela itself or its meteoric train.

This at any rate is certain—a flight of bodies travelling on the track of Biela's comet, and crossing the earth's orbit on November 27, could not possibly have been seen in the positions in which Pogson saw a cometic or cloudlike object. We have, Professor A. S. Herschel has pointed out, unmistakable evidence that Pogson saw one and the same object. For he rated the motion of the object on the first morning, and the observed rate accords perfectly with the position occupied by the object on the second morning.

Two observations of a comet do not afford the means of determining the path in which the comet is travelling. But if we combine Pogson's observations with some other assumption, as that the object he saw had crossed the earth's orbit on November 27 at a given hour, or that the period of the object is identical with that of Biela's comet, or the like, then an orbit can be determined.

Now Capt. Tupman, in a paper recently read before the Royal Astronomical Society, after showing that the meteors seen on the night of Nov. 27 were running in sensibly the same orbit as Biela's comet, proves conclusively that a body moving in the same orbit as those meteors, or in an orbit parallel to them, could not have been in the positions occupied by the object seen by Pogson. We must assume greater changes in the character of the orbit than appear admissible, in order to account for the observed positions; in particular, since the object seen by Pogson had an apparent motion nearly parallel to the ecliptic, the inclination of its orbit cannot possibly be so great as $12° 34'$, which is the inclination of Biela's comet.

On the other hand, Dr. J. Holetschek, in No. 1920 of the 'Astronomische Nachrichten,' combining Pogson's two observations, with Hubbard's values of (1) the longitude of the node, (2) the longitude of the perihelion, and (3) the inclination, deduces for the perihelion passage of Pogson's object the date December 23·368 (mean Berlin time) and the perihelion distance ·8339 (·8606 being Hubbard's value of the perihelion distance of Biela's orbit in 1872). It is noteworthy that Tupman obtains for the meteor-flights of last November and for Biela's comet the following elements respectively :—

	Meteors of Nov. 27.	Biela's Comet.
Perihelion passage	1872 Dec. 26·90	1872 Oct· 66·9 (?)
Longitude of perihelion	111° 48'	109° 24'
,, ,, ascending node	245° 57'	245° 54'
Inclination	13° 24'	12° 34'
Perihelion distance	·8265	·8718
Eccentricity	·7670	·7600
Motion	Direct	Direct

So that Holetschek's result would appear to indicate that the object seen by Pogson had been travelling about $3\frac{1}{2}$ days behind the meteors observed on November 27 last.

Professor von Oppolzer of Vienna, the eminent orbit calculator, shows in the same number of the "Astronomiche Nachrichten," that the same problem may be successfully treated· in a totally different manner. He assumes the period (or which amounts to the same thing,) the major axis of the object's orbit to be the same as that of Biela's comet, and that the object was moving from the earth in the interval between December 2 and 3, deducing elements nearly resembling those of Biela's comet.

It appears to me that the discordances obtained by different astronomers depend largely on the assumption that the object seen by Pogson, if identifiable at all with Biela's meteor-train, must in a special manner be identified with the cloud of meteors through which the earth passed on the night of November 27. But is there any valid reason for this assumption? It may seem at first sight that there is; that a cloud of meteors sufficiently dense to produce so remarkable a display should be visible, when it had passed beyond the earth, as a cloud of light in the telescopic field. But if we consider the real distribution of those meteors in space, we shall find reason to conclude that they were far too sparsely distributed to be visible under any circumstances, by the light they were capable of reflecting. Let it be remembered that the display lasted about six hours, and that during that period about 50,000 meteors at the utmost appeared above the horizon of any given place. But let us set 100,000 as the number of meteors so appearing, and the time at only four hours. Now the region of meteor-traversed atmosphere above the horizon plane of any station may be taken as a plano-convex lens, its plane circular face having a diameter certainly not less than 1,000 miles; and as the radiant was high above the horizon, we shall be within the truth in concluding that such a plane on the average presented (as supposed to be seen from the advancing meteors) an area equalling the 100th part of the area presented by the whole disc of the earth. So that if we take 10,000,000 for the total number of meteors falling on the earth during four hours, we shall certainly not underestimate the number (referring always to meteors large

The Lost Comet and its Meteor-Train. 107

enough to become visible to the naked eye). Now, the actual region of space traversed by the earth in four hours is a cylinder 260,000 miles long and having a cross section nearly 8,000 miles in diameter. Such a cylinder would have a volume of 12,500,000,000,000 cubic miles, and to each meteor of the 10,000,000 there would therefore correspond an average space of 1,250,000 cubic miles; that is, a space corresponding to a cube nearly 108 miles in length and breadth and height. Since such meteors as were seen on the night of November 27 have been estimated at less than an ounce in weight (in many cases only a few grains), it follows that their dimensions are inconsiderable. The largest can scarcely, when solid, be an inch in diameter. It will be conceived, therefore, how small must be the prospect of seeing a flight of bodies so exceedingly minute compared with the average space occupied by each. It is, indeed, easy to estimate the luminosity of such a flight regarded as a whole, if of given depth and at a given distance from the sun. Thus, suppose the flight of a million miles in depth, and at the earth's distance from the sun. Along a range of a million miles there would be less than 10,000 meteors. Now, granting each to have a disc one square inch in real area, we should have a total area of 10,000 square inches (that is, $8\frac{1}{3}$ feet square). And the ratio of this area to 108 miles square gives the ratio of the luminosity of the meteor-cloud (when of the given depth) to the luminosity of a surface illuminated by the sun at the earth's distance—(say, the moon for example). Now 108 miles square, or 11,664 square miles contain 11,664 ×

$(1,760)^2 \times (36)^2$ square inches, or roughly (for great nicety would be useless in such a problem) $10,000 \times (2,000)^2 \times (35)^2$ square inches; so that the ratio we require is 1 to $(70,000)^2$ or 1 to 4,900,000,000. That is, the luminosity of the meteor-cloud would be one-4,900,000,000th only of the moon's, and necessarily the meteor-cloud would be quite undiscernible. Hence we may be assured that if the object seen by Pogson was connected at all with the meteor-cloud through which the earth passed on November 27, he saw a very much denser part of the meteor cloud; and there is no reason why this dense portion or nucleus of the meteor-cloud may not have been at a considerable distance from the earth on the 27th of last November. This consideration would serve to remove some of the more perplexing circumstances of the recent observations.

JUPITER.

THE planet Jupiter has passed lately (this was written in 1873) through a singular process of change. The planet has not, indeed, assumed a new appearance, but has gradually resumed its normal aspect after four or five years, during which the mid-zone of Jupiter has been aglow with a peculiar ruddy light. The zone is now of a creamy-white colour, its ordinary hue. We have, in fact, reached the close of a period of disturbance, and have received a definite answer to questions which had arisen as to the reality of the change described by observers. Many astronomers of repute were disposed to believe that the peculiarities recently observed were merely due to the instruments with which the planet has been observed—not, indeed, to any fault in those instruments, but, in fact, to their good qualities in showing colour. A considerable number of the earlier accounts of Jupiter's change of aspect came from observers who used the comparatively modern form of telescope known as the silvered-glass reflectors, and it is well known that these instruments are particularly well suited for the study of colour-changes. Nevertheless, observations made with the ordinary refracting telescope were not wanting; and it had begun to be recognised that Jupiter really had altered remarkably in appearance, even before that gradual process of change which, by restoring his usual aspect, enabled every telescopist to assure himself that there had been no illusion in the earlier observations.

I propose now to discuss certain considerations which appear to me to indicate the nature and probable meaning of the phenomena which have recently been observed in Jupiter. It seems to me that these phenomena are full of interest, whether considered in themselves or in connection with those circumstances on which I had been led to base the theory that Jupiter is a planet altogether unlike our earth in condition, and certainly unfit to be the abode of living creatures.

I would first direct special attention to the facts which have been ascertained respecting the atmosphere of Jupiter.

It does not appear to have been noticed, as a remarkable circumstance, that Jupiter should have an atmosphere recognisable from our distant station. Yet, in reality, this circumstance is not only most remarkable, but is positively inexplicable on any theory by which Jupiter is regarded as a world resembling our own. It is certain that, except by the effects produced when clouds form and dissipate, our terrestrial atmosphere could not be recognised at Jupiter's distance with any telescopic power yet applied. But no one who has studied Jupiter with adequate means can for a moment fail to recognise the fact that the signs of an atmosphere indicate much more than the mere formation and dissipation of clouds. I speak here after a careful study of the planet during the late opposition, with a very fine reflecting telescope by Browning, very generously placed at my disposal by Lord Lindsay; and I feel satisfied that no one can study Jupiter for many hours (on a single night) without becoming convinced that the cloud-masses seen on his disc have a *depth* comparable with their length and bread. Now the depth of terrestrial cloud-masses would at Jupiter's distance be an absolutely evanescent quantity. The span of his disc represents about 84,000 miles, and his satellites, which look little more than points in ordinary telescopes, are all more than 2,000 miles in diameter. I am satisfied that anyone who has carefully studied the behaviour of Jupiter's cloud-belts will find it difficult to believe that their depth is less than the twentieth part of the diameter of the least satellite. Conceive, however, what the depth of an atmosphere would be in which cloud-masses a hundred miles deep were floating!

It may be asked, however, in what sense such an atmosphere would be inexplicable, or, at least, irreconcilable with the theory that Jupiter is a world like our earth. Such an atmosphere would be in strict proportion, it might be urged, to the giant bulk of the planet, and such relative agreement seems more natural than would be a perfect correspondence between the depth of the atmosphere on Jupiter and the depth of our earth's atmosphere.

But it must not be forgotten that the atmosphere of Jupiter is attracted by the mass of the planet; and some rather remarkable consequences follow when we pay attention to this consideration. Of course a great deal must be assumed in an inquiry of the sort. Since, however, we are discussing the question whether there can be any resemblance between Jupiter and our earth, we may safely (so far as our inquiry is concerned) proceed on the assumption that the atmosphere of Jupiter does not greatly differ in constitution from that of our earth. We may further assume that at the upper part of the cloud-layers we see, the atmospheric pressure is not inferior to that of our atmosphere at a height of seven miles above the sea-level, or one-fourth of the pressure at our sea-level. Combining these assumptions with the conclusion just mentioned, that the cloud-layers are at least 100 miles in depth, we are led to the following singular result as to the pressure of the Jovian atmosphere at the bottom of the cloud-layer:—The atmosphere of any planet doubles in pressure with descent through equal distances, these distances depending on the power of gravity at the planet's surface. In the case of our earth, the pressure is doubled with descent through about $3\frac{1}{2}$ miles; but gravity on Jupiter is more than $2\frac{1}{2}$ times as great as gravity on our earth, and descent through $1\frac{3}{8}$ mile would double the pressure in the case of a Jovian atmosphere. Now 100 miles contain this distance ($1\frac{3}{8}$ mile) more than seventy-one times; and we must therefore double the pressure at the upper part of the cloud-layer seventy-one successive times to obtain the pressure at the lower part. Two doublings raise the pressure to that at our sea-level; and the remaining sixty-nine doublings would result in a pressure exceeding that at our sea-level so many times that the number representing the proportion contains twenty-one figures.* I say *would* result in such a pressure, because in reality there are limits beyond which atmospheric pressure cannot be increased without changing the compressed air into the liquid form. What those limits are we do not know, for no pressure yet applied has changed common air, or either of its chief constituent gases, into the liquid form, or even produced any trace of a tendency to assume that form. But it is easily shown that there must be a limit to the increase of pressure which air will sustain without liquefying. For the density of any gas changes proportionately to the increase of pressure, until the gas is approaching the state when it is about to turn liquid. Now air at the sea-level has a density equal to less than the 900th part of the density of water; so that if the pressure at the sea-level were increased 900 times, either the density would not increase proportionally, which would show that the gas was approaching the density of liquefaction, *or else* the gas would be denser than water, which must be regarded as utterly impossible.

* The problem is like the well-known one relating to the price of a horse, where one farthing was to be paid for the first nail of 24 in the shoes, a halfpenny for the next, a penny for the third, two pence for the fourth, and so on. It may be interesting to some of my readers to learn, that if we want to know roughly the proportion in which the first number is increased by any given number of doublings, we have only to multiply the number of doublings by $\frac{3}{10}$ths, and add 1 to the integral part of the result, to give the number of digits in the number representing the required proportions. Thus multiplying 24 by $\frac{3}{10}$ths gives 7 (neglecting fractions); and therefore the number of farthings in the horse problem is represented by an array of 8 digits.

Or if any one is disposed, for the sake of argument, to assert that a gas *(ut ordinary temperatures)* may be as dense as water, then we need proceed but a few steps farther, increasing the pressure about 18,000 times instead of 900 times, to have the density of *platinum* instead of that of water, and no one is likely to maintain that our air could exist in the gaseous form with a density equalling that of the densest of the elements. We are still an enormous way behind the number of twenty-one figures mentioned above; and in fact, if we supposed the pressure and density to increase continually to the extent implied by the number of twenty-one figures, we should have a density exceeding that of platinum more than ten thousand millions of millions of times!

Of course this supposition is utterly monstrous, and I have merely indicated it to show how difficulties crowd around us in any attempt to show that a resemblance exists between the condition of Jupiter and that of our earth. The assumptions I made were sufficiently moderate, be it noticed, since I simply regarded (i.) the air of Jupiter as composed like our own; (ii.) the pressure at the upper part of his cloud-layer as not less than the pressure far above the highest of our terrestrial cumulus clouds (with which alone the clouds of Jupiter are comparable); and (iii.) the depth of his cloud-layer as about 100 miles. The first two assumptions cannot fairly be departed from to any considerable extent, without adopting the conclusion that the atmosphere of Jupiter is quite unlike that of our earth, which is precisely what I desire to maintain. The third is, of course, open to attack, though I apprehend that no one who has observed Jupiter with a good telescope will question its justice. But it is not at all essential to the argument that the assumed depth of the Jovian atmosphere should be even nearly so great. We do not need a third of our array of twenty-one figures, or even a seventh part, since no one who has studied the experimental researches made into the condition of gases and vapours can for a moment suppose that an atmosphere like ours could remain gaseous, *except at an enormously high temperature*, at a pressure of two or three hundred atmospheres. Such a pressure would be obtained, retaining our first two assumptions, at a depth of about fourteen miles below the upper part of the cloud-layer. This is about the 6,000th part of the diameter of Jupiter; and if any student of astronomy can believe that that wonderfully complex and changeful cloud envelope which surrounds Jupiter, has a thickness of less than the 6,000th part of the planet's diameter, I would recommend as a corrective the careful study of the planet for an hour or two with a powerful telescope, combined with the consideration that the thickness of a spider's line across the telescopic field of view would suffice to hide a breadth of twenty miles on Jupiter's disc.

But we are not by any means limited to the reasoning here indicated, convincing as that reasoning should be to all who have studied the aspect of Jupiter with adequate telescopic power. We have in Jupiter's mean density an argument of irresistible force against the only view which enables us even hypothetically to escape from the conclusions just indicated. Let it be granted, for the sake of argument, that Jupiter's cloud-layer is *less* than fourteen miles in depth, so that we are freed for the moment from the inference that at the lower part of the atmosphere there is either an intense heat or else a density and pressure incompatible with the gaseous condition. We cannot, in this case, strike off more than twenty-eight miles from the planet's apparent diameter to obtain the real diameter of his solid globe—solid, at least, if we are to maintain the theory of his resemblance to our earth. This leaves his real diameter appreciably the same as his apparent diameter, and as a result we have the mean density of his solid globe equal to a fourth of the earth's mean density precisely as when we leave his atmosphere out of the question. Now I apprehend that the time has long since passed when we can seriously proceed at this stage to say, as it was the fashion to say in text-books of astronomy, "therefore the substance of which Jupiter is composed must be of less specific gravity than oak and other heavy woods." We know that Brewster gravely reasoned that the solid materials of Jupiter might be of the nature of pumice stone, so that with oceans resembling ours a certain latitude was allowed for increase of density in Jupiter's interior. But in the presence of the teachings of spectroscopic analysis, few would now care to maintain, as probable, so preposterous a theory as this. Everything that has hitherto been learned respecting the constitution of the heavenly bodies, renders it quite unlikely that the elementary constitution of Jupiter differs from that of our earth. Again, it was formerly customary to speak of the possibility that Jupiter and Saturn might be hollow globes, mere shells, composed of materials as heavy as terrestrial elements. But whatever opinion we form as to the possibility that a great intensity of heat may vaporise a portion of Jupiter's interior, we know quite certainly that there must be enormous pressure throughout the whole of the planet's globe, and that even a vaporous nucleus would be of great density. For it is to be remembered that all that I have said above respecting the possibility of gases existing at great pressures applies only to ordinary temperatures—such temperatures, for example, as living creatures can endure. At exceedingly high temperatures much greater pressure, and therefore much greater density, can be attained without liquefaction or solidification. And in considering the effect of pressure on the materials of a solid globe, we must not fall into the mistake of supposing that the strength of such solid materials can protect its substance from compression and its effects. We must extend our conceptions beyond what is familiar to us. We know that any ordinary mass of some strong, heavy solid—as iron, copper, or gold—is not affected by its own weight so as to change in structure to an appreciable extent. The substance of a mass of iron forty or fifty feet high, would be the same in structure at the bottom as at the top of the mass; for the strength of the metal would resist any change which the weight of the mass would (otherwise) tend to produce. But if there were a cubical mountain of iron twenty miles high, the lower part would be absolutely plastic under the pressure to which it would be subjected. It would behave in all respects as a fluid, insomuch that if (for convenience of illustration) we suppose it enclosed within walls made of some imaginary (and impossible) substance which would yield to no pressure, then, if a portion of the wall were removed near the base of the iron mountain, the iron would flow out like water* from a hole near the bottom of a cask. The iron would continue to run out in this way, until the mass was reduced several miles in height. In Jupiter's case a mountain of iron of much less height would be similarly plastic in its lower parts, simply because of the much greater attractive power of Jupiter's mass. Thus we see that the conception of a hollow interior, or of any hollow spaces throughout the planet's globe, is altogether inconsistent with what is known of the constitution of even the strongest materials.

How, then, are we to explain the relatively small mean density of Jupiter's globe? On the supposition that his atmosphere is less than fourteen miles deep, we cannot do so; for there is nothing hypothetical in the above considerations respecting a solid globe as large as Jupiter's, excepting always the assumption that the globe is not formed of substances unlike any with which we are familiar. Even this assumption, though it is one which few would care to

---

* The effect of pressure in rendering iron and other metals plastic has been experimentally determined. Cast steel has been made to flow almost like water, under pressure.

maintain in the present position of our knowledge, amounts after all to an admission of the chief point which I am endeavouring to maintain: it is one way—but a very fanciful way—of inferring that Jupiter is utterly unlike the earth. Rejecting it, as we safely may, we find the small density of Jupiter not merely unexplained, but manifestly inexplicable.

All our reasoning has been based on the assumption that the atmosphere of Jupiter exists at a temperature not greatly differing from that of our own atmosphere. If we assume instead an exceedingly high temperature, abandoning of course the supposition that Jupiter is an inhabited world, we no longer find any circumstances which are self-contradictory or incredible.

To begin with, we may on such an assumption find at once a parallel to Jupiter's case in that of the Sun. For the Sun is an orb attracting his atmospheric envelope and the material of his own solid or liquid surface (if he has any) far more mightily than Jupiter has been shown to do. All the difficulties considered in the case of Jupiter would be enormously enhanced in the case of the Sun, if we forgot the fact that the Sun's globe is at an intense heat from surface to centre. Now we know that the Sun is intensely hot because we feel the heat that he emits, and recognise the intense lustre of his photosphere; so that we are not in danger of overlooking this important circumstance in his condition. Jupiter gives out no heat that we can feel, and assuredly Jupiter does not emit an intense light of his own. But, when we find that difficulties precisely corresponding in kind, though not in degree, to those which we should encounter if we discussed the Sun's condition in forgetfulness of his intense heat, exist also in the case of Jupiter, it appears manifest that we may safely adopt the conclusion that Jupiter is intensely heated, though not nearly to the same degree as the Sun.

We have thus been led by a perfectly distinct and independent line of reasoning to the very conclusion which I have advocated elsewhere on other grounds, viz., that Jupiter is in fact a miniature sun as respects heat, though emitting but a relatively small proportion of light. I would invite special attention to the circumstance that the evidence on which this conclusion had been based was already cumulative. And now a fresh line of evidence, in itself demonstrative, I conceive, has been adduced. Moreover I have not availed myself of the argument, very weighty in my opinion, on which Mr. Mattieu Williams has based similar conclusions respecting the temperature of Jupiter, in his interesting and valuable work called "The Fuel of the Sun." I fully agree with him in regarding it as a reasonable assumption, though I cannot go so far as to regard it as certain, that every planet has an atmosphere whose mass corresponds with, or is even perhaps actually proportional to, the mass of the planet it surrounds. If we make such an assumption in the case of Jupiter, we arrive at conclusions closely resembling those to which I have been led by the above process of reasoning.

Thus many lines of evidence, and some of them

absolutely demonstrative in my opinion, point to the conclusion that Jupiter is an orb instinct with fiery energy, aglow it may well be with an intense light which is only prevented from manifesting itself by the cloudy envelope enshrouding the planet.

But so soon as we regard the actual phenomena presented by Jupiter in the light of this hypothesis, we find the means of readily interpreting what otherwise would appear most perplexing. Chief among the phenomena thus accounted for, I would place the recent colour-changes in the equatorial zone of Jupiter.

What, at first view, could appear more surprising than a change affecting the colour of a zone-shaped region whose surface is many times greater than the whole surface of our earth? It is true that a brief change might be readily explained as due to such changes as occur in our own air. Large regions of the earth are at one time cloud-covered and at another free from clouds. Such regions, seen from Venus or Mercury, would at one time appear white, and at the other would show whatever colour the actual surface of the ground might possess when viewed as a whole. But it seems altogether impossible to explain in this way a change or series of changes occupying many years, as in the case of the recent colour-changes of Jupiter's belt. Let me not be misunderstood. I am not urging that the changes in Jupiter are *not* due to the formation and dissipation of clouds in his atmosphere. On the contrary, I believe that they are. What seems to me incredible, is the supposition that we have here to deal with such changes as occur in our own air in consequence of solar action.

I do not lose sight of the fact that the Jovian year is of long duration, and that whatever changes take place in the atmosphere of Jupiter through solar action might be expected to be exceedingly slow. Nay, it is one of the strongest arguments against the theory that solar action is chiefly in question, that any solar changes would be so slight as to be in effect scarcely perceptible. It is not commonly insisted upon in our text-books of astronomy—in fact, I have never seen the point properly noticed anywhere—that the seasonal changes in Jupiter correspond to no greater *relative* change than occurs in our daily supply of solar heat from about eight days before to about eight days after the spring or autumn equinox. It is incredible that so slight an effect as this should produce those amazing changes in the condition of the Jovian atmosphere which have unquestionably been indicated by the varying aspect of the equatorial zone. It is manifest that, on the one hand, the seasonal changes should be slow and slight so far as they depend on the sun, and that, on the other, the sun does not rule so absolutely over the Jovian atmosphere as to cause any particular atmospheric condition to prevail unchanged for years.

If, however, Jupiter's whole mass is in a state of intense heat—if, as appears to be the case, the heat is in fact sufficient to maintain an effective resistance against the tremendous force of Jovian gravitation—we can understand any changes, however amazing. We can see how enormous quantities of vapour must continually be generated in the lower regions to be condensed in the upper regions, either directly above the zone in which they were generated or north or south of it, according to the prevailing motions in the Jovian atmosphere. And although we may not be able to indicate the precise reason why at one time the mid zone or any other belt of Jupiter's surface should exhibit that whiteness which indicates the presence of clouds, and at another should show a colouring which appears to indicate that the glowing mass below is partly disclosed, we remember that the difficulty corresponds in character to that which is presented by the phenomena of solar spots. We cannot tell why sun-spots should wax and wane in frequency during a period of about eleven years; but this does not prevent us from adopting such opinions respecting the condition of the sun's glowing photosphere as are suggested by the behaviour of the spots.

It may be asked whether I regard the ruddy glow of Jupiter's equatorial zone, during the period of disturbance lately passed through, as due to the inherent light of glowing matter underneath his deep and cloud-laden atmosphere. This appears to me on the whole the most probable hypothesis, though, it is by no means certain that the ruddy colour may not be due to the actual constitution of the planet's vaporous atmosphere. In either case, be it noted, we should perceive in this ruddy light the inherent lustre of Jupiter's glowing mass; only in one case we assume that that lustre is itself ruddy, in the other we suppose that light, originally white, shines through ruddy vapour-masses. It is to be remembered, however, that whichever view we adopt, we must assume that a considerable portion of the light received, even from these portions of the planet's disc, must be reflected sunlight. In fact, from what we know about the actual quantity of light received from Jupiter, we may be quite certain that no very large portion of that light is inherent. Jupiter shines about as brightly as if he were a giant cumulus-cloud, and therefore almost as white as driven snow. Thus he sends us much more light than a globe of equal size of sandstone, or granite, or any known kind of earth. We get from him about three times as much light as a globe like our moon in substance, but as large as Jupiter, and placed where Jupiter is, would reflect towards the earth; but not quite so much as we should receive from a globe of pure snow of the same size and similarly placed. It is only because large parts of the surface of Jupiter are manifestly *not* white, that we seem compelled to assume that some portion of his light is inherent.

But the theory that Jupiter is intensely hot by no means requires, as some mistakenly imagine, that he should give out a large proportion of light. His real solid or liquid globe (if he have any) might, for instance, be at a white heat, and yet so completely cloud-enwrapped that none of its light could reach us. Or again, his real surface might be like red-hot iron, giving out much heat but very little light.

I shall close the present statement of evidence in favour

of what I begin to regard as in effect a demonstrated theory, with the account of certain appearances which have been presented by Jupiter's fourth satellite during recent transits across the face of the planet. The appearances referred to have been observed by several telescopists, but I will select an account given in the monthly notices of the "Astronomical Society," by Mr Roberts, F.R.A.S., who observed the planet with a fine telescope by Wray, 8 inches in aperture. "On March 26, 1873," he says, "I observed Jupiter about 8 p.m., and found the satellite on the disc. I thought at first it must be a shadow; but, on referring to the 'Nautical Almanac,' found that it was the fourth satellite itself. A friend was observing with me, and we both agreed that it was a very intense black, and also was not quite round. We each made independent drawings which agreed perfectly, and consider that the observation was a perfectly reliable one. We could not imagine that such an intensely black object would be visible when off the disc, and waited with some impatience to see the immersion, but were disappointed by fog, which came on just at the critical time." Another observer, using a telescope only two inches in aperture, saw the satellite when off the disc, so that manifestly the blackness was merely an effect of contrast.

In considering this remarkable phenomenon, we must not forget that the other satellites do not look black (though some of them look dark) when crossing Jupiter's disc, so that we have to deal with a circumstance peculiar to the fourth or outermost satellite. Nevertheless, we seem precluded from supposing that any other difference exists between this satellite and the others than a certain inferiority of light-reflecting power. I might indeed find an argument for the view which I have suggested as not improbable, that Jupiter is a heat-sun to his satellites, since the three innermost would be in that case much better warmed than the outermost, and therefore would be much more likely to be cloud-encompassed, and so would reflect more light. But I place no great reliance on reasoning so ingenious, which stands much as a pyramid would stand (theoretically) on its apex. The broad fact that a body like the fourth satellite, probably comparable to our moon in light-reflecting power, looks perfectly black when on the middle of Jupiter's disc, is that on which I place reliance. This manifestly indicates a remarkable difference between the brightness of Jupiter and the satellite; and it is clear that the excess of Jupiter's brightness is in accordance with the theory that he shines in part with native light, or, in other words, is intensely heated.

This completes the statement of the evidence obtained during the recent opposition of Jupiter in favour of a theory which already had the great advantage of according with all known facts, and accounting for some which had hitherto seemed inexplicable. If this theory removes Jupiter from the position assigned to him by Brewster as the noblest of inhabited worlds, it indicates for him a higher position as a subordinate sun, nourishing with his heat, as he sways by his attractive energy, the scheme of worlds circling round him. The theory removes also the difficulty suggested by the apparent uselessness of the Jovian satellites in the scheme of creation. When, instead of considering their small power of supplying Jupiter with light, we consider the power which, owing to his great size and proximity, he must possess of illuminating them with reflected light, and warming them with his native heat, we find a harmony and beauty in the Jovian system which before had been wanting; nor, when we consider the office which the Sun subserves towards the members of his family, need we reject this view on account of the supposition—

> That bodies bright and greater should not serve
> The less not bright.

Even the most ardent advocate of the theory of life in other worlds should at least not complain when he finds for one imagined world four others substituted.

SATURN AND ITS SYSTEM.

The planet Saturn is perhaps the most interesting of all the orbs in the heavens. Independently even of his ring-system, which gives him so singularly beautiful an aspect in the telescope, he holds a remarkable position as the centre round which circle as many dependent orbs as those which constitute the primary members of the Sun's family. There is something startling in the thought that in those remote depths, ten times farther away from the great centre of the system than we ourselves are placed, a system at once so beautiful and so elaborate should be pursuing its wide orbit. A universe is there, reduced by vastness of distance to a mere speck of dull light—a 'miracle of design' which has existed for ages, during which none on this earth recognized that aught distinguished the planet from its fellows, save characteristics of inferiority.

I propose to give a brief sketch of some of the most interesting facts which have been ascertained respecting this wonderful planet. I may remark, in passing, that although I have on several occasions discussed matters connected with the subject of the planet's condition, this is the first occasion on which I have described Saturn and its system in a general way since the time when I wrote the work bearing that name.

It is not wonderful, when we consider the dull aspect and slow motions of Saturn, that the ancients should have associated with this planet ideas of gloom and of malign influences. The alchemist assigned the metal lead, heavy and poisonous, to the most distant and most slowly moving planet known to them. The astrologer regarded Saturn as the most fatal of all the planets. Chaucer thus presents, in the address of Saturn to Venus, the characteristics of Saturn's influence: *

> 'My dere doughter Venus, quod Saturne,
> My cours that hath so wide for to turne,
> Hath more power than wot any man.
> Min is the drenching in the see so wan,
> Min is the prison in the derke cote,
> Min is the strangel and hanging by the throte,
> The murmure and the cherles rebelling,
> The groyning, and the prive empoysoning.
> I do vengeaunce and pleine correction,
> While I dwell in the sign of the leon.
> Min is the ruine of the high halles,
> The falling of the toures and of the walles
> Upon the minour or the carpenter:
> I slew Sampson in shaking the piler.
> Min ben also the maladies colde,
> The derk tresons, and the castes olde:
> My loking is the fader of pestilence.'

Travelling at a distance from the Sun varying from 823 millions to 921 millions of miles, or from nine to ten

---

* The word Saturnine sufficiently indicates the character ascribed to the planet's influence on the fates of men and nations.

times the Earth's, Saturn accomplishes a complete revolution around the Sun in rather less than thirty years. As the Earth goes once round the Sun while Saturn is traversing but about the thirtieth part of his orbit, it follows that year after year he is seen to advance but by a small distance along his track on the heavens. The Earth comes between Saturn and the Sun, and then Saturn is visible at night, and therefore favourably; then the Earth makes a complete circuit, and has to advance but a little way further before she is again between Saturn and the Sun. In fact, year after year, the return of Saturn to the midnight sky occurs about twelve days later, so that if in one year he is well seen in the summer, he will be well seen the summer after, and so on for several successive summers, before the year comes when he is well seen in autumn. Then for several more years (about seven) he is well seen in the autumn months. Next, for about seven years, he is well seen in the winter months. And lastly, for about seven successive years, he is well seen in the spring months. In 1873, he was actually at his nearest to the Earth, and highest above the horizon, at midnight on July 21st. In 1874, he held such a position on August 3rd. This year on August 16th; and so on. For ordinary observation, however, Saturn is as well placed as he can be about two months after opposition; for it is only the astronomer who is willing to wait until midnight for his observations of any celestial body.

. Two hundred and sixty-two years have passed since Galileo first examined Saturn with the telescope by which he had already discovered the moons of Jupiter. It must have been with singular interest that he prepared for his first telescopic view of the planet. Yet he could scarcely have expected what actually awaited him. There, in the small field of view of his telescope, was what appeared like a triple planet. Not a planet accompanied by two moons such as those which attend on Jupiter: these moons, seen in Galileo's telescopes, were the merest points of light, and scarcely to be distinguished from stars. What Galileo now saw was, however, very different. There seemed to be a central orb, and half overlapping it two others, somewhat smaller indeed, but still presenting considerable discs.* "When I observe Saturn," says Galileo, writing to the Grand Duke of Tuscany, "he seems to be triformed; with a glass magnifying more than thirty times, the central body seems the largest; the two others situated one on the east and one on the west, seem to touch the central body. They are like two supporters, who help old Saturn on his way, and always remain at his side. With a glass of lower magnifying power, the planet appears elongated and of the form of an olive."

In December 1610, and again during the winter of 1611-12, these two attendant orbs seemed to grow smaller and smaller, though retaining their position unchanged.

In the winter of 1612-1613, Galileo again examined Saturn, hoping to learn something more about these remark-

* What Galileo *thought* he saw may be represented by setting two shillings with a space an inch or so wide between them, and midway over that space a half-crown.

able supporters. But to his intense astonishment they were not to be seen. The planet shone with as fairly round a disc as Mars or Jupiter. Galileo was so startled at this strange event, that he began almost to doubt the evidence of his senses. "What is to be said concerning so strange a metamorphosis?" he wrote. "Are the two lesser orbs consumed, after the manner of the solar spots? Have they vanished and suddenly fled? Has Saturn perhaps devoured his own children? Or were the appearances indeed an illusion or fraud, with which the glasses have so long deceived me, as well as many others to whom I have shewn them? Now, perhaps, is the time come to revive the well-nigh withered hopes of those who, guided by more profound contemplations, have discovered the fallacy of the new observations, and demonstrated the utter impossibility of their existence. I do not know what to say in a case so surprising, so unlooked for, and so novel. The shortness of the time, the unexpected nature of the event, the weakness of my understanding, and the fear of being mistaken, have greatly confounded me."

Galileo afterwards saw the smaller orbs return into view; but he noticed that as they grew larger and larger they changed strangely in shape, until he finally saw them lose their globular appearance altogether, each assuming the figure of two arms stretched round the planet.

I shall not describe here, at length, the gradual process by which the true nature of the ring became recognized. Let it suffice to mention that Huyghens first, in 1656, announced that Saturn is not attended by two companion orbs, but by a mighty ring,—flat, so that when turned edgewise towards the Earth it cannot be seen in ordinary telescopes, and tilted towards the level of the path in which the planet travels, so that at two opposite parts of the path the ring, as seen from the Earth, appears to attain its greatest opening.

In passing, it may be mentioned that in 1656 the ring was closed—that is, turned edgewise towards the Earth—and that it opened out after 1656 so as to show the same flat side of the ring (the northern side) which is visible at present. This side remained in view, the ring, first opening out and then closing up, until December, 1671, when the ring was again turned edgewise towards the Earth, after which the southern face came into view. Now it is well to notice that though so many years have elapsed since Huyghens discovered the nature of the rings, there have not been many of these changes by which the northern and southern faces of the ring are brought alternately into view. To my idea, it gives a singularly impressive conception of the stately motion of Saturn in his orbit, to notice that during all the years which have passed since astronomers knew that Saturn is girdled about by a ring, the ring has swayed so slowly to and fro, (as seen from the Earth,) that the northern side has been turned only eight times towards the Sun, and the southern only seven. Two hundred and sixteen times the Earth has circled round the Sun, while Saturn has not yet swayed his ring through all its phases so many as eight times.

In 1675 Cassini found that the ring is divided by a

strong dark band into two concentric rings. But the English astronomer, William Ball, had discovered this feature ten years earlier. The interest of Cassini's observation consisted in the fact that it proved the band to be a division between two distinct rings, and not a mere dark streak upon one face of a flat ring.

Huyghens had, in the meantime, discovered a satellite attending on Saturn. This orb, which has received the name Titan, is distinguished among all the secondary members of the planetary system by its superior size. It is larger than the primary planet Mercury, and little inferior to the planet Mars. Cassini discovered in 1671 another satellite (now called Japetus) also large, though not nearly so large as Titan. We have no other means of estimating the magnitude of these bodies than by considering their brightness. But assuming them to resemble our own Moon, and the moons of Jupiter, in their power of reflecting sunlight, it would follow that Titan is about 4000 miles in diameter, and Japetus about 3000.

But perhaps the most remarkable circumstance respecting these bodies, is the enormous distance at which they travel around their primary. The outermost of Jupiter's moons travels at a distance of 1,190,000 miles from Jupiter. The distance of Japetus from Saturn is nearly twice as great, being no less than 2,210,000 miles. Titan travels at a distance of 760,000 miles from Saturn.

It is impossible to consider these enormous distances in the case of Jupiter's outer moon, and the two chief moons of Saturn, without being led to consider in what degree these orbs seem likely to subserve the purpose of supplying light to their primaries. It may be very unphilosophical to reason from final causes; *not* because of the objection urged by some, that we have yet to demonstrate that there is design in the scheme of the universe, but for a reason which others may accept willingly,—to wit, because however certain we may be that there is design in every portion of the universe, we are very far from being able to satisfy ourselves of the real purpose of any particular created object. Nevertheless, the mind of man is so constituted that it will inquire into final causes even where the inquiry may be hopeless, and will be ready to recognize final causes where, perhaps, the evidence is much less satisfactory than it appears. Now, certainly, it is natural for the astronomer to consider the moons of Jupiter and Saturn either as intended to subserve the same purpose as our own moon, *or* (if it can be shewn that they cannot subserve such a purpose) as created for some one or other of the special purposes which we seem to recognize among the celestial bodies of different orders. Taking Titan and Japetus as they are shewn to us by our telescopes—two orbs together equal in bulk to two such planets as Mercury—it is very difficult indeed to imagine that they subserve no useful purpose at all.

Now, if we consider the amount of light which Titan and Japetus can supply to their primary when they are 'full,' we shall, I think, be led to doubt whether they can have been intended to serve the same purpose as our Moon, and still less shall we be able to believe that they were meant, as Brewster and Chalmers have supposed, to compensate the Saturnians for their distance from the sun. Titan, when full, must appear to Saturn as an orb having somewhat less than two-thirds of our Moon's apparent diameter. Such an orb, if as bright (intrinsically) as our moon, would no doubt be a useful light-giver. But it must be remembered that the moons of Saturn, being as far from the Sun as Saturn is, are like him very faintly illuminated. They are illuminated by only about one-ninetieth part of the light which our Moon receives! accordingly, whereas the disc of Titan must be about four-ninths of our Moon's, the luminosity of this small disc is only one-ninetieth of our Moon's, so that the total quantity of light supplied by Titan to Saturn is only 4-810ths, or about a 200th part of that which we receive from the full moon.

This would seem to shew, at least to those who recognize design in the works of the Almighty, that Titan was certainly not intended to serve the same purpose to Saturnians that our Moon serves to the inhabitants of earth.

But if this seems strongly shewn in the case of Titan, it is much more strongly shewn in the case of Japetus. For Japetus is smaller than Titan, and almost exactly three times as far away. As a moon, it has a diameter equal to little more than one-seventh of our Moon's. The disc it shews is but about the forty-third of our Moon's, and its lustre being one-ninetieth (like Titan's), the total quantity of light which it supplies to its primary is only equal to about the 3850th part of that which we receive from the full moon. It may readily be shewn, indeed, that our Earth supplies more than eight times as much light to the planet Venus (when our Earth is seen at her brightest from Venus) as Japetus supplies to its primary.

In passing we may notice that another satellite called Hyperion—between Titan and Japetus—is so much smaller than Japetus (though probably about a thousand miles in diameter) as to supply less than half as much light to Saturn, probably about 1-9000th part of the light which we receive from the Moon.

Thus we seem led to the conclusion that *these* moons, at any rate, are not intended to compensate the Saturnians for their great distance from the Sun. That three orbs should have been created, to supply together about the 200th part of the light which our Moon supplies, and that this provision should have been intended to compensate the Saturnians for the circumstance that they get from the Sun only about one-ninetieth part of the light which we receive, are propositions too improbable, as it seems to me, to be reasonably entertained. When it is added, that all the eight Saturnian moons together would supply—if all full together—only about the sixteenth part of the light which we receive from the full moon, it seems abundantly demonstrated, I conceive, that whatever purpose the Saturnian satellite-system was intended to subserve, it was *not* intended to compensate the Saturnians for the effects of their great distance from the great centre and luminary of the planetary system.

On December 23, 1672, Cassini discovered a satellite

travelling within the orbit of Titan; and in March, 1684, he discovered two other satellites travelling yet nearer to Saturn. It affords striking evidence of the patience with which these astronomers of the seventeenth century worked, that in order to discover these two satellites Cassini had to employ telescopes one hundred and one hundred and thirty-six feet long (without tubes, however). In other words, the distance of the object-glass from the observer's eye was more than twice as great as the length of the gigantic tube of the Rosse telescope. Observing under such conditions must have been the most tedious work conceivable. It would be exceedingly difficult to get an object into the field of view, and even more difficult to keep it there. The modern observer, who, with well appointed equatorial, has but to set his telescope by the divided circles, and can then by setting the clock going, be saved all further trouble—the telescope simply travelling after the object by means of the clock-motion—may look with some degree of contempt on the rough appliances of his predecessors: yet he has so much the better reason for looking with cordial admiration on the patient and zealous spirit with which the astronomers of former times conducted their labours.

More than a century passed before any further discovery of importance was effected. On August 19th, 1787, Sir W. Herschel thought he could recognise a sixth satellite travelling very close to Saturn's rings. But it was not until he had completed his forty-feet reflector that he could assure himself on this point. On August 27th, 1789, the first evening after this powerful instrument had been completed, Herschel turned it towards Saturn. As soon as the planet was brought into the field he plainly perceived six stars shining around Saturn. Five of these were the satellites already discovered; and in less than two and a half hours Herschel had satisfied himself that the sixth was also a satellite.* Soon after Herschel discovered a seventh satellite, travelling yet closer to the outer ring.

It remains only to be mentioned, in order to complete the record of satellite discovery, that an eighth satellite, travelling between the paths of Titan and Japetus, was discovered independently by Bond in America, and Lassell in England. It is probably the smallest of the whole family; and there is something so remarkable in the circumstance that this tiny orb should thus be found travelling between the two giant satellites, Titan and Japetus, that we may almost be permitted to entertain the suspicion that in reality Hyperion is but one of a ring of small satellites travelling between the orbits of Titan and Japetus.

Before returning to the consideration of the Saturnian

---

* It has been asserted that the sixth satellite was discovered with one of the twenty-feet reflectors, and Sir John Herschel has been quite seriously taken to task for maintaining that the discovery was due to the forty-feet telescope. The above are the actual circumstances, as recorded by Sir W. Herschel himself. It seems wholly impossible to regard the doubtful view which he obtained in 1787 as the actual discovery of the satellite. According to all the rules usually adopted in these cases, the true discovery dates from those two and a half hours of observation, during which Herschel first satisfied himself that the faint speck of light near Saturn was not a fixed star.

rings, it may be well for us to consider the nature of Saturn's family of satellites. We have in this scheme what may be regarded as no inaccurate picture, in miniature, of the Solar System itself. Of course, there are differences in points of detail, since Nature does not repeat herself detail for detail in such cases. Yet we find some striking features of resemblance. Thus the Sun's family consists of eight members, and so also does Saturn's. Among the planets there are two which are prominent among the rest by their great bulk; and in Saturn's family we find also Titan which we can compare with Jupiter, and Japetus which we can compare with Saturn.

Certainly, if we consider what the Saturnian satellite family really is, that the orbs composing it are all large in reality, however minute they may appear either when viewed with the telescope or when considered with reference to such orbs as Jupiter or Saturn; that the span of the complete system is no less than 4,400,000 miles, or more than five times the Sun's diameter; that even Japetus, which moves the slowest, circles on his orbits with a rapidity which exceeds a hundred-fold the velocity of our swiftest express trains—we cannot but regard this system of secondary orbs as a most important portion of the scheme ruled over by the Sun. If we are compelled to believe that the purpose intended to be fulfilled by these bodies is not the illumination of the Saturnian nights— and for my own part I can arrive at no other conclusion— we seem bound to believe that they were created for some other purpose of importance. It does not seem at all unlikely, on this view of the subject, that they are themselves the abodes of living creatures of various orders. I have before shewn reasons for believing that Saturn may be a source whence heat is supplied to these eight orbs, whereas it seems unlikely that he is himself a world fit to be the abode of living creatures. Again, though the satellites supply Saturn with very little light, yet they are capable of supplying each other with no inconsiderable amount, and must frequently present phenomena of great beauty and interest as viewed from each other. Thus a variety of reasons suggest the probability that we are to look among the Saturnian satellites, and not to Saturn himself, for places fit to be the abodes of living creatures.

We have seen that in the latter half of the seventeenth century Saturn's ring had been found to be divided. Sir W. Herschel, notwithstanding the great telescopic power which he applied to the examination of the rings, was unable to do more than satisfy himself of the existence of the great division. It was suspected in his day that other divisions exist,—not that any had been seen, but that the discussion of the nature of the ring-system had led to the inference that it must consist of many distinct rings. But Herschel could not detect signs of the existence of any other divisions than the great one.

But during the present century many skilful observers have recognized other divisions. One such division separates the outer ring into two of nearly equal width. This division seems to be permanent; but it is most difficult of detection, and can only be seen with telescopes of the first quality and on nights when the atmospheric conditions are very favourable. Other traces of division have not continued to be recognizable, and are therefore probably not permanent. It has been remarked that "if each division thus detected were considered as a satisfactory indication of a permanent division through a complete circumference, it would follow that the system consists not of two or three, but rather of thirty or forty concentric rings. Strange as such a conclusion might appear, and manifold as are the conditions of instability the complexity of such a system would introduce, we should have no resource (on the assumption of the solidity of the rings) but either to accept this solution of the question, or to reject the testimony of most accurate and skilful observers—of such men as Encke, the Struves, Captain Kater and Jacob, Mr. Dawes, and the astronomers of the Collegio Romano. The telescopes also through which such divisions have been repeatedly seen, have been among the most celebrated instruments of modern times."

But the most singular discovery yet made respecting this remarkable ring-system remains to be described. On November 15th, 1850, Bond, of America, discovered a dark ring inside the inner bright one; and a few days later Dawes, in England, independently discovered this ring. The colour of the dark ring is a deep purple; or rather, since, as we shall presently see, the ring is semi-transparent, and therefore a portion of its apparent colour is that which it transmits, we may say, without committing ourselves to any theory as to the true seat of the colour, that the region occupied by the ring presents a deep purple colour. The nearer part of the dark ring can be traced over the disc of the planet, but the outline of the planet can be recognized *through* the ring. This portion of the ring does not shew a purple tinge, but has been compared to a crape veil. A division has at times appeared in the dark ring, which also appears at times to be separated from the neighbouring bright ring.

Professor Bond, of America, noticed at about the same time a very remarkable darkening of the inner bright ring, on its inner edge, close to the dark ring. The peculiarity about this darkening was, that instead of being exactly similar in shape to the outlines of the several rings, its outline formed a longer oval, as though the darkened part were wider in those places which lie upon the seeming longer axis of the rings. If the rings were *really* oval, as they appear through the effects of foreshortening, this peculiarity would be explicable; but as the rings are circular, and every part in turn comes into the position indicated, for the rings rotate and moreover Saturn himself carries them into varying positions as seen from the Earth, the appearance is altogether inexplicable as a mere shade or darkening. If, between the bright ring and the dark ring, there were a ring of an intermediate tint, that ring, being concentric with the others (else it could not rotate), would present similar outlines, whether the whole system were more or less foreshortened. This not being the case, one outline of the darkened part being always more elliptical than the other, we must, in explaining the darkening, find an interpretation which will explain this peculiarity. I believe the explanation enforced upon us by this consideration, is simply that the inner part of the bright ring is transparent, or rather, that we can see through this part, for, as will presently appear, we have no reason for believing that the actual substance of any part of the ring-system is transparent in the same sense that glass or crystal is transparent. I have shewn in my treatise on Saturn that if the inner part of the bright ring consists of a multitude of concentric zones between which the dark sky beyond can be seen from our terrestial station, the observed appearances would necessarily be seen. The explanation, to be adequately understood, requires such an illustration as is given in the ninth plate of that work; but its general principle may be understood by any one accustomed to drawing, who will attend to the following description. Suppose several white hoops to be lying one within the other (and quite concentrically) on a dark flat surface; the hoops being not shaped like those used by girls, but like the iron hoops which boys use. (A piece of cane bent into a circle would make such a hoop.) Now, if we looked at such a set of hoops from above, we should see so many white concentric circles on a dark ground. But let the point of view be not directly above, so that we look slantwise at the set of hoops. Then we shall see a number of similar white ovals on a dark ground. Now, if these ovals were mere oval *lines*, that is if the hoops were mere threads, the dark spaces between them would seem to grow narrow where the ovals were narrowed, and in just the same degree; but as the ovals are formed by stout hoops the case is altered, the dark spaces are *more* narrowed where the ovals are flattened. Nay, if the hoops are pretty close to each other, a very little foreshortening will make them seem actually to touch where the ovals are flattened, while where the ovals are lengthened out the dark background is visible. (If the reader will draw such a set of hoops, as they would actually be seen, he will at once perceive that this is so.) Now, without supposing that the rings of Saturn are composed of such hoops, I find myself led to the conclusion that the matter forming the rings runs into hoop-like shapes, and that where Bond saw the darkening, above described, these hoop-formed portions were far enough apart to let the dark sky beyond be seen where the ovals of the rings were most lengthened, the spaces closing up by foreshortening where these ovals were most narrowed. It is demonstrable, indeed, that, if the appearance observed by Professor Bond was not a mere illusion (which in the case of so practised an observer is altogether unlikely), it can be explained in this way and no other. So that the peculiar darkening seen by Bond is an independent proof of the multiple nature of the ring-system—a proof as complete as though Bond's telescope had been powerful enough to reveal the several rings forming this part of the bright inner ring.

Saturn's ring-system, regarded as a whole, is a structure so remarkable that we seem invited to consider it with a special degree of attention, in order that if possible we may form some idea of its real nature. If there were no other circumstance remarkable about it but its mere vastness, it would even then be well deserving of our closest scrutiny. But that a ring system so symmetrical and beautiful should girdle a planet completely about, that it should accompany the planet on its path around the Sun, that it should be as definite a portion of the planet's system as the belts on the planet's real globe, or as the satellites which circle about that orb, these are circumstances which render the study of the ring-system specially interesting. For we cannot but recognize the fact that such a system, swayed as it must be by the mighty attraction of Saturn's mass, must present a number of relations of a very complex and perplexing kind.

Let us in the first place briefly consider the dimensions of the rings and of the globe round which they circle.

Saturn's globe is somewhat compressed, its greatest diameter being 73,000 miles, its least diameter 66,000 miles. Remembering that the Earth's mean diameter is about 7900 miles, we see how vastly the planet exceeds the Earth in volume. Roughly the volume of Saturn is seven hundred times that of the Earth, his mass about ninety times the Earth's, for the materials of which he is constructed are on the average of much smaller specific gravity than those forming the Earth's globe.

The utmost span of the rings—that is, the diameter of the outer boundary of the outer ring—is about 167,000 miles, the breadth of this ring about 10,000 miles. The great division between the rings has a width of about 1600 miles. The inner bright ring has a breadth of about 17,500 miles, and the dark ring is about 8500 miles wide. If we add together those breadths, we find for the width of the entire system 37,600 miles, or rather more than half the equatorial diameter of the planet. The inner diameter of the system of rings—that is, the diameter of the inner boundary of the inner ring, is therefore about 91,800 miles; and a space of about 9400 miles intervenes between the dark ring and the body of the planet. The thickness of the ring-system has not been satisfactorily determined. It is probably less, perhaps very much less, than one hundred miles.

Now it would obviously be impossible to consider here at length the reasoning which has been applied to ascertain the nature of the rings. This subject alone forms in my treatise on Saturn a chapter nearly twice as long as the whole of the present essay; yet only those parts of the subject are there treated which are suitable for the general reader. Here then I must give the merest sketch of the matter.

Before the subject was treated by the mathematician, many singular theories were suggested concerning the rings. Maupertuis thought that the tail of a comet passing near Saturn had been attracted from its course by the planet's mass, and has since continued to circle as a ring around Saturn. Buffon considered that the equator of Saturn must once have extended to the outer edge of the ring, and that the equatorial portion was thrown off by the centrifugal force (that imaginary force which has been the parent of so many unphilosophical fancies) while the rest of the planet has contracted to its present dimensions. Mairan entertained a view somewhat resembling Buffon's; he supposed that the rings are the remains of outer shells formerly existing around Saturn, which have been broken up by some vast convulsion.

But when mathematicians had obtained some degree of mastery over the problems suggested by the action of gravity—in particular when they had begun to recognize how the peculiarities of the Moon's motion are accounted for by the law of gravitation—they began to inquire into a number of other problems of the same sort. Amongst these, the questions suggested by the Saturnian rings come naturally to be dealt with.

Let it be remembered that in considering the Moon's motions the mathematician has to shew how the various influences exerted upon her, cause the Moon to travel on a path continually varying in shape and position, her own motion in this path being also variable. And mathematicians had satisfied themselves that in whatever way the Moon's motions may be thus affected, there is no risk whatever that she will be so perturbed on her path as to come into collision with the Earth at any future time. In the case of Saturn's rings the mathematician had to inquire how, supposing these rings to be solid formations, they circle as they do around Saturn; and whether solid rings so circling would be safe from destruction.

The great mathematician Laplace, who was the first to

deal successfully with this problem, arrived at the conclusion that the two great rings known in his day cannot possibly be two solid rings. He shewed that they must be divided into several rings, otherwise they could not continue to circle safely, as they do, around the planet's globe. But he shewed that another very strange relation must hold, in the case of each member of this multiple ring-system. Every single ring must be eccentrically weighted. A perfectly uniform ring would be soon destroyed by the attractions to which it would be subjected.

There for awhile the problem rested. But when the dark ring was discovered, mathematicians again began to examine the subject. For the transparency of this ring suggested the idea that it, at least, might be a fluid ring. Professors Bond and Pierce in America discussed the chances which a fluid ring would have of continuing to circle safely around so mighty an attracting body as Saturn. In discussing this matter, Professor Pierce had to go over the same ground as Laplace; and pushing his inquiries further, (which he was enabled to do by the great advance which had in the interval taken place in the mastery of such mathematical problems as were involved) he found that the ring-system must be composed of many more rings than even Laplace had imagined.

On March 23rd, 1855, the subject of the Saturnian ring-system (in the particular mathematical aspect we have spoken of) was chosen by the University of Cambridge as the subject of the Adams Prize Essay. In 1857 the prize was adjudged to Professor J. Clerk Maxwell. He shewed that the eccentricity indicated by Laplace as a necessary feature of the structure of each ring, must be so considerable, that the ring-system could not possibly appear as it actually does. Moreover, the slightest cause would be sufficient 'to destroy the nice adjustment of the load, and with it the stability of the ring.'

Next, Professor Maxwell also discussed the probability that the rings may be fluid. He found that oceanic rings poised in mid-space around a mighty attracting mass like Saturn, would inevitably be wave-tossed, and that the waves would so increase that the rings would be broken up into separate fluid masses.

We thus see that an inquiry instituted with the object of explaining how solid continuous rings could be maintained, as the Saturnian rings manifestly are maintained, about a vast and massive central orb, ended in demonstrating that the rings are not continuous, but must consist at present—even if they have not consisted always —of a multitude of separate bodies, which may be either solid or fluid. Of course there is nothing in this conclusion to prevent us from believing that the rings may be partly vaporous.

But a rather singular result appears to follow from the inquiries which Professor Maxwell further instituted into the conditions under which rings of satellites would exist. He finds reasons for believing that such rings would gradually grow wider, by an extension inwards, and thus be eventually though very slowly (and perhaps not completely) destroyed. It certainly seems reasonable to believe that in the dark ring we have evidence that some such process is actually taking place. For, though we find that this ring must have been in existence long before it was discovered, (indeed many hundreds of years must needs have been required for the formation of so vast a ring), yet it is very difficult to believe that it can have been so conspicuous when Herschel examined Saturn with his great reflectors as it is at the present time. He could scarcely have overlooked the part which shows outside the planet's disc, had this been the case, for now under favourable atmospheric conditions this part can be seen with a four-inch telescope. Nor is it at all likely that he would, in that case, have mistaken the part which extends across the disc for a dark belt on Saturn, as actually happened. It seems almost certain, then, that during the last sixty or seventy years this dark ring has been continually growing more and more conspicuous—in other words, that it has been growing wider, and that more and more satellites of the uncounted millions forming the ring-system, have been compelled to take up their abode within the domain of this particular ring.

It is a circumstance well worthy of attention that the great division between the rings, instead of being black as it was formerly supposed to be, is found to be merely very dark brown or brownish purple. This shews that within the zone (1500 miles wide) which forms this division there must be at all times many satellites, perhaps stragglers from those belonging to the adjacent bright rings.

Another very singular circumstance has been noticed when the rings have been turned edgewise. At this time the fine bright line forming the side-view of the ring-system has been seen to be bordered by a faint misty light, growing more conspicuous towards the inner edge of the ring-system. It has been inferred, and the inference seems just, that this appearance is caused by satellites travelling (either through perturbations or from the effects of collisions) above or below the general level of the ring-system.

This essay has already extended to a greater length than I had proposed when I began; and I must refrain from entering into any general consideration of the ring-system regarded as a Saturnian appendage. I shall merely remark, therefore, that I have been able to shew by a careful mathematical examination of the subject, the results of which are presented pictorially and tabularly in my treatise on Saturn, that the shadows thrown by the rings must cover wide Saturnian regions for many years continuously, and this in the very heart of the Saturnian winter. Thus in Saturnian latitude 40°, corresponding to the latitude of Madrid on our earth, the sun begins to be eclipsed about three years after the autumnal equinox.* For a while there are only morning and evening eclipses —that is, the days already shortening with the approach of winter are still further shortened by eclipses caused by

---

* It will be remembered that the Saturnian seasons are more than seven years in length, and that from the autumnal to the vernal equinox is a period of nearly fifteen years.

the rings. These morning and evening eclipses gradually grow longer and longer, until about a year has passed, by which time they last through the whole of the Saturnian day, now transformed to night. This state of things continues for nearly seven years—more exactly (according to my calculations) for six years 236 days—during the whole of which time the sun is altogether concealed from view, unless now and then for a moment he can be partly seen between the satellites which compose the rings. From the blackness of the shadow thrown by the rings, however, it is very unlikely that gaps through which the sun may thus be seen are at all common. After these $6\frac{3}{8}$ years of what must be regarded as practically total eclipse, the morning and evening eclipses begin again, and gradually last for a shorter and shorter time, until about three years before the vernal equinox. Then for about twenty years, which includes the long Saturnian summer, the sun is not eclipsed by the rings; moreover, as he begins to illuminate the visible side of the rings, at the Saturnian vernal equinox, it follows that during the Saturnian summer nights the ring appears as a band of brightness on the Saturnian sky, except where the broad shadow of the planet falls upon it.

The circumstances here considered seem to accord with what has been already noticed in the case of the satellites. The ring-system does not seem calculated to render Saturn's globe a more convenient place for living creatures. On the contrary, a portion of that small supply of light which Saturn receives from the Sun is intercepted by the rings precisely at the period when, according to our ideas, it would be most desirable that the supply would be increased; while again throughout the Saturnian winter nights the ring-system supplies no light whatever, but blots out many hundreds of stars from view.

The just inference would appear to be that either Saturn is altogether uninhabited, or that the creatures inhabiting the planet are so different from any with which we are acquainted, that we can form no estimate of their requirements. To use Sir John Herschel's words, " We shall do wrong to judge of the fitness or unfitness of their condition from what we see around us, when perhaps the very combinations which convey to our minds only images of horror, may be in reality theatres of the most striking and glorious displays of beneficent contrivance." I would venture to point out that the view which I advocated respecting Jupiter and Saturn in the "Expanse of Heaven," would at once remove all doubts as to the beneficence of the arrangements described above. If Saturn is a secondary sun to his satellites, the ring-system would not only interfere in no way with his action in this respect, but might well be the very source whence a large part of Saturn's energy as a sun may be derived. The downfall of satellites from time to time out of the ring-system, after collisions or excessive perturbations, would at least be a source of heat not to be neglected in considering Saturn's position as a subordinate sun.

I shall draw this essay to a close by quoting a description of the colours observable in Saturn's system when suitable telescopic power is employed. It is from the pen of Mr Browning, the well-known optician. "The rings," he says," are yellow-ochre shaded with the same and sepia ; the globe, yellow-ochre and brown madder, orange and purple, shaded with sepia ; the crape-ring, purple madder and sepia ; the great division in the rings, sepia. The pole and the narrow belts, situated near to it on the globe, pale cobalt blue. These tints are the nearest I could find to represent those seen on the planet ; but there is a muddiness about all terrestrial colours, when compared with the colours of objects seen in the skies. These colours could not be seen in their brilliancy and purity, unless we could dip our pencil in a rainbow, and transfer the prismatic tints to our paper."

A GIANT SUN.

To those who are acquainted with the teachings of astronomy respecting the mighty ruler of our planetary scheme, the title of this essay may appear strange. For assuredly our sun must himself be considered as a giant orb—giant in size, as Sir John Herschel says in his charming "Familiar Lectures," and giant in strength, but withal a benevolent giant, being "the almoner of the Almighty, the delegated dispenser to us of light and warmth, the immediate source of all our comforts, and indeed of the very possibility of our existence." How, then, it may be asked, can any other orb be called by way of distinction a giant sun, as though the sun which rules our day were but a dwarf? It seemed fitting that, in speaking of Jupiter in the "Expanse of Heaven," I should describe his mighty orb as a miniature sun; for vast as is the bulk of Jupiter, he seems dwarfed into insignificance when compared with the sun's inconceivably magnificent globe. A thousand Jupiters would not make up the volume of the sun, nor would the mass of a thousand Jupiters outweigh his, if masses so mighty could be balanced against each other. But to speak of any other orb as a giant sun, would seem to imply that there exists in the universe a globe bearing

A Giant Sun.

some such relation to the sun as the sun bears to Jupiter, or Jupiter to the relatively minute orb on which we live.

Incredible as the idea of such a globe may be, however, it is with precisely such a globe that I propose now to deal. Mighty as is the orb of the sun, I am to speak of an orb more than a thousand times vaster. Grand as is the scheme ruled by the sun, and inconceivable as are the forces exerted by the sun upon the orbs which circle round him, I am to describe a sun which exerts forces many times more mighty on orbs which themselves probably exceed our sun in mass and volume. Magnificent as is the conception that our sun with his attendant family of planets is sweeping through space at the rate of two or three hundred miles in each minute of time, the sun of which I am about to write carries a far mightier train through space at a rate many times greater.

If the reader of these lines had turned his eyes towards the south at about nine o'clock on a clear evening in the beginning of Febuary 1871, he would have seen two orbs which far outshone all others in the heavens. High up in the sky, and not far from the twin stars, Castor and Pollux, the planet Jupiter was shining with a steadfast lustre which distinguished him almost as markedly as his superior brilliancy from all the stars in his vicinity. Low down and almost vertically beneath the kingly planet, was a star which, though not matching Jupiter in actual brilliancy, surpassed him in beauty. For this star—the famous Dog-star of the ancients—glows with a light which continually changes in apparent colour. At one moment it appears unmistakably red, at another a pure green, at another a sapphire blue—though these colours last but for an instant, while, during somewhat longer intervals, the light of the star is white. Poets in all ages have noticed this peculiarity of the light of Sirius, from Homer who compared the fiery lustre of the arms of Diomede with the splendour of the autumn star, "When new risen from the waves of ocean,"* to our poet-laureate, who sings of Arac and his brothers, that

> "As the fiery Sirius alters hue
> And bickers into red and emerald, shone
> Their morions, wash'd with morning, as they came."

It is difficult to conceive that this orb, brightly as it shines, so far surpasses in volume the magnificent planet which, in 1871, outshone it in the higher heavens, that the very drawing by which astronomers are in the habit of

---

* In the lines referred to Homer seems to describe Sirius as shining more brightly when newly-risen than at any other time; and a commentator remarks unhesitatingly, and as though recording some well-attested astronomical fact, that Sirius "shone brightest at its rising." I am not sure that the words of Homer will bear this interpretation, since the word translated "brightly" may equally bear the meaning "splendidly,"—that is, may not relate to the quantity of light actually received from the star, but to the beauty of the star's appearance. It is, of course, not the case that Sirius (either as seen here or in any country) shines most brightly when newly risen; though certainly the star appears more beautiful when near the horizon, its changes of colour being then better marked and succeeding each other more rapidly. A similar remark applies to Arcturus, Vega, and Capella, the three stars which come next to Sirius in brilliancy. Indeed the remark applies to all stars bright enough to shew well through the denser air close by the horizon.

indicating the insignificance of our earth compared with the sun, might be employed to indicate the inferiority of Jupiter as compared with Sirius. Yet even this fact (for such it is), amazing as it must appear, sinks into insignificance beside the fact that Sirius is a sun many times more splendid than our own. That beautiful star, which even in the most powerful telescope man can construct, appears as a mere point of light, is in reality a globe emitting so enormous a quantity of light and heat, that if it were to take the place of our sun every creature on this earth would be destroyed by its fiery rays.

Before proceeding to consider the discoveries relating to Sirius which have rewarded the labours of modern astronomers, it may be interesting to inquire briefly into the ideas of the ancients respecting this splendid orb—the more so that, if we are to accept the descriptions given by ancient writers as literally exact, we must conceive that the star has, during the last two thousand years, undergone a change of the most marvellous kind.

It is remarkable that the ancients should have regarded Sirius as comparable with the sun in regard to the influence which it exerts upon the earth. For instance, Sirius was supposed to produce the unhealthy weather prevalent in many parts of Italy during the autumnal months. Yet the influence of the star was not in all countries regarded as baneful; for the Egyptians ascribed the inundations of the Nile to Sirius, and were thus led to worship the star as a deity. The *dog-days* began at the part of the year when the star rose just as the sky was beginning to grow too bright for any stars to be seen. So that the mischievous effects assigned to these Canicular Days were associated, not with the time when the star shone most conspicuously at night, but with the season when it was known that Sirius was above the horizon in the day-time.

But if it is perplexing to understand how the ancients came to regard the rays of Sirius as thus potent, either for evil or for good, it is even more difficult to understand how Manilius was led to anticipate the results of modern astronomical research by boldly suggesting that Sirius is a sun comparable with our own in splendour. Sherburne thus translates the words of Manilius about Sirius:—

> " 'Tis strongly credited this owns a light
> And runs a course not than the sun's less bright,
> But that removed from sight so great a way
> It seems to cast a dim and weaker ray."

The question whether, as some suppose, Sirius has changed in colour since the days of the ancient astronomers, is of extreme interest and importance. Unfortunately the evidence is far from satisfactory. If the ancients had been a little more careful in describing the phenomena of the heavens, it is probable that many results which are at present being slowly evolved by careful and laborious observation, would admit of being at once and satisfactorily determined. Amongst these must be included the question whether any of the larger stars are changing in colour. Whatever changes are taking place are unquestionably slight, and proceed very slowly. They are therefore not easy to detect; for it is difficult to prove that the observer's estimate of colour has remained unchanged during the whole series of observations. The difficulty is still greater when different observers have been at work; for two persons can scarcely be found whose estimates of all hues and tints are exactly alike. But it is not impossible that in considerable intervals of time—for instance, in two thousand years—changes too marked to be thus misapprehended may take place. A star with a well-marked red or yellow tint may become white or green, or a white star may become ruddy or blue, and so on. So that if the ancients had left us a clear statement of the hues of all the leading stars, we might have been enabled to determine very satisfactorily whether any of these orbs had changed in colour or tint.

Now at a first view of the accounts given by the ancients respecting Sirius, it appears plain that the star must have changed in colour. At present Sirius, when high above the horizon (as seen, therefore, in southern latitudes), is unmistakably white. But Aratus and Ptolemy, Seneca and Cicero, Virgil, Horace, and Ovid, agree in using terms which, as ordinarily understood, imply redness or even a ruddy purple tint. Nay, Ptolemy says distinctly that Sirius was of the same colour as the star Antares (the Scorpion's Heart), now sometimes described as a *red* Sirius; and Seneca said that the redness of Sirius was more marked than that of Mars. But unfortunately we have no evidence to shew that the redness here referred to was other than that red lustre with which the star glows from time to time when near the horizon. If one of these authors had but stated what is the colour of Sirius when high enough above the horizon to shine without scintillation, it is probable that a conclusion, bearing most significantly not merely on questions respecting the stars, but on the condition of our own sun, would have been established. If we accept the conclusion that Sirius was a red star two thousand years ago, we cannot but look with some misgiving on the question whether our own sun may not one day change likewise in colour—a question of grave importance to the human race. For the colour of a sun is closely related to the quality of the rays which it emits. We receive at present from our sun, in certain proportions, rays which produce the effects of heat, and light, and chemical action; and these several effects correspond with the parts of the solar spectrum coloured, respectively, red, and yellow, and indigo. Or rather, the rays from the red and orange part of the solar spectrum are more heating than light-giving, and produce scarcely any chemical action whatever;* the rays from the orange-yellow, yellow and yellow-green part excite more light than heat or chemical action; and the rays from the blue, indigo, and violet

---

* The photographer takes advantage of this circumstance to obtain chemical darkness (so to speak) without the inconvenience of optical darkness. For by means of orange-coloured glass he can exclude all light which would produce the least change in his chemicals. Orange yellow hangings are as well suited as black hangings would be for a photographic dark room. It is owing to the same peculiarity that we are not always quite satisfied with the photographs of our ruddy cheeked children.

portion excite more chemical action than light, and scarcely any heat whatever. Hence, if our sun changed in colour, his rays would supply more heat or else produce a more intense chemical action than at present; and it is by no means clear that such a change would be advantageous to the inhabitants of this earth.

Before leaving this part of our subject, it may be mentioned, as bearing on the probability whether Sirius has changed in colour or not, that certain variable stars do change systematically in colour—though in a period so short, that they are somewhat removed from comparison with Sirius and his supposed change during the past two thousand years. The Wonderful Star (Mira) in the Whale becomes yellowish as it loses brightness, and as its lustre returns gradually resumes its whiteness.

Let us now turn, however, to the researches of modern astronomers into the nature and physical condition of this magnificent orb.

Owing to the superior brilliancy of Sirius, it was natural that astronomers should be led to regard this star as nearer to us than any other in the heavens. But Sirius is not well placed for observation from European stations, and accordingly when astronomers first attempted to estimate the distance of a fixed star, they did not select Sirius for the experiment. One notices in their remarks respecting Sirius, however, a sort of tacit assumption, that at whatever distance they might find any actually observed star to lie, Sirius must be regarded as at a less distance.

But as the great problem (the most difficult observational problem ever attacked by astronomers) began to be mastered, it was recognised that Sirius is by no means the nearest of the fixed stars. Nay, this general conclusion began to be recognised, that the brightness of a star is no sufficient criterion of relative proximity. The first star whose distance was actually determined was one which can only be just seen on clear moonless nights by persons having ordinary powers of eyesight. And though the star next dealt with (the nearest of all so far as is known) is a very brilliant orb, yet its lustre falls far short of that of Sirius. In fact, according to the first published estimate of the distance of Sirius there are three stars so minute as to be actually invisible to the unaided eye, which yet lie nearer to us than this brightest of all the fixed stars.

It would appear, however, from the careful researches applied to the matter in recent times, that the distance of Sirius had been over-estimated, and that as a matter of fact this star must be set third in order of distance,— among those stars at least whose distances astronomers have attempted to determine. According to these later estimates, while the distance of the nearest of all stars (so far as is known) must be set at some twenty-two millions of millions of miles, the distance of Sirius is about eighty millions of millions of miles.

I have spoken of the erroneous estimate of the distance of Sirius. It may be well, in passing, to consider the nature and extent of the probable error. We have heard no little astonishment expressed because astronomers have detected an error of some three millions of miles in their estimate of the sun's distance. It appears inexplicable to many that such an error as this is in reality altogether trivial—the real wonder being that astronomers should have come within several millions of miles of the truth. But if the error in the estimate of the sun's distance appears startling, what will be thought of an error which must be estimated by millions of millions of miles? Such, however, is the case as respects Sirius. If the estimate of the star's distance which formerly was accepted (and even now appears in many of the best astronomical treatises extant) were correct, the distance of Sirius would amount to about 130 millions of millions of miles; the corrected estimate is as above mentioned 80 millions of millions. The difference is some half a million times larger than the sun's distance from the earth.

It may be asked, then, by the reader, whether there must not have been some gross blundering on the part of astronomers. Nay, if unfamiliar with the actual nature of the problem which astronomers have had to deal with, he may even be disposed to believe that there is something after all in the outcry of those loud-voiced persons who denounce the Astronomer Royal and the Royal Observatory, and who assert that every shilling devoted by Government to the support of observational astronomy is thrown away. A few words of explanation, however, will probably remove this impression.

What the astronomer has to do in order to determine the distance of a star is to notice whether in the course of the year the star seems to shift its apparent place on the celestial sphere. The earth circuits her wide path round the sun once in each year, and therefore the astronomer really sees each star from a shifting point of view. So that each star must be really seen in different directions at different seasons of the year, only most of the stars are so far off that this change of direction is altogether inappreciable. In the case of Sirius the change is just appreciable and that is all that can be said. As Sir John Herschel has stated, "Sirius and Arcturus, the two brightest stars visible in our hemisphere, stand barely within the limits of any estimation approaching to certainty." The annual displacement of Sirius may be thus illustrated :—On a clear moonlight night let the reader notice the apparent diameter of the moon. Next let him try to conceive that diameter divided into about 3,800 equal parts. Then the greatest displacement of Sirius is equal to one of those minute portions. Sirius in fact appears to circle round a minute oval path on the heavens, having for its longest diameter a space equal to about the 3,800th part of the moon's apparent diameter. Now the error of the earlier estimate (supposing that estimate erroneous) consisted in setting the displacement of Sirius at about the 6,300th part of the moon's diameter,—the difference between the two estimates corresponding to about the 9,500th part of the moon's apparent diameter. If the reader will but conceive the moon's apparent diameter divided into about 100 parts, and one of these parts again into 100 parts, he will be able to form an idea of the exceeding minuteness of the quantity by which astronomers suppose that their first estimate was erroneous. But most probably the truth lies between the two estimates, so that the actual error of each is only about half this exceedingly minute quantity.*

Let us assume as the probable distance of Sirius, a value between those which have been mentioned above,— to wit, 100 millions of millions of miles.

If astronomers could measure the disc of Sirius, their knowledge of the star's distance would of course enable them at once to calculate the real diameter of the star. But in the most powerful telescope Sirius appears as little more than a mere point of light; and it is well known to astronomers that even the almost evanescent dimensions of the disc are not real, but merely optical. In fact, the

---

* It must be stated clearly, however, that though no discredit whatever can attach to astronomers for failing to determine exactly quantities which are in reality all but evanescent, yet no more reliance must be placed on the estimates of star-distances than shall appear to be justified by the accordance of different and independent determinations. In the present instance the results not being accordant, we cannot possibly admit that the distance of Sirius has been satisfactorily determined. A similar remark applies to the case of that star barely visible to the unaided eye, which I have mentioned as the nearest of all the stars in the northern heavens. The mean of the best recent observations differs markedly from the value which had been judged so trustworthy that Sir John Herschel quoted it with confidence in his "Outlines of Astronomy." The star has, in fact, been set at two-thirds of the distance formerly assigned to it. So long as such discrepancies exist we cannot speak with any confidence of a star's distance. But this very star is the nearest *but one* of all the stars astronomers have dealt with. So that the startling, but inevitable conclusion is deduced that there is *but one star* in the heavens of whose distance astronomers have any definite ideas. This star is the one known as Alpha Centauri; and hitherto all observations agree in placing it at about twenty-two millions of millions of miles from the earth.

more powerful and perfect the telescope the smaller does Sirius appear, though its light is greatly increased. Sir William Herschel tells us that "when Sirius was about to enter the field of view of his forty-feet reflector, the light resembled that which announces the approach of sunrise," and when the field of view was fairly entered "the star appeared in all the splendour of the rising sun, so that it was impossible to behold it without pain to the eye." In the great Rosse telescope Sirius blazes with an even greater splendour. Yet neither of these instruments could "raise a disc" on the star.

Nor need we wonder at this, if we consider the circumstances of the case. We have already seen that the wide sweep of the earth on her path causes Sirius to shift but by about the 5,000th part of the moon's apparent diameter (taking a quantity intermediate between the two values mentioned above). Now this signifies that, as seen from Sirius, the whole span of the earth's orbit—though upwards of 180,000,000 miles in extent—would be reduced to about the 5,000th part of the moon's apparent diameter. It follows of course that, as seen from the earth, a globe 180,000,000 miles in diameter, at the distance of Sirius, would be so reduced as to have an apparent diameter equal to about the 5,000th part of the moon's. Now enormous as is the bulk of Sirius, no astronomer supposes for an instant that the star is comparable to such a globe as I have here mentioned. Such a globe would have a diameter exceeding our sun's some 210 times, and therefore a volume exceeding his some 9,500,000 times, which is utterly incredible. Assigning to Sirius a diameter exceeding our sun's 10 times (and therefore a volume, exceeding his 1,000 times), it would result that, as seen from the earth, Sirius has an apparent diameter equal to less than the 100,000th part of the moon's; and no telescope in existence could show so minute a diameter as a real measurable quantity. The nominally available power of the great Rosse telescope (6,000) would, indeed, show Sirius with a diameter equal to about the 16th part of the moon's—a quantity which a good eye could appreciate in the case of a globe shining no more brightly than the moon does. But the intrinsic lustre of Sirius resembles that of the sun when shining in full splendour, and there is no man living who could recognise as a *disc* an orb shining as the sun does, but with an apparent diameter equal only to the 16th part of his.

How, then, it may be asked, can astronomers claim to know that Sirius is an orb exceeding our sun in magnitude?

Practically it is impossible for astronomers to determine the dimensions of Sirius; but by comparing the amount of light received from him with that received from our own sun, they can form tolerably safe conclusions as to the probable dimensions of the star. They have only to inquire how far from us our own sun should be placed in order to shine just as brightly as Sirius, and to compare that distance with the actual distance of Sirius, in order to infer whether the sun or Sirius is the larger orb, and by how much one exceeds the other.

The only estimate which need be here considered is

that which results from combining together the best modern estimate of the light of the full moon as compared with the sun's, and the best modern estimate of the light of Sirius as compared with that of the full moon. The former estimate is due to the indefatigable German light-student, Dr Zöllner; the latter we owe to Sir John Herschel, the estimate having been made during his stay at the Cape of Good Hope. According to these estimates the light of Sirius is such that some 4,200,000,000 of stars, each as bright as Sirius, would be required to supply as much light as we receive from the sun. Now the distance of the sun is about 91,500,000 of miles; and we have assigned as the most probable distance of Sirius 100 millions of millions: 100,000,000 contain $91\frac{1}{2}$ nearly 1,100,000 times and Sirius is *so* many times farther from us than the sun. So that the sun's light at the distance of Sirius would be reduced in the proportion of this number multiplied into itself or about 1,200,000 millions of times; and *so* many orbs as large and bright as the sun would be wanted at the distance of Sirius to supply the same amount of light as the sun actually supplies to us. We have seen, however, that only 4,200,000,000 orbs as large and bright as Sirius would be needed to that end. Hence the light of Sirius must exceed the light of the sun (at equal distances) in the same degree that 1,200,000 exceeds 4,200, or about 286 times. Assuming an equal degree of intrinsic brightness—so that a square mile of the surface of Sirius is supposed to give out as much light as a square mile of the sun's surface—it follows that at equal distances the disc of Sirius exceeds the disc of the sun 286 times in size, and that therefore the diameter of Sirius exceeds that of the sun 17 times. If this be the case—and this relation must *à priori* be regarded as more probable than any other—the bulk of Sirius exceeds that of the sun 4,860 times.

If I had adopted the earlier estimate of the distance of Sirius, I should have obtained the result that Sirius gives out 400 times as much light as the sun, and has a volume exceeding his 8,000 times. These are the values adopted by Sir John Herschel in his "Familiar Essays." On the other hand, by adopting the latest estimate of the distance of Sirius, I should have obtained (as in my "Other Worlds") the result that Sirius gives out 192 times as much light as the sun, and exceeds him 2,688 times in volume. It will be admitted that even this, the least of our estimates, is sufficiently stupendous to justify the title of the present paper.

The only circumstance which could excite doubt as to the justice of the inference that Sirius is a giant sun, would be the possibility that the star is not composed of the same materials—the same elements—as our sun. Were no evidence obtainable on this point, it might be questioned whether Sirius is not a brilliant light rather than a glowing body. Unphilosophical as the idea of light without a body in which the light is manifested may appear at the present day, yet not very many years ago it would have been held that the idea is admissible. Indeed Dr Whewell in his "Plurality of Worlds" definitely lays down the proposition that the size and mass of a star cannot safely be inferred from the quantity of light it emits. Now, however, apart from the known fact that light cannot exist or be sustained without the motion of material particles (so that the continuance of a mighty light implies the existence of a vast mass) we have distinct evidence respecting the constitution of many stars, Sirius being among the number. The spectrum of Sirius (that rainbow-tinted streak into which its light is spread out, so to speak, by means of the spectroscope) resembles that of our own sun in all essential respects, a circumstance showing that Sirius, like our sun, is a glowing mass, whose light before reaching us has passed through the vapours of many elements. Dr Huggins, our chief authority in such matters, speaks thus respecting Sirius:—"The spectrum of this brilliant white star is very intense; but owing to the star's low altitude, even when most favourably situated, the observation of the finer lines is rendered very difficult by the movements of the earth's atmosphere." Three if not four known elements can be recognised as existing in the atmosphere of Sirius, viz., hydrogen, iron, magnesium, and sodium. But doubtless many others could be identified but for the unfavourable circumstances mentioned by Dr Huggins, for he adds that "the whole spectrum is crossed by a very large number of faint and fine lines."

The study of Sirius by means of the spectroscope has led to a very remarkable discovery respecting the motion of this mighty orb. It had been already known that Sirius is in rapid motion through space; simply because astronomers could see that year by year the star is changing its position on the celestial sphere. I have spoken above of the minute change of place noted in the course of each year as the earth circuits round the sun; but the reader is not to infer that the star does not shew any signs of a real motion of its own. The astronomer, in looking for the small change of place repeated each year, does not allow his observations to be vitiated by a change (sometimes comparatively large) which continues progressively year after year. He makes a proper correction for the progressive change so as to be able to determine satisfactorily the amount of the recurrent change. In the case of Sirius, while the recurrent change is scarcely perceptible, even with the most delicate instruments, the progressive change is not only considerable enough to be detectible by its effects in a year, but as it accumulates year after year, the astronomer need only compare observations made at considerable intervals (as ten, fifty, or a hundred years) to ascertain the rate of apparent motion with any desired degree of accuracy. It chances, indeed, that the accounts left by ancient astronomers, rough though those accounts were, sufficed in the very infancy of modern exact astronomy to shew that Sirius is in motion; for Halley announced so far back as 1718 that Sirius must be held to be moving slowly southwards on the heavens, if the observations of the Alexandrian astronomers are to be accepted. The rate of this motion has since been determined with extreme exactness. It is such that in the course of about 1,433 years Sirius traverses a space equal to the apparent diameter of the moon, moving southwards and westwards on the heavens, the southwardly exceeding the westwardly motion in the proportion of about five to two. Now, since we know something about the star's distance, this result enables us to infer something as to the star's real rate of motion. The displacement is a reality, the star *must* be moving athwart the line of sight —either directly or on a slant course. The smallest velocity capable of explaining the displacement is that estimated on the supposition that the star is moving squarely across the line of sight. Now, it can easily be calculated that if this is the case, and the distance of the star equal to the greatest of the values mentioned above, then the star must be moving athwart the line of sight at the rate of nearly twenty-six miles in every second of time. On the other hand, supposing the true distance of the star to correspond to the later and smaller estimate above mentioned, the rate of motion is about fifteen miles in every second of time. Taking the mean value of the distance, we infer for the rate of motion athwart the line of sight, a velocity of no less than twenty miles per second.*

* Should any astronomical reader compare this paragraph with Dr. Huggins' remarks on the same subject in the *Philosophical Transactions for* 1868 (p.550), he will recognise some considerable discrepancies. These arise from the circumstance that Dr. Huggins (who treats of this matter only in passing) has by inadvertence taken the westwardly motion of Sirius at a fifteenth of its true value. This causes the value twenty-four miles per second to result where the above paragraph

So far all is simple enough. Direct observations of the plainest nature, applied on the most obvious principles, have told us all we require to know as to the displacement of Sirius on the heavens. But I have said that the spectroscope has given information respecting the motion of Sirius; and the account of this portion of the work relates to one of the most remarkable achievements of modern science.

We have seen that the actual displacement of Sirius on the heavens supplies no information whatever as to the direction in which he is crossing the line of sight. He may be moving directly or squarely across that line with the velocity above determined; but he may, on the contrary, be moving on a line greatly slanted with respect to the line of sight, and his real velocity may therefore be very much greater. In the latter case all that part of his velocity which tends to carry him either towards or from us must escape recognition by ordinary means. The case may be compared to that of a train bearing a light in the night-time. An observer of such a train can readily detect any motion which causes the light to be seen in a changing direction; but that part of the motion which brings the light nearer to him or removes it farther from him he cannot detect, except in so far as it causes the

mentions twenty-six miles per second. Then this velocity is increased to forty miles per second instead of being reduced to 13·3 miles per second, to correspond to the later or reduced estimate of the distance of Sirius. I mention these points, not to call attention to slips such as will continually occur in stating relations of the sort, but to prevent the reader from being in doubt as to where the truth lies.

light to appear larger or smaller than at first. Now no conceivable velocity of approach or recess in the case of Sirius would cause the star to appear appreciably brighter or fainter even in the course of hundreds of years. If we set the star's distance at a hundred millions of millions of miles, what effect can an approach or recession through even many hundreds of millions of miles produce on the star's apparent brightness? Nay, we can readily infer from the seeming displacement of the star how utterly ineffective any corresponding motion of approach or recess would be in affecting the star's light. We have seen that in 1,433 years the star shifts on the heavens by a space equal to the moon's apparent diameter. Now it follows from this that if the motion of recess or approach be as great as what may be termed the thwart motion, the distance of the star would change in 1,433 years in the proportion in which the distance of the farthest point of the moon's globe exceeds that of the nearest point, or about as 60 exceeds 59; the corresponding change of lustre, therefore, in that long interval of forty-three generations would be smaller than the most skilful astronomer could estimate, even though the change occurred within an hour—so that he could test the different degrees of lustre with one and the same telescope, and under like conditions of atmosphere, eyesight, and so on.

It is this apparently intractable problem, however—the problem of measuring the rate at which a star is approaching or receding—which the spectroscope has enabled men to solve. The actual principles on which the method of observation depends need not here be explained, because they have already been considered at some length in a paper entitled the "Gamut of Light," in my treatise, "Orbs around us." But I may so far recapitulate what I have there said, as to note that if we are approaching Sirius or receding from him, either through his motion or the sun's, or through the combined effects of both motions, the waves of light which travel to us from Sirius must appear shortened or lengthened, precisely as sea-waves would seem narrower or broader according as a swimmer travelled against or with their onward course. Now the light from a star contains all degrees of wave-length from the longest light-waves (which correspond to the red end of the spectrum) down to the shortest (which correspond to the violet end); so that amidst all these wave-lengths the observer could no more recognise such a change as would result from approach or recess than the swimmer of our illustrative case could recognise the apparent shortening or lengthening of waves in a storm-tost sea where waves of all dimensions were abroad. But if light-waves of any specified length can be in any way distinguished from the rest, the case (as respects them) corresponds to that of a swimmer crossing a long and uniform succession of rollers. Now the dark lines in the spectrum of a star, when they can be certainly identified with the lines belonging to the spectrum of some known element, supply this very knowledge of the true wave-lengths. Dr Huggins had identified certain very well marked lines in the spectrum of Sirius with the well-known lines of hydrogen. If he could find that these lines in the star's spectrum are measurably displaced either towards the red or the violet end of the spectrum, he could infer that the wave-lengths of the star's light are measurably lengthened or shortened through a recession or approach on the part of the star. This he actually effected. He found that one of the hydrogen lines of the star was displaced in such a way as to indicate a lengthening of the light-waves corresponding to a recession at the rate of forty-one miles per second. But a part of this recession was due to the earth's orbital motion at the time of observation, and another part is due to the sun's own motion through space. There remains, after these portions have been deducted, a motion of recession in space amounting to about twenty-six miles per second. This rate of motion—or rather a recession from the sun at the rate of twenty-nine miles per second—is absolute, not being affected in any way by our estimate of the distance of Sirius. Combining the recession in space with the estimated *thwart* motion of twenty miles per second, we deduce a real motion in space amounting to about thirty-three miles per second.*

But the circumstance which remains to be mentioned respecting Sirius before this paper is drawn to a conclusion, is perhaps more remarkable than any yet referred to.

* Of course the two motions must not be simply added together, since they are not in the same direction. The actual motion is represented by the diagonal of an oblong whose sides represent the motion of recession and the thwart motion.

When astronomers compared together the places of Sirius as recorded in a long series of observations, they found what appeared like a periodic displacement of the star. In the first instance, they had examined only the recorded positions of the star as respects east and west; and the observed displacement in this direction suggested that in reality Sirius is circling around another orb, or rather that Sirius and some other orb are circling around a common centre, in a period of fifty years. When it was found that the star appears to drift to north and south of its mean place in a manner according very closely with this hypothesis, astronomers naturally began to regard the theory as rendered highly probable by a coincidence which could scarcely be regarded as accidental.

But no star had been seen where this theory required that a star should be; and moreover the theory required an orb whose bulk should be about two-thirds of the enormous bulk of Sirius, and it was to be inferred that so large an orb would shine with a lustre comparable with that of Sirius himself. On this last point, however, it was well remarked that we have no sufficient reason for believing that all the orbs which people space are luminous. However, a search was instituted for the star which the theory seemed to require. Nor was the search unsuccessful. With a telescope $18\frac{1}{2}$ inches in aperture, made by himself, the eminent American optician, Alvan Clark, detected a faint star close by Sirius, apparently, though actually (on a moderate computation), at least 2,000 millions of miles from him. The movements of this star have been held by some astronomers to accord fairly with the requirements of the theory just mentioned; though I must admit that I fail to find a very close resemblance between the actual motion of the faint companion and those which the theory requires. But we now have a choice of disturbing companions, since the late Mr Goldsmidt (who far surpassed even our own "eagle-eyed Dawes" in keenness of vision) not only saw Clark's star with a telescope only four inches in aperture, but actually succeeded in detecting five other companion stars.

We can best explain the faintness of these stars by supposing that they are opaque bodies which shine only by reflecting the light which they receive from their sun Sirius. But if so, they must be globes of enormous real dimensions, the least of them probably exceeding our own sun many times in volume, while the greatest (so we may conclude from the disturbance Sirius himself undergoes) must be so large and massive that a thousand such orbs as our sun would not equal it either in bulk or mass. We have here, then, a system differing altogether in character from our solar system, the largest member of which is but equal in mass to about the 1,300th part of the sun. The complete Sirian system, may even outweigh Sirius himself, and its mass added to his must exert an attractive influence throughout an enormous portion of the stellar system. It would seem, indeed, not wholly impossible that Sirius holds a higher rank in the scale of creation that our sun and other similar orbs—that compared with him these are as secondary orbs compared with primaries.

Without insisting on this, however, we may assert with confidence that whether we consider his volume, his bulk, or the mighty energy evidenced by his brightness, Sirius well merits the title under which he has been here described. Of all the orbs with which astronomers have to deal, he seems worthiest to be called *par excellence* the giant sun.

THE STAR-DEPTHS.

THE awe with which the thoughtful student of astronomy in our day contemplates the star-depths can scarcely exceed the simple wonder of the Chaldæan herdsman, who gazed on the mysterious vault of heaven and watched the constellations as they passed with stately motion along their nocturnal arcs. Brought up from our youth to regard the fixed stars as the peers of our own sun, and the sun as an orb exceeding more than a million times in volume this earth on which we live, the grandeur of these conceptions is yet in part marred by their familiarity. The ancient astronomer, even though he might believe, with Aristarchus of Samos, that the stars are golden studs upon the crystal dome of heaven, and the sun scarce larger than the Peloponnesus, must yet have been penetrated with a profound sense of the mystery surrounding all he saw. We have learned so much, that we are apt to feel as though all knowledge were within our grasp. The orbs of heaven have been weighed and analyzed, they have been tracked on orbital paths around each other, they have been counted and gauged and charted, until it would seem as though their domain had been completely explored and mastered. It was not so with the ancients. They might guess and theorize, but they *knew* scarce anything of the stars. And out of their want of knowledge sprang a sense of awe, which probably surpassed in intensity the feeling with which even the most thoughtful astronomers of our own day regard the orbs tenanting the depths of heaven.

It is my purpose in the present paper to attempt to restore to the sidereal system something of that mystery which pervaded it of old. I wish to shew that some, at least, of those views which had seemed most thoroughly established, have but a slight foundation, if any, on which to rest; and that so far from having penetrated the secret of the star-depths, we stand as yet but on the threshold of that mighty domain which belongs to the astronomy of the future.

Since the establishment of the Copernican theory, the extension of the sidereal system as recognized by astronomers, has been progressively increasing. I do not refer here merely to the increase of telescopic power, and the corresponding increase of the range of astronomical vision. That increase of range could only tell us what might readily have been guessed without it—namely, that the vast spaces which lie beyond the range of any given telescopic power are not untenanted by stars. But the feature to which I would especially invite attention is the increase of the estimated scale on which the sidereal system is built,—the increase in our estimate of the size and brightness of individual orbs, and the yet more surprising increase in our estimate of the distances which separate orb from orb.

The first step in this progress was the most remarkable of all. It was very justly urged by Tycho Brahé, that, if the Copernican theory were true, the stars must be regarded as immensely more distant than astronomers had ever ventured to imagine. Tycho Brahé did not, indeed, know how far the Earth actually is from the Sun; but he knew that the extent of her orbit or of the Sun's orbit, according as the Sun or the Earth is fixed, must be measured by millions of miles. "Is it credible," he asked, "that although moving in an orbit so enormous in extent, the Earth as seen from the nearest star would seem absolutely unchanged in position?" Yet this must be the case if the Copernican theory be true. For not one of the stars seems to move, as the Earth completes the circuit spoken of by Copernicus; and if no star moves as seen from the Earth, the Earth must appear at rest as seen from each star in the heavens. Each star must therefore lie at so enormous a distance, that the wide extent of the Earth's orbit is reduced to a mere point. "Such a conception," Tycho reasoned, "seems wholly inadmissible; and therefore the Copernican theory must be erroneous."

This reasoning was valid, although the conclusion was incorrect. We must not class the objections urged by Tycho Brahé against the Copernican system, with those unmeaning arguments by means of which the Ptolemaists had long defended their position. Undoubtedly the conclusion that the stars are suns comparable in splendour with our own, was not one to be lightly accepted. And yet no other conclusion could be adopted, if the motion of the Earth around the Sun were once admitted. We have just seen that the Earth's orbit, viewed from each of the fixed stars, would be reduced to a mere point. The Sun, then, which lies within that orbit, and whose relative dimensions were perfectly well known even in Tycho's time, would *à fortiori* be but a point as seen from even the nearest of the stars. If he were visible at all, it would merely be on account of the enormous intrinsic brilliancy of his light. But the stars are points of light, and the intrinsic brilliancy of *their* light also must be enormous, in order that they may be barely visible. Their seeming minuteness is at once seen to be no proof of real minuteness, when the fact is recognized that the Sun would appear at least as minute if viewed from the neighbourhood of a fixed star.

The mistake of Tycho Brahé consisted in his failing to consider that the whole question was one of evidence. If Copernicus and his followers could prove their case, any conclusions legitimately deducible were to be accepted, without any reference to the startling character of the views they might point to. When Tycho began to see the heavens opening out before him, and all the stars taking rank as suns, the blaze of splendour was too fierce—his mental vision was unprepared to contemplate so glorious a display, and he would fain have dropped a veil over that unbearable effulgence.

But the men who followed him were more daring.

Boldly grasping the weapons which Tycho Brahé had collected for an attack upon the Copernican theory, they turned those weapons against the Ptolemaists. Seizing the only available vantage-ground—that one peculiarity of the Solar System, without which the theories of Newton himself would never, in all probability, have had existence—the great astronomer Kepler found in the seemingly capricious motions of the planet Mars the means of abolishing at once and for ever the 'cycles and epicycles,' the 'centrics and eccentrics,' in which astronomers had so long put faith. Then Newton pushed the attack yet farther, setting forth the real significance of those laws which, in Kepler's hands, had seemed empirical. And lastly, one proof followed after another, until the new theories had become so firmly established that no one who comprehends their position has since ventured to attack them.

But in the meantime, while the confirmation of the Copernican theory was demonstrating as real those wonders at which Tycho Brahé had stood appalled, fresh light was thrown on the real dimensions of the universe of stars. For it was found, as research after research was directed to the point, that the Sun's distance had been hugely underrated, and that therefore even Tycho's estimate of the stars' distances and dimensions, according to the Copernican theory, fell far short of the truth. More and more scrutinizingly astronomers searched the evidence bearing on the subject of the Sun's distance; wider and wider grew the limits beyond which they proved that that distance must lie; but as yet they could find no sign *how far* those limits were exceeded. From a few millions of miles the estimated distance had grown to tens of millions—forty, fifty, eighty millions. At length the limit was nearly reached, and for the first time in the history of science men were able to say, *not*, as hitherto, that the Sun's distance certainly exceeds such and such a number of miles, but that it approaches, more or less closely, to such and such a value.

The first rough estimate set the Sun's distance between eighty and one hundred millions of miles. Gradually obtaining better and better means of measuring the vast gulf which separates us from our ruling luminary, astronomers have found 91,500,000 to represent, with sufficient accuracy, that enormous distance. Precisely as the estimate of the Sun's distance in Tycho Brahé's day had thus been enlarged, so had his estimate of the distances which separate the stars from us been overpassed, enormous and even inconceivable as he had deemed them.

It is this great fact, then, that I take as chief guide in passing beyond the limits of the Solar System to survey the star-depths; the fact, namely, that seen from the nearest fixed star the Earth's orbit, though more than 180 millions of miles in diameter, is reduced to dimensions absolutely inappreciable by all ordinary modes of measurement. Let the reader turn, on any clear night, to the constellation of the Great Bear, and let him regard the middle star of the Bear's curved tail—the middle horse of those three which are supposed to draw the celestial Plough. Close by that orb he will see a faint orb, which was known in old times as "Jack by the middle horse." It would be a fact altogether amazing in its significance, if the wide sweep of the Earth's path round the Sun were, at the distance of the nearest star, reduced to a circle of diameter seemingly no greater than the distance separating these two orbs, which appear to lie so close together on the celestial sphere. But that tiny distance exceeds five hundred times the apparent diameter of the Earth's path, as it would appear if it could be viewed from the nearest star, Alpha of the Centaur.

Even the mighty instruments of our own day, wielded with all the skill and acumen which a long experience has generated, have not sufficed to enable us to measure the distances of more than about a dozen stars. Nor probably will it ever be possible for man to count by the hundred the number of stars whose distances are known. Of all the millions of stars revealed by the telescope, not the ten-thousandth part will have their true position *in space* assigned to them, however roughly. The real architecture of the stellar system must remain for ever unknown to us, except as respects a relatively minute portion, lying within certain limits of distance from the Earth.

But while the direct measurement of the star-depths is thus out of our power, we are able, by carefully studying the scene presented to us, to learn much respecting the way in which the sidereal system is constructed, and also respecting the nature of the bodies which compose that system.

In the first place, we have, in the movements of the stars, a means of estimating certain general relations; and in particular, of determining whether, as had been supposed, the apparent brightness of the stars is likely to afford a good general test of their distance.

It will be clear that if two stars are travelling along in the same direction and at the same rate, we could at once estimate their relative distance by comparing the amount of their seeming motions. If one was twice as far from us as the other, it is obvious that the more distant orb would seem to move but half as quickly as the nearer. To take a simple illustrative instance—the nearer of two men walking at equal rates in the same direction, but one twice as far from the observer as the other, would not merely be reduced in seeming height to one half the seeming height of the other, but his steps being correspondingly reduced in seeming extent, he would appear to move but one half as fast.

Of course the actual motions of the so-called fixed stars are not of such a nature as to afford precise information as to the star distances. The stars are moving in all conceivable directions, and at very different rates. In the case of any given star, the seeming motion can tell us little respecting either the real motion or the star's distance. But the average seeming motions of a set of stars may give us more trustworthy information; because in taking an average we get rid, to a great extent, of the effects of errors affecting individual cases. For example, if we class together all the stars of the sixth magnitude—the faintest, that is, which the unaided eye can see—and, adding all their seeming motions together, divide the resulting sum-total among all the stars of this order, we may regard the resulting mean motion as very fairly representing the true mean for the sixth magnitude stars. I say nothing, here, of the special rules according to which this summing up and distribution should be effected—let us suppose both operations effected with strict attention to mathematical considerations. Then we have the average seeming motion of the order of stars we are dealing with, and we can compare its amount with that belonging to other orders.

Clearly we should expect that if, on the whole, brightness affords satisfactory evidence as to distance, the average seeming movements of faint stars should bear a certain and a small proportion to the average seeming movements of bright stars. But the very first result of such a process of distribution as I have spoken of, is to shew that no such proportion holds. On the contrary, the average seeming motions of the fainter stars are about as large as the average seeming motions of the stars belonging to the leading orders of magnitude. To make the comparison more complete, I have taken the stars of the first, second, and third magnitude to form one set, and those of the fourth, fifth, and sixth, to form a second; then, on comparing the average seeming movements for the two sets, I have, to my surprise, found these movements strictly equal.

It is easy to see why this result may fairly be regarded as surprising. For let us consider its real significance. We have seen that the seeming rate of a star's motion affords evidence as to the star's distance, and evidence which may at least as safely be trusted as that afforded by seeming brightness. Judging then from the result just arrived at, we should infer that the stars of the three leading orders of magnitude are, on the average, no nearer to us than the stars of the next three orders. This would be to trust solely to the evidence derived from the stellar motions. We cannot, however, altogether neglect the evidence derived from brightness. We must believe that the brighter stars are, on the whole, somewhat nearer to us than the fainter ones. If we would combine the two forms of evidence, we must infer, I conceive, that among the orbs which surround us on all sides, there are some which are distinguished among the rest by their superior size and brightness. These must be few in number, compared with all the stars that the unaided eye can see. The inferior orbs must be spread more richly throughout surrounding space; and hence some among them must lie nearer to the Sun than any of those larger orbs which are his real peers. The larger apparent motion of these nearer stars, suffices, when averages are taken, to make up for the circumstance that distance must inevitably affect the average apparent rate of motion, as well as the average brightness. That this interpretation is just, is confirmed by the circumstance that it is among the fainter stars that the most remarkable motions are observed.

The important conclusion to which we are forced, as I judge, is that we must divide the stars into two chief classes —leading orbs like our own sun, and minor orbs more profusely spread throughout space. On only one point is there any doubt. There *must* be a great range of stellar magnitudes, a much wider range than has been usually supposed. But it is not quite clear whether our sun belongs to the class of smaller, or to that of larger orbs. I have spoken hitherto as though he were certainly one of the leading stars, and this is the view usually accepted. But there are reasons for believing that our sun may be a small star by comparison with the greater number of those which exist in his neighbourhood. For if we consider the small number of stars whose probable dimensions are known, we find reason for believing that, whereas the least of these orbs is fully one-fifth of our sun, the largest exceeds our sun two or three thousand times in magnitude. And to this must be added the circumstance, that many stars, which cannot be included in the list of those whose distances are known, have yet been so far dealt with that the astronomer is quite sure that their distances are greater than any of the measured distances. All such stars are certainly larger than we should judge them to be if their distances were measurable. This we know: what we are ignorant of is, *how much larger* they may be. So far then as can be judged, our sun is inferior, both in magnitude and in brightness, to the greater number of the orbs which surround him.

But to return to what I have spoken of as proved—the existence, namely, of a very wide range of difference amongst star-magnitudes; let us inquire whether we have evidence of even greater variety in the constitution of the star-depths.

So soon as we have passed the range of the unaided eye, we have lost all means, or even hope, of measuring distances. We are then immersed amid really fathomless depths, and all we can hope to do is to form some conception respecting the *relative* dimensions of the objects brought into our view.

There is indeed a theory about the star-system, which is based on a different idea respecting the difficulties which the astronomer has to contend with. I refer to the theory, which finds a place in all our text-books of astronomy, that the star-system has the form of a cloven flat disc. This theory was formed by Sir William Herschel, when he was as yet unaware of the vastness and complexity of the star-system. The very words used in describing his process of research, indicate that the great astronomer was full of confidence in the power of his great telescopes to fathom all the profundities of the sidereal system. He called his method star-gauging, he spoke of the distance at which the boundary of the star-system lay in this or that direction, and he discussed the numerical results he had obtained, without doubting that those results really enabled him to determine the architecture of the galaxy.

But as the work progressed Sir William Herschel grew less confident. He began to recognize signs of a complexity of structure which set his method of star-gauging at defiance. It became more and more clear to him also, as he extended his survey, that the star-depths were in fact unfathomable—not only by his gauging telescope, (commonly known as the twenty-feet reflector,) but even by that mighty mirror which was one of the chief wonders of the world, until the great Rosse telescope dwarfed it into relative insignificance. At length Sir William Herschel definitively abandoned the principles on which his star-gauging had been based; and his observations, as well as his theoretical researches, were thenceforth directed to the determination of the general laws which prevail amid the star-depths. It cannot be questioned that, with those principles, he gave up also the theory of the star-system which he had based upon them. But, singularly enough, the theory remains, and seems likely to remain, in our text-books of astronomy; while the far more wonderful views to which the later labours of Sir William Herschel pointed, have been almost wholly neglected.*

If we consider, in the first place, the views of Sir William Herschel respecting the Milky Way, we shall find that the variety which we have recognized among the isolated stars, is altogether slight by comparison with the amazing variety of magnitude, of arrangement, and

---

* Struve, the highest authority of recent times on the subject of the stellar system, with the single exception of Sir John Herschel, accounts for this strange circumstance by noting that Sir William Herschel nowhere announces, in so many words, that the cloven disc theory of the stellar system must be abandoned, though the great astronomer did very clearly abandon the principles which had led to the enunciation of that theory. It may be added that the theory is very simple, and very easily understood, whereas the subsequent inquiries and views of Sir William Herschel deal with very complex relations.

probably of constitution, to be recognized among the orbs which form the Galaxy. It is only necessary to understand rightly the change which took place in Sir William Herschel's views, to see that this conclusion must be accepted by those who regard the opinion of that great astronomer as decisive in questions relating to the stellar system.

Herschel's earlier labours had proceeded on the hypothesis of a generally uniform distribution of the stars; and according to this hypothesis, those rich regions of the Galaxy in which stars of all magnitudes are spread with unspeakable profusion, had implied simply an enormous extension of the stellar system in the direction in which these glories are seen. The smaller and also more profusely scattered stars were not to be regarded as in reality smaller and in reality spread more richly in space, but as lying farther away than the brighter, and occupying a more extensive region.

But Herschel abandoned the theory of a generally uniform distribution of stars. In fact, instead of adopting any general *à priori* theory, by means of which to interpret the aspect of the star-groups, he changed his plan of proceeding altogether, and endeavoured, by means of a careful study of the laws of star-grouping, to arrive at consistent theories respecting the real distribution of the stars throughout space. This was undoubtedly the safer course; and we might be disposed to wonder that Herschel had not adopted it in the first instance, were it not for the circumstance that the theory he actually adopted when he began his labours, had been so long regarded an unquestionably sound one.*

When Herschel began to reason from observed appearances, he was quickly led to abandon the theory of a uniform distribution of the stars. He saw that the Milky Way, for instance, is by no means to be regarded as a zone of stars resembling, in their arrangement, those which form our constellations. 'The stars we consider as insulated are surrounded,' he says, 'by a magnificent collection of innumerable stars, called the Milky Way. For though our sun, and all the stars we see, may truly be said to be in the plane of the Milky Way, yet I am now convinced, by a long inspection, and continued examination of it, that the Milky Way itself consists of stars very differently scattered from those which are immediately about us.' †

---

* It would be unfair, however, to omit mention of the fact that Michell had clearly shewn, a quarter of a century before Herschel began his labours, that the theory of a uniform distribution of the stars is untenable.

† I have here to correct statements which will be found in more than one place in writings of my own. Although I had carefully gone through the whole series of Sir William Herschel's papers four or five years ago, I failed to notice that his views had undergone a complete change. Having then been led, by researches of my own, to feel grave doubts respecting the generally accepted theory of the star-system, or rather to feel absolutely certain that that theory is unsound, I have spoken of it as Herschel's, when discussing the objections which I have had to note against it. A more careful study of Herschel's own words has shewn me that, though the theory was undoubtedly enunciated by him, he was the first to abandon it. I believe the mistake I fell into is common with those who have given to Herschel's papers but a single perusal. Even the laborious Struve fell into the same error; and it was only after a careful re-examination of Sir William Herschel's papers, that he wrote, "Nous parvenons au résultat, peut-

And he noted, in a special manner, *how* he judged that certain portions of the Milky Way were constituted. For speaking of the great clustering aggregations, which can be observed along various portions of the Galaxy, he expressed his belief that these aggregations are globular in form.

Now if the stars seen within a certain circular region in the heavens, are enclosed in reality within a globular space, we can infer the relative distances of the nearest and farthest stars within the region. We cannot tell which stars are nearer, and which are farther, neither can we tell the actual distances of any stars within the circular region but we *can* assure ourselves that the distances of the farther stars do not exceed the distances of the nearest in more than a certain proportion. If we look at a spherical balloon far away in the upper regions of air, we may be quite unable to tell how far off the balloon is or how large it is, or therefore by how much the distance of the farthest part of the balloon exceeds the distance of the nearest part; but though we cannot tell *by what amount*, we can tell quite certainly *in what degree* the distance of the farthest part exceeds the distance of the nearest. For this relation depends only on the apparent size of the balloon, and remains precisely the same whether the balloon is near and small, or far away and large. Supposing the balloon had

être inattendu, mais incontestable, que le système de Herschel, énoncé en 1785, sur l'arrangement de la Voie Lactée, s'écroule de toutes parts, d'après les recherches ultérieures de l'auteur ; et que Herschel luimême l'a entièrement abandonné.'

no car, nor carried any object of known dimensions, as a man or pony or sheep, we might believe that the farthest point of the silken covering was ten yards, or ten feet, or but ten inches farther away than the nearest point; but we should be in no doubt whatever as to the relative distances of these two points. In fact, if we were to hold up a small ball, as a marble or a bagatelle-ball, so as just to hide the balloon, the relation between the distances of the farthest and nearest points of the ball would be exactly the same as the relation between the distances of the farthest and nearest points of the balloon. And in precisely the same way, if one were to hold up a ball so as to hide one of the great globular clustering aggregations of stars in the Galaxy, we should know that the distance of the farthest star in that aggregation exceeds the distance of the nearest star, in the same degree that the distance of the farthest point of the ball exceeds that of the nearest.

This result is so important, that I need make no excuse for having thus, at some length, urged its real nature upon the attention of the reader. For let us consider what the lesson thus taught us respecting these star-clusters in reality implies. In these clustering aggregations we commonly see stars of all orders, from certain not very conspicuous orbs—say stars of the seventh or eighth magnitude—down to stars so faint that they are barely visible, even in the most powerful telescopes with which the Herschels, Rosse, Lassell, and Bond, have explored the depths of space. Nay, in some of these clusters, there are regions in which, after the highest powers of the largest telescopes have been applied, faint patches of cloudy light remain still unresolved into stars. Now according to the theory first entertained by Herschel, the faintest stars in these clusters, and especially the faint unresolved star-dust, (if one may so speak,) would be regarded as many times farther away than the stars of the seventh or eighth magnitude belonging to the same cluster. There would, in fact, be stars of all orders of distance, corresponding to the various orders of apparent magnitude, from the seventh downwards. But when once it is admitted that these clustering aggregations are globular in their general form, we can no longer admit such an interpretation of the various orders of magnitude seen among the stars which form the clustre. The fainter stars are certainly not many times farther away than the brighter, certainly not twice as far away, nor half as far again. The relative minuteness of these fainter orbs, and their relative closeness to each other, are *real* and *not merely apparent* phenomena. Stars which the earlier theory would have taught us to regard as not smaller nor more closely set than the brighter, but about ten times as far off, are shewn to be a thousand times smaller, and set a thousand times more closely;* stars which the earlier theory would have placed one hundred times farther away than the brighter

* The average distances separating star from star would be in this case but ten times smaller, and in the following but a hundred times; but the number of stars included in a given region of space would be, respectively, a thousand and a million times greater; and these relations may properly be described in the words used in the text.

stars in a cluster, are now found to be a million times smaller, and set a million times more closely.

It will be seen at once that the wonderful variety of structure recognized by the telescopists in the richer regions of the Milky Way, receives quite a new interpretation when the later views of Sir William Herschel are accepted. Few who have not studied the Galaxy with the telescope, can be aware of the real complexity of that marvellous system of stars. I know, indeed, of nothing which is better calculated to impress the observer with a sense of the real magnificence of the stellar system, than a view, even through a telescope of moderate power, of the glorious star-depths in the constellations Cygnus, Aquila, and Perseus. In telescopes of great power, these regions and others, more especially some in the southern heavens, present a display so marvellous, that all description must fail to convey any just conception of its splendour.

I have had occasion lately to study somewhat attentively the laws according to which the stars are distributed in the more densely aggregated regions of the Milky Way; for I have constructed a circular chart, two feet in diameter, in which all the northern stars which can be seen with a telescope two and three-quarter inches in aperture, are included. In all there are 324,198 stars in this chart, and therefore about one hundred and fifty times as many as can be seen with the unaided eye on the darkest and clearest night. It is wonderful, indeed, when contemplating this immense congregation of stars, to consider that the same portion of the heavens, if surveyed completely with the gauging telescopes of the Herschels, would shew twenty or thirty times as many stars. But even among the stars which smaller telescopes exhibit, there are signs of definite laws of arrangement too well marked to be regarded as merely accidental—that is, as implying no real connection between the stars thus seemingly associated.

When larger telescopes are applied to the same rich regions of the heavens, fresh peculiarities are brought into view. Father Secchi of Rome speaks thus of the distribution of stars within a certain very bright portion of the Milky Way in the constellation Sagittarius, as revealed by the powers of the fine refracting telescope of the Roman Observatory:—'There are large stars and lucid clusters; then a layer of smaller stars certainly below the twelfth magnitude; then a nebulous stratum with occasional openings.' But what startled him and all to whom he shewed it, was the regular disposition of the stars in figures* so geometrical that it is impossible to regard them as accidental. 'They are for the most part like the arcs of a spiral; one can count as many as ten or twelve stars of the ninth and tenth magnitude—following each other on the same curve like the beads on a rosary; sometimes they seem to diverge from a common centre, and, strangely enough, it usually happens that either at the centre of the

* Thus far the quotation is from Webb's charming little work entitled 'Celestial Objects for common Telescopes,' who has summarised Secchi's remarks; the remainder of the passage in inverted commas, is translated from a quotation given by Webb in the same work. (*Note*, p. 267.)

rays, or at the beginning of the branch of a curve, there is a larger star of a red colour. It is impossible to regard such an arrangement of the stars as accidental."

The accounts given by Sir John Herschel of various parts of the Milky Way, as seen in the southern hemisphere, afford even more remarkable evidence of the singularly varied and complex nature of the star-grouping in those richer parts of the Galaxy. The following passage serves to give some idea of the nature of this evidence. I quote the passage as it appears in Herschel's splendid work entitled 'Observations made at the South Cape,' so far, at least, as respects the sequence of the remarks; here and there certain technical phrases have been omitted or changed, since the passage otherwise would not be suited to these pages: 'After passing the dark interval between the two streams of the Milky Way,' in Centaurus, 'the coming on of the Milky Way is thus described'—Herschel is here quoting from his note-books: '"The edge of a great nebulous projection of the Milky Way of great extent, running horizontally. The northern half of the field of view has stars on a black ground. After this the Milky Way becomes very nebulous, in great cirrous masses and streaks." "Further on commences a series of great nebulous and semi-nebulous Milky Way patches over the whole breadth of the zone."' Then occur several remarkable clusters, '"among alternations of vacuity and richness most surprising, and baffling all description;" as the main body of the Milky Way comes on, the frequency and variety of these masses increase.' . . . . Further on, the following remarks occur: "The Milky Way is here composed of separate, or slightly or strongly connected clouds of semi-nebulous light; and, as the telescope moves, the appearance is that of clouds passing in a scud, as sailors call it." "I could fill a catalogue with the clusters of the sixth class which are here. The Milky Way is like sand, not strewed evenly as with a sieve, but as if flung down by handfuls, (and both hands at once,) leaving dark intervals, and all consisting of stars of the fourteenth, fifteenth, . . . to the twentieth magnitude, and down to nebulosity, in a most astonishing manner." Again, "after an interval of comparative poverty, the same phenomenon, and even more remarkable. I cannot say it is *nebulous*. It is all resolved, but the stars are inconceivably numerous and minute. There must be millions on millions, and all most unequally massed together; yet they nowhere run to *nuclei* or *clusters much brighter in the middle*." This extraordinary exhibition terminates' nearly on the meridian marking the eighteenth hour of right ascension, 'where the Milky Way resumes its usual appearance.'

If we regard the Milky Way as a whole we are equally struck with the evidence of complexity of structure. As described indeed in many text-books of astronomy, the aspect of the Milky Way might be regarded as according well with the theory that the stellar system is shaped like a cloven flat disc. For we are commonly told that the Milky Way is a zone, or band, circling the whole of the celestial sphere, and divided along one half of its length into two distinct streams. But as a matter of fact, this description is very far indeed from accurately presenting the characteristics of the Milky Way. Both portions of the descriptions are indeed equally untrue. For, in the first place, the Milky Way does not circle the heavens, but is in one place cloven right across by a wide dark rift. And in the second place, one can only say of a very small portion of the Milky Way that it is double. Near the constellation Cygnus, in the northern heavens, the Milky Way is double; but one of the branches, after proceeding somewhat beyond the head of Ophiuchus (the Serpent-bearer) bends away from the other branch and is presently lost altogether. Now at the opposite side of the heavens, near the constellation Crux, (or the Cross,) the Milky Way is again double; but tracing the second branch on the side towards the place where the second branch on the other side loses itself, we presently find the southern second branch becoming subdivided into several branches, and these forming a region of interlaced streaks, accompanied by patches of light, which seemed to be quite disjoined from all the branches. This strangely complex region spreads out towards the constellation Libra, where it loses itself; but a well-marked branch bending round towards the adjacent continuous stream seems to end in three well-marked patches. Over the whole of this region, the complexity of the Milky Way, as seen by the naked eye, is fairly comparable with the complexity of the telescopic aspect of the same region as described by Sir John Herschel.

Even in our northern heavens, however, there are regions which are singularly complex, and as it were variegated. 'It is indeed,' says Professor Nichol, 'only to the most careless glance, or when viewed through an atmosphere of imperfect transparency, that the Milky Way seems a continuous zone. Let the naked eye rest thoughtfully on any part of it; and if circumstances be favourable, it will stand out rather as an accumulation of patches and streams of light, of every conceivable variety of form and brightness; now side by side, now heaped on each other; again spanning across dark spaces, intertwining and forming a most curious and complex net-work; and at other times darting off into the neighbouring skies in branches of capricious length and shape, which gradually thin away and disappear.'

Thus far I have been dealing only with the general laws of star-distribution. I have endeavoured to shew that instead of a system of suns spread with a general uniformity throughout space, we have to deal with orbs differing widely from each other in magnitude, and distributed throughout space in the most varied manner. Streams and branches of stars, strangely shaped groups, forming, as regards their seeming arrangement, the most complex reticulations; islands of light and lakes of darkness, resulting from the aggregation of stars towards certain regions and their segregation from others;—these, and other phenomena of a similarly perplexing nature, serve at least to shew that the star-system has not that simplicity of structure so commonly assigned to it in our text-books of astronomy. But we have still to consider details. Among the wonders of the star-depths, there are to be noted phenomena even more wonderful than those general features which have hitherto been dealt with. Coloured stars; double and multiple stars; periodic, variable, and temporary stars; the various orders of star-clusters, star-cloudlets, and star-mist; these are among the wonders of the star-depths. With them we have now to deal, considering them rather for the evidence they afford respecting the richness and variety of the sidereal system than with special reference to the features of individual objects belonging to these various classes. With respect to some of them, indeed, my chief task will be to shew reasons for believing that they really do belong to the star-depths; and not, as has hitherto been commonly judged, to regions of space lying far beyond the bounds of our own star-system.

Let us pause for a moment to survey the ground over which we have passed.

We have considered the scale on which the stellar universe has been formed, and the general varieties of structure observable within the range of telescopic vision. We have seen that, compared with distances separating star from star, the dimensions of our Sun, and even of the system over which he bears sway, sink into utter insignificance. And then, endeavouring to picture to ourselves the manner in which these star-ranges are distributed—the plan on which this system of magnificent distances is formed—we have seen reason to believe that a variety of distribution prevails which renders the scheme of stars singularly difficult to interpret aright. So long as we could believe in uniformity either of dimensions or distribution, we could deduce certain conclusions as to the structure of the great star-system. Varieties of appearance were then at once explicable, as due either to the various distances at which the particular regions under survey were placed, or else to the various depths to which the telescopic sounding-line penetrates before reaching the limits of the star-system. But so soon as we are led to doubt whether any sort of uniformity exists within the star-depths, we lose at once the means of readily interpreting the scene disclosed to us in the telescopic survey of the heavens. A region which appears singularly rich in stars may be a true star-cluster—a subordinate star-system—or it may be a region where the line of sight passes through an almost interminable range of stars. Seemingly minute stars may form schemes of suns far smaller than our own, or than any of the leading orbs of the heavens; or they may be orbs surpassing even Sirius in magnitude and splendour, but set at depths compared with which his enormous distance is relatively as insignificant as the distance of our moon compared with the dimensions of the Solar System. A cloud of light in the star-depths may be a vast mass of nebulous matter, or it may be a scheme of stars as magnificent as the most splendid of all the star-clusters discernible with the telescope.

It does not follow that in the presence of these sources of perplexity we need wholly despair of solving the problems presented by the star-depths; but it becomes more necessary than ever to exercise extreme caution at each step of our progress. We must avail ourselves of every method of research or inquiry which promises to throw the least light on the very difficult questions we have to deal with. 'In the midst of so much darkness,' wrote Sir John Herschel to me on this point, 'we ought to open our eyes as wide as possible to any glimpse of light, and to utilize whatever twilight may be accorded to us, to make out though but indistinctly the forms that surround us.'

It is not in this place indeed that this searching analysis should be undertaken. My purpose in writing these lines is not to exhibit in detail the reasoning by which certain conclusions may be attained, but rather to present an account of what is known or may be inferred respecting the stellar depths. But it is well that the reader should notice that the facts to be described have an interest other than that which they derive from their intrinsic importance, inasmuch as it is to them chiefly that we are to look for hints to guide us in the attempt to solve the noblest problem ever attacked by man.

We have already had abundant reasons for believing that 'one star differeth from another in glory,' not merely as seen upon the heavens, but in reality, and to an extent which corresponds with the variety of dimensions recognized among the members of the Solar System itself. Let us now briefly consider the evidence we have of an equally remarkable variety of condition and constitution among the stars composing our galaxy.

In the first place, we can infer from the different colours of the stars, that their condition, and the condition also of worlds dependent upon them, must differ to a corresponding extent. Even the naked eye recognizes remarkable diversities of star-colour; but it is only when the telescope is directed to the work of survey that the true extent of these diversities is fully recognized. Confining our attention for the present to single stars, it is to be noticed that every variety of pure colour—that is, of the hues seen in the prismatic spectrum—from bluish and greenish, (not full green or blue,) through yellow, orange, ruddy, and full red, even to the deepest ruby, may be recognized among isolated stars. But no isolated stars of a full blue or green colour have yet been detected.*

Here we have an instance of variety of condition which cannot but be regarded as highly significant. In whatever way we explain the colour of a red or orange star on the one hand, or of a greenish or bluish star on the other, we cannot but admit that they must differ markedly in condition and that the condition of either must be markedly different from that of a white star. A red star may be heated in different degree than a white star, or it may be surrounded by absorbing vapours different in character from those which surround an orb of the latter class, or the

---

* This, however, has been questioned, since some observers (and notably the late Admiral Smyth) have considered certain isolated stars to be decidedly blue or green. The general opinion is in favour of those who assert that the blue or green hues of these stars are not well marked, and that a peculiarity of vision has led the before mentioned observers into error.

difference of aspect may be explicable in some other manner; but it is not conceivable that any explanation can present two such stars as alike, or nearly alike, in their physical condition. And so of other distinctions of colour.

We are not left in doubt, however, on this point; for the spectroscope exhibits to us the nature of the characteristic difference between stars which differ in colour. Father Secchi has been able, in fact, to arrange the stars of different colour into four distinct types, according to the character of the rainbow-tinted streak into which the spectroscope spreads out their light.

First in order are the stars usually considered white, but in reality shining with a somewhat bluish light. Such are Sirius, Vega, Altair, Rigel, and Regulus, as well as all the stars of Charles's Wain, except Dubhe. The spectrum of a star of this order 'shews rays of all the seven colours, and is sometimes crossed by very numerous and mostly very fine lines, but always by four broad and very dark lines. Of these four lines one is in the red, another in the greenish blue, and the remaining two in the violet. All the four are due to hydrogen.* The spectra of these stars shew also the lines of sodium, iron, and magnesium. 'Nearly half the stars in the heavens,' (that is, of those visible to the unaided eye,) 'are included in this type, and their spectra may be examined even with a telescope of small power.'

* From Dr Schellen's fine work on Spectrum Analysis, translated by Jane and Caroline Lassell, and edited by Dr Huggins, F.R.S. See further, "The Expanse of Heaven."

The second type of fixed stars is that to which our sun belongs. 'In this class,' says Secchi, 'most of the yellow stars are included, as for instance, Capella, Pollux, Arcturus, Aldebaran, Dubhe in the Great Bear, Procyon, &c. The dark lines are very strongly marked in the red and in the blue portions of their spectra, but are almost entirely absent in the yellow.' The well-known dark lines in the solar spectrum illustrate this peculiarity; yet it should be noted that though well-marked dark lines are absent from the yellow part of the spectrum, fine lines are present there in great numbers. 'The close conformity to the solar spectrum undoubtedly leads to the conclusion,' says Dr Schellen, 'that these stars are composed of similar elements, and possess a physical constitution in other respects analogous to that of our Sun.' We have seen that about one half the stars hitherto observed belong to the first type. Secchi considers that the second type includes about two-thirds of the remainder; so that already five-sixths of all the observed stars have been taken into account.

The third type includes all the stars shining with a well-marked red tint. As an example, the brilliant but variable star Betelgeux, which marks the right shoulder of Orion, may be cited. The star Alpha Herculis, in the head of the Kneeling Hero, also belongs to this type. "The spectra of such stars appear like a row of columns illuminated from the side, producing a stereoscopic effect; and when the bright bands are narrower than the dark ones, the spectrum has the appearance of a series of grooves. Red stars of even the eighth magnitude have been examined spectroscopically with Secchi's admirable instrument, and shew a similar constitution, while no spectrum could be obtained from white stars of the same magnitude." The spectrum of stars of the third type resembles in a remarkable degree the spectrum of a solar spot, a circumstance which has led Secchi to regard these as spot-covered suns.

Stars of the fourth type, like those of the third, have a spectrum presenting a columnar appearance; but the number of the columnar bands is less, and the brighter side of each band is towards the violet end of the spectrum, whereas in stars of the third type the reverse is the case. Into peculiarities such as these, however, we need not here enter at length, because they do not affect those general relations with which we are here dealing.

Now, passing from the consideration that these varieties of the stellar spectrum indicate corresponding varieties of elementary structure in the suns which people space, let us consider for a moment how the condition of inhabited worlds circling around other suns than ours must be affected by the nature of the light emitted by the orbs which rule them.

Our sun sends forth rays which supply three very different requirements of living creatures, animal and vegetable, peopling our earth. Without light, we should all before long perish miserably; and the sun's rays supply us with light. Without heat, we should be even more quickly destroyed; and the sun's rays provide ample supplies of heat. But besides light and heat, we require, directly and indirectly, that chemical action of the solar rays which has been called *actinism*. Without this action the air we breathe would be loaded before long with pestilential vapours, which would destroy the lives of men and animals; plants would wither, and presently die; the whole earth, in fact, would soon be the abode of death, as surely, though perhaps not so quickly, as though the sun had ceased to supply either light or heat.

Now at present, these three forms of energy are exerted in certain proportions, admirably suited to our requirements. Dividing the solar rays according to the position they occupy with reference to the spectrum—we have from the red rays, and from dark rays beyond the red, the chief supply of heat; from the whole visible spectrum, but chiefly from the yellow portion, comes the supply of light; and lastly, the violet rays, and the dark rays beyond the violet, afford the chief supply of actinism. If any change were to pass over our sun whereby the proportion of heat and light and actinism were appreciably modified, we should undoubtedly suffer sooner or later. If the modification were considerable, all plants and animals would probably perish. But if our sun's rays were so affected that he was visibly changed in colour—either to our own eyes, or to the inhabitants of some far distant world whence our sun is seen as a star—there can be no question that *this* change would result in a considerable modification of the proportion in which heat, light, and actinism reach our earth. For we have seen that varieties of stellar colour imply varieties in the stellar spectra, some stars having the red or heat end relatively more brilliant than the rest of the spectrum, others having the yellow or light portion in relative excess, others the violet or actinic portion. Since, then, the creatures living on this earth would unquestionably suffer if our sun were so changed as to resemble stars of certain colours, it follows that the creatures in worlds circling around stars of those colours must differ in many important respects from those existing on our own earth. So that the varied tints seen amid the star-depths supply evidence of a corresponding variety in the scenes displayed by the unnumbered myriads of worlds circling around other suns than our own.

In passing from isolated suns to double and multiple star-systems, I scarcely know whether to dwell chiefly on the varieties of arrangement observable in these systems or on the singularly-marked and beautiful colours seen among them, as the more striking illustration of the complexity of the scheme according to which the universe has been formed. But as the subject of colour has already been discussed, it may be well to consider the former relation more particularly at this point.

If we consider only the double stars, we find a perfectly marvellous variety of arrangement as respects magnitude and distance. In some pairs the component stars are equal, in others we find every degree of disproportion in the magnitudes of the components, from a slight inequality down to such an enormous disproportion as in the case of Sirius or Antares, where the chief star is a brilliant of the leading order, (a 'double first,' as it were,) and the companion is barely visible in powerful telescopes. As respects distance, it is not possible to speak quite so confidently—at least, in any specified instance; since a pair whose components appear to be very close together may in reality be separated by a distance exceeding that which separates a 'wide double.' But among so many thousands of double stars which have come under telescopic scrutiny, this difficulty need not perplex us, since the laws of averages assure us that peculiarities of arrangement will not *prevail* in a large array of instances. So that we may feel assured that the observed immense variety in the distance of double stars—whether in the actual observed distance, or in the relation between this distance and the seeming magnitudes of the component stars—corresponds to an equally immense variety in the real distances. Then the subject of colour enters into the question of arrangement (apart from the evidence it supplies as to elementary constitution,) and here again we find the most surprising variety. We have pairs of white, yellow, orange, and red stars; then we have red and white pairs, red and yellow, red and orange, and so on, with all such combinations, the larger or smaller star having either colour of any such pair; again, we have white and blue, white and green, white and violet, red and blue, red and green, red and violet, and so on, the larger star in all such cases being white, yellow, orange, or red, and the smaller blue, green, violet, or purple. We have also small companion stars, coloured lilac, fawn, dun, buff, ashen grey, livid, olive, russet, citron, and so on, to say nothing of colours so peculiar that no ordinary name can be given to them.*

If we regard a pair of stars as forming a double sun round which, or rather round the common centre of which, other orbs revolve as planets, we are struck by the difference between such a scheme and our own Solar system; but we find the difference yet more surprising, when we consider the possibility that in some such schemes each component sun may have its own distinct system of dependent worlds. In the former case, the ordinary state of things would probably be such that both the suns would be above the horizon at the same time and then probably their distinctive peculiarities would only be recognizable when one chanced to pass over the disc of the other, as our moon passes over the sun's disc in eclipses. For short intervals of time, however, at rising or setting, one or other would be visible alone; and the phenomena of sunset and sunrise must therefore be very varied, and also exquisitely beautiful, in worlds circling round such double suns. But where each sun has a separate system, even more remarkable relations must be presented. For each system of dependent worlds, besides its own proper sun, must have another sun, less splendid, perhaps, (because farther off,) but still brighter beyond comparison than our moon at the full. And according to the

---

* For such a colour the celebrated astronomer, W. Struve, invented the pleasing name, '*olivaceasubrubicunda,*' respecting which the author of 'Celestial Objects for common Telescopes' remarks that it matches Gruithuisen's '*stickstoffsauerstoffatmosphäre,*' and (an English chemist's invention) the *iodide of methylodiethylamylammonium.*

position of any planet of either sytem, there will result for the time being either an interchange of suns instead of the change from night to day, or else double sunlight during the day, and a corresponding intensified contrast between night and day. Where the two suns are very unequal, or very differently coloured, or where the orbital path of each is very eccentric, so that they are sometimes close together, and at others far apart, the varieties of condition in the worlds circling around either, or around the common centre of both, must be yet more remarkable. 'It must be confessed,' we may well say with Sir John Herschel, 'that we have here a strangely wide and novel field for speculative excursions, and one which it is not easy to avoid luxuriating in.'

If it be supposed that in some instances the smaller component of a double system shines either wholly or to a considerable degree by reflecting the light of its primary, we shall find yet further reason for wonder at the diversity of structure within the star-depths. For unquestionably the largest of all the planets which circle around the Sun would not be visible even under the most powerful telescopic scrutiny, at the distance of the nearest fixed star. Nay, an opaque orb as large as our Sun, if placed where Jupiter is, would not reflect a tenth part of the light necessary to render it visible at such a distance.

But such considerations as these become perfectly bewildering when extended to triple, quadruple, and generally to multiple star-systems. It will afford some idea of the amazing variety of arrangement observable among such systems, that even among the host of triple stars already observed by astronomers, not two have been found which closely resemble each other in arrangement, while, so soon as we pass to more complex systems, we find that each fresh object of the class differs utterly from all which have been previously observed.

In considering the actual condition of the region of space occupied by a triple, quadruple, or multiple star-system, we find ourselves surrounded on all sides by sources of perplexity—so long, at least, as we compare the worlds in such regions with our own earth, or with any member of the Solar system. All the most marked characteristics of life on our earth must be wanting in those worlds which circle around the component suns of multiple systems. There can be no year, strictly so called, no orderly succession of seasons, no regular alternation of day and night, in many cases *no night at all*, save for brief periods at exceedingly long intervals. Placed at such a distance from any star of one of these systems that that star appears as a sun, the others also must supply an amount of light sufficient of itself to banish night. More commonly, indeed, each star of such a system, while above the horizon, would be a sun shining more brightly than our sun does to the inhabitants of many planets of his scheme. But where there are three or four such suns, the simultaneous absence of all from the sky must be an uncommon event—as uncommon, for instance, as those occasions when none of Jupiter's satellites can be seen. The inhabitants of worlds such as these can but seldom witness the spectacle of the starlit sky; and the study of any orbs beyond their own system must be a task of infinite difficulty, since it can only be pursued for a few occasional hours of darkness, separated by many months of persistent daylight.

The consideration of these multiple systems leads us on, step by step, to the various orders of star-clusters. For we can point to multiple systems of greater and greater richness, and as it were compactness, until we arrive at orders which we are compelled to regard as veritable star-clusters. Yet it is to be noticed that we might have approached the study of star-clusters in a different direction. For we have already had occasion to consider the various degrees of stellar aggregation in different parts of the heavens; and some of the regions of aggregation, while indubitably features of the galaxy regarded as a whole, are yet so well defined, and so clearly separated from the surrounding more barren regions, that we cannot refuse to regard them as vast star-clusters. We can thus either proceed from the smaller star-clusters—to which we have been led by the study of multiple star-systems—onwards to larger and yet larger groups of stars, until we have arrived at the aggregations just mentioned; or we can pass from these through the successive orders of a diminishing scale until we arrive at multiple star-systems.

Yet here it is well to remark that a difficulty presents itself which can only be removed by the theory, to which we have been already led by other considerations, that the great aggregations of stars are not (or at least, all of them are not) to be regarded as formed of orbs necessarily comparable with Sirius and Arcturus, Capella, Vega, and Aldebaran, in real magnitude and splendour. For we can pass from the single suns onwards to double suns, multiple systems, star-clusters, and stellar aggregations, thence to less and less condensed and more and more extended aggregations, until we arrive at unaggregated star-groups, consisting, in fact, of the single orbs with which we set out. Now it is to be observed that we seem to be brought to the single stars by a course which is not a mere retracing of our steps. For supposing we regard star-clusters as intermediate between the least condensed aggregations on the one hand, and single stars on the other, we pass onwards from these least condensed aggregations to single stars, without going through any of the steps of our progress *towards* the aggregations. Obviously there can have been no true progression here. And we are compelled to believe that by following the course indicated, we arrive at quite another order of star-groups than those which form our constellations, although in appearance the less densely aggregated star-groups may resemble systems of true suns, like Sirius and Arcturus, Aldebaran and Capella.

But the fact is that, again and again, as we contemplate the wonders of the star-depths, we find ourselves thus tracing out perplexing sequences, one class of objects merging into another class seemingly altogether distinct, and this class into yet another, until we are bewildered by the multiplicity of analogies whereof some at least must be deceptive.

For instance, I have spoken of the various orders of star-clusters by which we may be led to the vast stellar aggregations; and there can be no question whatever that an apparently perfect sequence can be traced from sharply-defined clusters such as the magnificent object '13 Messier' in the constellation Hercules, to such groups as the Pleiades, or Præsepe in Cancer, or the splendid star-clusters near the sword-hand of Perseus, these groups being undoubtedly mere condensations in rich star-regions. It also cannot be doubted that we can pass from such a cluster as the one in Hercules, to others less rich in numbers, but equally compact, and so to clusters continually poorer and poorer (numerically) until we arrive at mere multiple systems, and so to quadruple, triple, double, and single stars. But it is equally certain that we can pass from the globular star-clusters to others oval in shape, and more and more closely set,* until at length we arrive at the nebulæ, properly so called—that is, spots of cloudy light which have not been resolved into separate stars by any telescopic power yet applied. Here, then, a progression as real as either of the preceding seems to lead us to objects which have been commonly regarded as wholly distinct from any *portions* of the galactic system, and probably analogues of the whole of that system.

* The connection between shape and closeness of star-setting is certain, though most perplexing. Sir John Herschel writes:—'It may be generally remarked, as a fact undoubtedly connected in some very intimate manner with the dynamical conditions of their subsistence, that the elliptic nebulæ are, for the most part, beyond comparison more difficult of resolution than those of globular form.

But it may be urged that this progression may relate simply to distance, and that therefore we need not regard it as forming a new and distinct sequence. To illustrate the matter, suppose that we could recognize among the companies of persons proceeding along a road,—many different kinds of groups—and that we arranged these different orders into a perfect sequence; then, taking any given order, we should find the various groups belonging to this order presenting different aspects according to their distance. Say the order comprised sets of persons travelling six together; then a set of six close by would differ in appearance from a set of six far away; and we might form many sets of six at different distances into a perfect sequence, according to their varying appearance.

Now according to this view of the matter the various orders of regularly-shaped nebulæ, even down to those which no telescope can resolve, would be star-clusters lying at great distances. And since the star-clusters, properly so called, must be regarded as belonging to our own galactic system, it would follow that all the orders of nebulæ belong to that system. We should at least find it it very difficult to say up to what point this complete sequence of objects belonged to our star-system, and where external star-systems began to be in question) and still less easily could we explain how complete external systems should thus be linked, as far as appearances extend, with mere portions, and relatively minute portions, of our own star-system.

So that whether we consider distance to be solely

in question, or that the various orders of nebulæ are associated with star-clusters, as forming parts of a real sequence of objects, we alike find reason for believing that the nebulæ, or irresolvable star-clusters, belong to our own galactic system.

But at this stage a very striking and beautiful argument can be adduced to indicate the real place of the nebulæ— so long regarded as external galaxies—in the scheme of our own galactic system.

If we were to mark down on a globe the place of every nebula yet known to astronomers, we should not find that the marks were spread in a random manner over the sphere. On the contrary, we should find them aggregated in a well-defined manner into two large regions, separated by a wide ring-shaped region of nebular poverty. An interesting circumstance, this, whatever opinion we may form as to the nature of these star-cloudlets. Placed as we are, in the midst of a region of star-space, which appears to our conceptions as spherical, the existence of two great clusters of nebulæ in opposite regions of this seemingly spherical space, is a significant phenomenon, and one which any theory of the universe, to be established on a firm basis, is bound to account for. But the circumstance becomes yet more significant when we notice *where*, on the star sphere, the intervening zone of barrenness is situated. If the globe had been originally free from marks, and we sought to indicate by a circular streak the central circle of this ring-shaped vacancy, the streak would occupy the very place which astronomers have assigned as the central circle of the Milky Way. Now I shall not pause here to dwell on the significance of this fact, though I regard it as one of the most significant in the whole array of facts hitherto learned respecting the galaxy. The special argument I wish at present to insist upon is of a more delicate, though not less significant kind. The star-clusters, which as we have seen are associable with (or rather not separable from) the nebulæ, are also connected, as respects distribution, with the galactic circle. But whereas the irresolvable star-cloudlets are withdrawn from the galactic region the star-clusters are aggregated over that region. This, however, is not all. If we consider the various intermediate classes between the brightest globular clusters and the faintest of the irresolvable star-cloudlets, we find that their relation to the Milky Way corresponds with their order in the series : the brightest and most obviously stellate clusters are found almost exclusively within the Milky Way; the next order of clusters are chiefly in the Milky Way, but a few are met with outside its borders; the next order are but slightly aggregated towards the Milky Way; the next are pretty evenly distributed over the heavens; the next are slightly segregated from the Milky Way; and lastly, the actually irresolvable star-cloudlets, though counted by thousands, have scarcely ten of their order near the galactic zone.

It is not difficult to recognize the significance of these facts, though it may be exceedingly difficult to give their exact interpretation. Any doubts we might before have had, respecting the reality of the sequence of association linking together the most stellate clusters with the faintest star-cloudlets, must be removed, when we find in their distribution a law of sequence corresponding exactly with that recognized in their aspect. That they all form part and parcel of one and the same scheme, appears to me to be an inference as inevitable as it is important. The whole aspect of the universe, or of that which is for us the universe—that is, the region of space to which our range of research extends—is at once altered when we are led to regard the star-cloudlets, which have so long been looked upon as external galaxies, as forming, instead, subordinate features of our own star-system. Nor is the conclusion one which should lead us to entertain less exalted ideas of the real universe, although at first sight we seem to have blotted from existence thousands of star-systems, each as important as our own galaxy. For as certainly as we must recognize the fact that the external galaxies are at least not demonstrated realities, so surely must we regard the ideas which have been entertained respecting our own galaxy as falling far short—infinitely short, I had almost said—of the reality. Its unnumbered myriads of suns are reinforced, according to these new conceptions, by thousands of star-systems. Its imagined limits are shewn to be only the limits of certain portions of its extent. We find the Milky Way of the Herschels— already chosen as the apt emblem of the infinite power of the Creator—presented to us as the merest fragment of the great star-system to which our Sun belongs, the merest drop in the infinite star-depths. In place of an unlimited series of star-universes like our own, we find that our own star-universe is unlimited, or at least ungaugable by the most powerful telescopes man has yet constructed.

I have said in the preceding paragraph that the nebulæ have not been demonstrated to be external galaxies, assigning thus the lowest possible degree of significance to the argument which I myself regard as *demonstrating* that they form part and parcel of our own star-system. But it cannot be too often repeated that the reasoning of Sir John Herschel respecting the Magellanic clouds has in effect finally established the fact of which I have just attempted to give an independent demonstration. I have already indicated the bearing of his reasoning on our ideas respecting the distribution of stars throughout the galactic system; but the evidence he adduces is yet more striking as respects the nebulæ. For within the two Magellanic clouds are found all orders of nebulæ, from the most obviously stellate orders, to those which Sir John Herschel's fine telescope failed wholly to resolve. All classes of these objects, then, exist within the regions of space occupied by the Magellanic clouds—regions which we have already seen to be roughly globular in shape, and unquestionably far within the limits of distance enclosing our own star-system.

But perhaps the most surprising of all the facts yet ascertained respecting the mysterious star-depths surrounding us on all sides, is the circumstance that inconceivably vast spaces are occupied by gaseous matter, shining with a faintly luminous light. I have spoken hitherto of nebulæ as star-cloudlets, and unquestionably large numbers of these objects are really composed of stars, and give forth the same sort of light (in general respects) as our sun, and other single stars. But others have been shewn by the researches of our great physicist, Dr. Huggins, to be composed of luminous gas or vapour. The famous nebula in Orion is among the number thus constituted, so are the dumb-bell nebula in Vulpecula, the ring nebula in Lyra, and other well-known objects. In the southern hemisphere the great nebula in Argo has been shown to be gaseous, (by Captain Herschel,) and the fine irregular nebula in the greater Magellanic Cloud is another of these gaseous masses. The strange objects called the planetary nebulæ are also all gaseous, so far as these researches have yet extended.

Here again we find a distinct association between the distribution of the gaseous nebulæ, and the features of the galaxy. The irregular nebulæ, such as the one in Orion, the great Argo nebula, and the great nebular masses in Sagittarius and Cygnus, are all on, or else close by, the Milky Way, with one solitary exception, the nebula (already mentioned) in the greater Magellanic cloud, that wonderful region which includes all forms of celestial objects. The planetary nebulæ also show a decided tendency to aggregation along the galactic zone of the heavens. Added to this is the noteworthy circumstance that all the irregular gaseous nebulæ seem to cling around the stars forming certain very remarkable star-groups. For example, the Orion nebula clings round the group of stars of which the well-known set of four called the trapezium is the central aggregation. The Argo nebula is described by Sir John Herschel as ushered in by a marvellous array of stars, of which it forms in a sense the climax. And so of all these regions of irregular nebulous matter; they are all, without exception, rich in stars. Of the association of this gaseous matter with our own star-system there can be no question whatever.

And here in passing, I may be permitted to make a few remarks on the bearing of Dr. Huggins's noteworthy discovery, on the famous nebular hypotheses of Sir W. Herschel and Laplace. These hypotheses, (for they must by no means be regarded as forming one and the same hypothesis,) were intended to account on the one hand for the various orders of objects seen in the star-depths, and on the other for the various signs of a process of growth or development in the Solar System. Herschel sought to shew how irregular nebulous masses might develop into solar systems. Laplace endeavoured to prove that our Solar System has been developed from rotating nebulous masses.

That the reasoning of Sir W. Herschel as to the really nebulous character of many of the cloud-like objects he observed has been abundantly confirmed and justified by Dr. Huggins's discovery, cannot reasonably be questioned. It needs but a careful comparison of Herschel's remarks with Dr Huggins's account of his own discoveries, to see that in this case, as in so many other instances, Sir W. Herschel rightly analysed what his telescopes had revealed

But when we pass from Herschel's interpretation of what he actually saw, to his speculations respecting the unknown—to his views, in fact, respecting the past history of the objects revealed to him—we do not find any fresh reasons in Dr. Huggins's discovery for accepting, or at least insisting upon, the nebular origin of suns. We have vast gaseous masses intermingled with and surrounding groups of stars, and apparently spread with exceptional richness where these stars or suns are most densely aggregated. But this is not what we should expect to find if stars were formed out of this gaseous matter. On the contrary, we should expect that where stars were most numerous, there the nebulous matter would have been most completely used up, so to speak—exhausted, as it were, in the work of star-making. Nor again can we recognize in the substances which appear to constitute the gaseous nebulæ the fitting materials for making stars. So far as the spectroscopic analysis of the gaseous nebulæ extends, their chief constituent would appear to be the gas nitrogen, the element next in importance in their constitution being the gas hydrogen, while a third element, as yet not identified, seems to be present in their substance. I would not insist too much on this evidence; but it must not be forgotten that it is all the evidence we have: and it must be regarded as at least an unsatisfactory basis on which to rear the hypothetical development of suns like our own, in whose orb exist the glowing vapours of iron, copper, and zinc, sodium, antimony, and mercury, barium, carbon, silicon, and sulphur, and probably every single element known to our chemists.

As respects the nebular hypothesis of Laplace, Dr. Huggins's discovery must be regarded as wholly silent. In the mere existence of vast masses of glowing gas, we have no evidence whatever of those regularly rotating spheroids of vapour which Laplace's hypothesis requires as the primal forms of stars or suns.

These objections are not urged because of the special difficulties which have been recognised by some in the bearing of the nebular hypotheses on religious questions. It has indeed always seemed to me a circumstance to be regretted, that religious questions should have been in any way associated with the scientific difficulties involved in this particular question. There is always this objection to such associations, that in forming them we are apt to associate scientific errors with religious teachings; and these truths seem to suffer when the scientific errors are exposed. Thus well-meaning men have again and again injured the cause they were most eager to serve, by calling in to its aid unsuitable allies. But although I can see no religious reasons for casting discredit on the theory that processes have gone on and are going on upon an infinitely vast scale, resembling those which we see daily going on around us upon a finite scale, yet it does appear to me that there are many excellent scientific reasons for doubting very gravely whether all the suns which people space were originally formed from masses of glowing gas.

To return, however, to the wonders of the star-depths.

Hitherto I have considered only the various forms of matter which occupy surrounding space. Stars and star-systems, star-clusters and star-aggregations, star-cloudlets and star-mist—all these, and probably yet other forms of matter, spread throughout the immeasurable depths which surround us on all sides—form a scene altogether amazing in splendour and sublimity. But how infinitely are the wonders of this scene enhanced, when we recognize in every part of its extent the existence of the most stupendous vitality!

In the first place, we know that those wonderful processes, taking place, as recent discoveries shew, in the central orb of our system, must have their analogues in the economy of every star of the universe. Not one star, indeed, may resemble our sun very closely in details; but in general respects, every self-luminous orb in the universe must be, like the Sun, the scene of the most amazing activity. For no otherwise can the continuance of their intense luminosity be maintained. We have, indeed, in the case of many stars, direct proof of a degree of activity far exceeding even that recognized in the case of our own sun. For many stars vary in lustre to an extent so remarkable as to be scarcely comparable with those minute changes of lustre which our sun undergoes as his spots alternately wax and wane in number and extent; while one or two—as the star Mira in the Whale, and the star Eta in the Ship—undergo changes so remarkable, that it is almost impossible to conceive that these orbs can be the centres of schemes of inhabited worlds.

The motions taking place within the star-system are also altogether amazing when rightly apprehended. Contemplating the stars on a still night, the idea of infinite repose is suggested by their serenity of aspect. Judging the stars again by the ordinary tests of motion, the astronomers of old had abundant reason to regard them as the very emblems of fixity. But in the light of modern astronomical research, we have this lesson forced upon us, that every one of these bright orbs, and all the millions that are unseen save by telescopically strengthened vision, are urging their way so swiftly through space, that the most rapid motions familiar to us must be regarded as absolute rest by comparison. We know with what startling rapidity an express train rushes past a quiet country station. In its swift motion and heavy mass, it seems the embodiment of might and energy. Yet the swiftest express train moves but at the rate of about one mile in a minute of time, and its bulk is utterly insignificant compared with that of the smallest member of the Solar System. What inconceivable energy must we recognize, then, in the motion of our sun through space, at a rate of hundreds of miles per minute, the whole of his attendant family (each member of which is travelling rapidly around him) accompanying him in his swift rush through the interstellar depths? Yet even this wonderful energy of motion seems little when compared with the flight of Sirius, an orb a thousand times larger than the Sun, and travelling many times more swiftly. And we have abundant reasons for believing that amongst the stars revealed by powerful telescopes there are thousands as large as Sirius, and millions as large as our Sun — all with their attendant systems speeding with inconceivable rapidity on their several courses!

I would ask, in conclusion, whether we have now better reason than the astronomers had of old time to consider the mysteries of the universe as fully revealed to us and interpreted. We know much that was unknown until of late, and we have been able to understand some matters which once seemed inexplicable; but the star-depths, as we see them now, are even more mysterious, as well as far more wonderful, than as displayed to the astronomers of old.

STAR GAUGING.

The account of Sir W. Herschel's labours and views presented in our text-books of astronomy, is unfortunately so inexact, that the title itself of this paper will appear strange to many readers. We not only hear nothing about Sir W. Herschel's employment of two different methods of star-gauging in such treatises, but we actually find neither of his methods presented correctly, inasmuch as the properties of the two methods are assigned to a single nondescript method, the incongruities thus arising being apparently altogether overlooked. It is partly with the hope of rendering better justice to the greatest of observational astronomers than has heretofore been accorded to him, that I now write, but partly and chiefly in order to prepare the way for submitting to the notice of students of the heavens a method of research which promises to throw light on the noblest but most difficult of all the problems of astronomy, the determination of the laws according to which the sidereal universe has been constructed. It was this problem which Sir W. Herschel regarded as the end and aim of all his astronomical researches, even of those which seemed to bear little upon it. He observed other objects for practice and to test his telescopes,—the stars alone he studied as the final aim of his researches,—"A knowledge of the construction of the heavens," he wrote in 1811, after more than a quarter of a century of stellar study, " has always been the ultimate object of my observations."

I cannot but express some degree of surprise at the fate which has befallen the noble series of papers in which Sir W. Herschel presented his researches to the world. As I have elsewhere pointed out, little " has hitherto been done to bring the records of his labours properly before the student of astronomy. His papers, merely collected into a volume, would form a most important addition to astronomical literature; but, if suitably edited, and illustrated by the work of his son, and of others who have succeeded him in his own field of work, the volume would do more to advance the study of sidereal astronomy than any work which has been published during the last century." With very few exceptions, what has hitherto been done in making Herschel's words and work public, has been an injustice to his memory. It seems to have been supposed that his papers could be treated as we might treat such a work as Sir J. Herschel's " Outlines of Astronomy ;" that extracts might be made from any part of any paper without reference to the position which the paper chanced to occupy in the complete series. Nay, it seems to have been thought a tribute of respect to his memory thus to quote his words without question or debate. The idea does not seem to have occurred to any one (with the solitary exception of Wilhelm Struve), that it is but an ill compliment to the great astronomer to assume that he laboured from 1784 to 1818 upon a subject scarcely touched before his day, without making any such progression towards new knowledge that his earlier views had to be corrected in the light of later researches. It seems to have mattered little that he himself in so many words expressed the fact that his views had altered: he had said such and such things in 1784 and 1785; and those things the world was bound to accept as his teaching, whatever he might say thereafter to the contrary. And if anyone should express doubts as to those earlier views, and should endeavour to strengthen his position by quoting Sir W. Herschel in 1818 against Sir W. Herschel when thirty-two years younger, it was the fashion to denounce such attempts as altogether rash and presumptuous. This is as though every writer on astronomy should present Kepler's youthful fancies about the relations between the regular solids and the planetary orbits as the matured views of that astronomer, and denounce as irreverent any attempt to suggest that, on the whole, the laws of elliptic motion subsequently discovered by him were better worthy of respectful consideration.

We owe, I conceive, to French writers part of the misconception which has arisen respecting Herschel's labours. It pleased Arago to forsake in Herschel's favour the usual attitude of French men of science with respect to foreigners. He published a work, purporting to be an Analysis of Herschel's Life and Labours. In this work the earliest ideas of Sir W. Herschel respecting the constitution of the heavens,—the views which he entertained before he had made any systematic observations whatever, —are presented with an unfortunate perspicuity. I refer to Herschel's paper of 1784, about which I shall presently have to speak more at length. It is here we find the first enunciation of the famous grindstone theory of the universe, at least the first remarks of Sir W. Herschel on that theory, for it is to Wright of Durham that the first enunciation of the theory is really due. This theory Arago presents, making use of the relations which in 1784 Sir W. Herschel expected to find. At p. 456 Arago says, "the galactic system is a hundred times more extended in one direction than in another," and he then refers to a picture of a certain solid figure illustrating Herschel's ideas in 1784 respecting the shape of our system. But as Wilhelm Struve justly remarks, the only section based on Herschel's observation (presented in the paper of 1785) shows the greatest extension as exceeding the least not in the proportion of 100 to 1, but only as $5\frac{1}{2}$ to 1 ; while the solid figure pictured in 1784 did not in any way relate to observations made by Herschel. It is not too much to say that Arago probably limited his real study of Herschel's papers to the paper of 1784, dipping into the others to gather thence the more striking passages, in full confidence that they accorded well with the views enunciated in 1784, and consequently without any attempt to understand the gradual progression of Herschel's ideas respecting the universe.

The effect of this has been disastrous. All the French writers and most of the continental writers,—Guillemin,

Flammarion, and the rest,—follow Arago unhesitatingly. Too many of our English writers of text-books have borrowed directly from French authors. A few others have presented original analyses of Herschel's papers, but still such analyses have only been sound for the earlier papers (1784 and 1785), while the blending of matter taken from later papers introduces the same real confusion of ideas as in Arago's work, though not always accompanied with the same unfortunate perspicuity of statement.

Passing over such occasional reference to Sir W. Herschel's labours as we find in the pages of writers of a higher order than those just mentioned, it may be said that the elder Struve alone, of all astronomers who have dealt with Herschel's papers, clearly recognized the change which took place in the great astronomer's views as his labours proceeded. We owe this, I believe, to the fortunate chance which led Struve to go over a second time, with close attention, the series of papers which he had probably before read once through (no astronomer would be worthy of the name who had not done so), but without a careful consideration of the bearing of the several papers on Sir W. Herschel's progressive researches. While on a visit to England he received from Sir J. Herschel a volume containing not only the complete series of the elder Herschel's papers, but many valuable manuscript notes by the great astronomer. Struve had already carried out a series of researches into the laws of stellar distribution; and he was under the impression that his results were opposed to those which Sir W. Herschel had obtained. On carefully re-reading Herschel's papers, however, he found that his own results were in agreement with those to which Herschel had been led during the later portion of his observing career. In fact, Struve had overlooked, as I believe every first reader of Herschel's papers invariably does overlook, the fact that Herschel not only adopted new views of the heavens as his labours proceeded, but abandoned the very principles which he had taken for his guidance in the earlier part of his career. It was the merest accident that Struve, already engaged in the careful study of stellar distribution, received the interesting present just mentioned, which led to the re-examination of the great master's papers on the heavens. Yet Struve, a skilful astronomer, an excellent mathematician, a laborious student, and doubtless a careful reader, might fairly have been expected to derive correct impressions from his first reading of those papers. The fact that he did not, that by his own account the second reading almost reversed the ideas he had derived from the first, renders less surprising the fact (for such it is) that men like Nichol, Grant, and even Sir John Herschel, among those who have published their impressions, and others of the utmost eminence in astronomy who have not done so, have entertained altogether erroneous ideas respecting the relations which exist between the earlier and the later views of Sir William Herschel. There are many who have read every paper by the elder Herschel on the constitution of the heavens, who would be quite unable to explain by what steps he was led to abandon the principles on which he based his first method of star-gauging, in favour of those which formed the basis of his second method. Nay, I happen to know that not a few of those who have read Herschel's papers have not recognized the distinction between the two methods, even if they are aware that Herschel ever employed more than one mode of star-gauging.

For my own part, I have not found five successive readings of Herschel's series of papers, and the analysis of some passages, as carefully as one analyses the most concentrated portions of a process of mathematical reading, to be one whit more than the proper mastery of Herschel's papers require. They are not, by any means, easy to understand. Sir W. Herschel was seldom at the pains to indicate that he had changed his views, being, for the most part, satisfied with presenting his newly-adopted opinions without any special reference to those he had before entertained. Where he did refer to any change of opinion, he did not enter into details, but simply noted that the views he had formerly entertained had given place to others, the results of a more complete acquaintance with the facts. Nor was Sir W. Herschel a particularly lucid writer; we shall see, as we proceed, that at times, in order to understand his meaning, we have to examine the context more carefully than is usually necessary in scientific or explanatory writing.

In 1774, Herschel enunciated his general views respecting the sidereal system, and the method which seemed to him, at that time, the best for attempting to ascertain the true figure of the system. This, *his first method of star-gauging*, has been described, though not with strict accuracy, in most of our text-books of astronomy. If we suppose that our sun is a member of a system of suns scattered with a certain general uniformity throughout a region of space having a certain well-defined figure, then a method exists by which it is possible to determine that figure, provided only that a telescope can be constructed which is powerful enough to reach to the limits of the system in all directions. For manifestly the farther the system extends in any given direction, the greater will be the number of stars lying towards that direction (since we have supposed a certain general uniformity of distribution); so that if we use the same telescope with unchanged "power," and direct it in turn to every part of the heavens, then, by counting the number of stars brought into view in these different directions, we can determine the relative extension of the system along those directions —in other words, we can determine the shape of the system.

This is the famous method of gauging the heavens. I give another description of it (borrowed from the pages of that fine work, Grant's history of "Physical Astronomy"), because the method should be very carefully considered by the reader. Grant speaks of the plan as a "remarkable method, devised by Herschel for ascertaining the configuration in space of this great sidereal system, by examining the heavens at different distances from the Galactic Circle, and numbering the stars visible in the field of view of his telescope. Assuming that the stars are uniformly distributed throughout space, and that the telescope suffices to penetrate to the utmost limits of the sidereal stratum constituting the Milky Way, it is manifest that the number of stars visible in the field of view of the telescope would increase with the length of the visual line, and would thereby afford an indication of the distance from the observer to the exterior surface of the Milky Way. Hence, by comparing together the lengths of the various lines formed in this manner, and taking into consideration their respective distances from the Galactic Circle, the actual configuration in space of the Milky Way may be ascertained. Such is a brief outline of the celebrated method of gauging the heavens, which Herschel *practised to a vast extent in the early period of his researches* on the constitution of the Milky Way." Here the italics are mine. I invite special attention to Grant's recognition of a change in Herschel's methods of research towards the latter part of his career as an observer. It is remarkable that, notwithstanding this, Grant failed to notice how and in what respects Herschel modified the views to which his earlier method of star-gauging had led him.

It will be noticed that this plan of star-gauging consisted essentially in applying one and the same telescopic power to different parts of the heavens. It involved the assumption of a general uniformity of stellar distribution within the limits of our system. And it required that the telescope should penetrate to these limits,—at least, if in any part of the heavens this was not the case, the shape of the system towards that part could not be determined.

It is necessary to notice, however, that the general uniformity of distribution by no means implied the non-existence of clustering aggregations of stars, or of streams, branches, and nodules of stars within the limits of the system. On the contrary, Herschel, so early as 1785, clearly indicated his recognition of such varieties; and all that he insisted upon at that time was that such peculiarities were themselves so distributed as to produce within the system, regarded as a whole, a general uniformity of distribution.

It is absolutely essential, if we would understand Herschel's earlier views, to take his own preliminary description, which somehow appears to have escaped the notice of commentators,—unless we suppose the difficulty of grasping Herschel's real meaning to have caused them to misunderstand the passage.

"It will be best," Herschel says, "to take the subject from a point of view at a considerable distance, both of space and of time. Let us suppose, then, numberless stars of various sizes scattered over an indefinite portion of space in such a manner as to be almost equally distributed throughout the whole. The laws of attraction, which no doubt extend to the remotest region of the fixed stars, will operate in such a manner as most probably to produce the following remarkable effects":—

"Form I. In the first place, since we have supposed the stars to be of various sizes, it will frequently happen that a star being considerably larger than its neighbouring ones, will attract them more than they will be attracted by others that are immediately around them; by which means they will be, in turn, as it were, condensed about the centre; or, in other words, form themselves into a cluster of stars of almost a globular figure, more or less regularly so, according to the size and original distance of the surrounding stars."

"Form II. The next case, which will also happen almost as frequently as the former, is where a few stars though not superior in size to the rest, may chance to be rather nearer each other than the surrounding ones; for here also will be found a prevailing attraction in the combined centre of gravity of them all, which will occasion the neighbouring stars to draw together, not, indeed, so as to form a regular, or globular figure, but, however, in such a manner, as to be condensed towards the common centre of gravity of the whole irregular cluster. And this construction admits of the utmost variety of shapes, according to the number and situation of the stars which first give rise to the condensation of the rest."

"Form III. From the composition and repeated conjunction of both the foregoing forms, a third may be derived,[*] when many large stars, or combined small ones are situated in long-extended, regular, or crooked rows, hooks, or branches; for they will also draw the surrounding

---

[*] Here the words "may be derived" are not intended to imply doubt as to the fact that the groups of the third form exist. The context shows that Herschel means that *we may deduce* the existence of the

ones, so as to produce figures of condensed stars, coarsely similar to the former, which gave rise to these condensations."

"Form IV. We may likewise admit of still more extensive combinations when, at the same time that a cluster of stars is forming in one part of space, there may be another collecting in a different, but perhaps not far distant quarter, which may occasion a mutual approach towards their common centre of gravity."

"Form V. In the last place, as a natural consequence of the former cases, there will be formed great cavities, or vacancies, by the retreat of the stars towards the various centres which attract them ; so that upon the whole, there is evidently a field of the greatest variety for the mutual and combined attractions of the heavenly bodies to exert themselves in."

After considering the possibility of catastrophes during the evolution of the forms here described, Herschel proceeds to consider the position of the terrestrial observer in his " own retired station, in one of the planets attending a star." He shows that to such an observer, placed in a far extending stratum " or branching cluster of millions of stars, such as may fall under Form III.," considered above, the following appearances will be presented :—To the naked eye, " The heavens will not only be richly scattered

third form from considering that both the other forms must be compounded and repeatedly conjoined. It is important to notice this, because " Form III." is the key of the whole passage, being the form which Herschel attributed to our Milky Way at this stage of his researches.

over with brilliant constellations, but a shining zone or Milky Way will be perceived to surround the whole sphere of the heavens, owing to the combined light of those stars which are too small, that is too remote, to be seen." Let this passage be particularly noted before we proceed, as on its right comprehension depends our entire judgment as to Herschel's earlier views. He here presents the sidereal system as a far-extending stratum or branching cluster of millions of stars, of Form III., and therefore including within its limits many subordinate clusters and nebulæ of Forms I. and II.; while he regards the light of the Milky Way as resulting from the extension of the system towards that zone much farther than in other directions.* This must be borne carefully in mind in reading what immediately follows. "Our observer's sight," proceeds Herschel, "will be so confined that he will imagine this single collection of stars, of which he does not even perceive the thousandth part, to be the whole contents of the heavens. Allowing him now the use of a common telescope he begins to suspect that all the milkiness of the bright path which surrounds the sphere may be owing to stars. He perceives a few clusters of them in various parts of the heavens, and finds also that there are a kind of nebulous patches; but still his views are not extended so far as to

---

* In fact, his views at this stage corresponded closely with those which had been advanced by Lambert nearly a quarter of a century earlier. In the papers of 1784, Herschel presents views more nearly resembling those which Wright of Durham had advanced half a century earlier, and which Kant adopted a year or two before Lambert advanced his more correct views.

reach to the end of the stratum in which he is situated, so that he looks upon these patches as belonging to that system which to him seems to comprehend every celestial object. He now increases his power of vision, and applying himself to a close observation, finds the Milky Way is indeed no other than a collection of very small stars. He perceives that those objects which had been called nebulæ are evidently nothing but clusters of stars. He finds their number increase upon him, and when he resolves one nebula into stars he discovers ten new ones which he cannot resolve. He then forms the idea of immense strata of fixed stars, of clusters of stars, and of nebulæ, till going on with such interesting observations he now perceives that all these appearances must naturally arise from the confined situation in which he is now placed. *Confined*, it may justly be called, though in no less a space than what before appeared the whole region of the fixed stars; but which now has assumed the shape of a crookedly branching nebula, not one of the least, but perhaps very far from being the most considerable of those numberless clusters that enter into the construction of the heavens."

It cannot be denied that the passage just quoted is not very easy to understand. At one stage, or rather throughout the greater part of the passage, it seems abundantly clear that Herschel is describing our sidereal system as including multitudes of subordinate clusters and nebulæ. But then at the end, he describes it as itself a nebula, greater than some, but less than others, of numberless clusters, composing the sidereal heavens. And the perplexity which the passage as a whole thus occasions, is accompanied by a perplexity arising from the variety of meaning which may be attributed to the different sentences. For instance, where he says that the observer "forms the idea of immense strata of fixed stars, of clusters, and of nebulæ," he might (so far as the grammatical interpretation of the sentence is concerned) mean either (1) the idea of immense strata, composed of fixed stars, clusters, and nebulæ, or (2) the idea of immense stellar strata, star-clusters, and nebulæ. The latter has been the meaning usually adopted—if, at least, this particular sentence has been discussed at all. Such a meaning accords with the theory (the familiar Grindstone Theory) commonly attributed to Herschel. Nevertheless it should be manifest, from the passage just quoted (regarded as a whole), that Herschel not only recognized star-strata, including within their limits subordinate clusters and nebulæ, but that he regarded our sidereal system as a star-stratum of that kind. How, then, are we to remove the difficulties I have noted in the passage as a whole, and in its several parts? It must certainly be by taking a meaning which covers both the two views which appear contradictory, for no one will for a moment admit that Sir W. Herschel really held contradictory views. Accordingly, we must believe *both* that Herschel held our galaxy to be a stratum, including in its limits star-clusters and nebulæ, *and* that he regarded it as one among many systems of its own order, that is, one among many star-clusters and nebulæ, and of a higher order than those (spoken of under the same name; but really) subordinate to, and included within, itself and its fellow systems.*

That this is Herschel's meaning we perceive clearly from a passage following almost immediately after the one just quoted. "It will appear," he says, "that many hundreds of nebulæ, of the first and second forms, are actually to be seen in the heavens, and their places will hereafter be pointed out; and many of the third form will be described." Thus, there can be seen in the heavens many hundreds of clusters and nebulæ of one kind (Forms I. and II), and also many clusters of a higher order (Form III.), within which the others exist as subordinate parts—or, in other words, we can see the clusters and nebulæ which form part of the architecture, as it were, of our own

* The case is one of those to which I have referred above, where we have to reason from the context in order to understand Herschel's true meaning. And it would be unfair, I think, to blame the ordinary commentator for failing to apply such reasoning to Herschel's voluminous papers. What, however, does seem unfortunate, is the course adopted by our text-book writers, in selecting passages from Herschel's papers at random, notwithstanding these difficulties, and stringing them together as Herschel's matured views. It is as though a person not very familiar with a language were to pretend to analyse a book in that language by selecting from the book all the sentences he was able to understand. I may note, in passing, that the author of one of the best treatises on observational astronomy in existence, has been led into a most curious misapprehension. Herschel had expressed a belief that the stellar stratum extends one hundred times farther in the direction of its general level than at right angles to that level: but later (in the paper I am quoting from above) he assigned $5\frac{1}{4}$ to 1 as the proportion. Now the late Admiral Smyth, at p. 310 of his "Bedford Cycle," presents a picture of the sidereal system, showing that he had combined these two different results into one, thus giving to our system length, breadth, and thickness as 1, $5\frac{1}{4}$, and 100.

sidereal system; while we can see, but not in such great numbers, external nebulæ of the same order in the scale of creation as our own galaxy. Herschel, in fact, describes ten nebulæ of the latter order, speaking of them as external Milky Ways. Instances of the fourth order "will be related," he proceeds; "a few of the cavities mentioned in the fifth will be particularized, though many more have already been observed: so that upon the whole, I believe it will be found that the foregoing theoretical view, with all its consequential appearances, as seen by an eye enclosed in one of the nebulæ, is no more than a drawing from nature, wherein the features of the original have been closely copied; and I hope the resemblance will not be called a bad one, when it shall be considered how very limited must be the pencil of an inhabitant of so small and retired a portion of an indefinite system, in attempting the picture of so unbounded an extent."

In further confirmation of this interpretation of Herschel's views at this stage of his labours I will now quote a passage which is perfectly irreconcilable, I venture to affirm, with the simple theory of the sidereal system so commonly attributed to Sir W. Herschel.

"If," he says, "it were possible to distinguish between the parts of an indefinitely extended whole, the nebula we inhabit might be said to be one that has fewer marks of profound antiquity upon it than the rest. To explain this idea, perhaps, more clearly, we should recollect that the condensation of clusters of stars has been ascribed to a gradual approach; and whoever reflects upon the number of ages that must have passed before some of the clusters could be so far condensed as we find them at present, will not wonder if I ascribe a certain air of youth and vigour to many very regularly scattered regions of our sidereal stratum. There are, moreover, many places in the stratum where there is the greatest reason to believe that the stars, if we may judge from appearances, are now drawing towards various secondary centres, and will in time separate into different clusters so as to occasion many subdivisions. Hence we may surmise that when a nebulous stratum consists chiefly of nebulæ of the first and second form, it probably owes its origin to what may be called the decay of a great compound nebula of the third form; and that the subdivisions which happened to it in the length of time occasioned all the small nebulæ which spring from it to lie in a certain range, according as they were detached from the primary one. In like manner our system, after numbers of ages, may very possibly become divided so as to give rise to a stratum of two or three hundred nebulæ; for it would not be difficult to point out so many beginning or gathering clusters in it. This view of the subject throws a considerable light upon the appearance of that remarkable collection of many hundreds of nebulæ which are to be seen in what I have called the nebulous stratum of Coma Berenices. It appears from the extended and branching figure of our nebula, that there is room for the decomposed nebulæ of a large, reduced, former great one to approach nearer to us in the sides than in other parts. Nay, possibly, there might originally be another very large joining branch, which in time became separated by the condensation of the stars: and this may be the reason of the little remaining breadth of our system in that very place; for the nebulæ of the stratum of Coma are brightest and most crowded just opposite our situation, or in the pole of our system. As soon as this idea was suggested, I tried also the opposite pole, where, accordingly, I have met with a great number of nebulæ, though under a much more scattered form."

I apprehend that this conception even of the possibility that the two great nebular systems lying (roughly) towards the galactic poles, may be the fragments of branches formerly belonging to our own sidereal system, which is itself tending towards a dissolution into such fragments, cannot in any way be reconciled with the absurd cloven-grindstone theory which is advanced over and over again in our text-books as the outcome of Sir W. Herschel's labours.

I could quote several other passages from the fine paper of 1785, in confirmation of the thesis, that, even at this early stage, Sir W. Herschel not only recognized great variety of structure within the limits of our sidereal system, but also regarded large numbers of clusters and nebulæ as forming parts of that system. I will, however, content myself with two short passages; one indicating his ideas respecting the relation between our Milky Way and star-clusters, the other showing what orders of nebulæ he alone regarded as probably external systems, resembling our own in extent and importance. "Some parts of our system seem indeed," he says, in the former, "to have already suffered greater ravages of time than others, if this way of expressing myself may be allowed. For instance, in the body of Scorpio is an opening, or hole, which is probably owing to this cause. . . . . This opening is at least four degrees broad; but its height (*sic*) I have not yet ascertained. It is remarkable that the nebula 80 Messier, which is one of the richest and most compressed clusters of small stars I remember to have seen, is situated just on the western border of it; which would almost authorize a suspicion that the stars of which it is composed were collected from that place, and had left the vacancy. What adds not a little to this surmise is, that the same phenomenon is once more repeated with the cluster of stars 4 Messier, which is also on the western border of another vacancy, and has, moreover, a small miniature cluster, or easily resolvable nebula following it at no very great distance." The other passage runs thus:—" There are some very remarkable nebulæ which cannot well be less, but are probably much larger than our system; and being also extended, the inhabitants of the planets that attend the stars which compose these nebulæ, must likewise perceive the same phenomena; for which reason these nebulæ may also be called Milky Ways *by way of distinction.*"

It was to a sidereal system which he regarded as thus complex in structure and in shape that Sir W. Herschel applied his first method of star-gauging. He believed himself to be gauging, not, as has been so commonly supposed, a simple cluster of stars belonging to the same order in the scale of creation as the clusters and nebulæ discernible in the telescopic scrutiny of the heavens, but a great clustering aggregation of stars, star-clusters, and nebulæ, belonging to the same order as certain of the more remarkable and extended of the nebulæ.

In what sense, then, it may be asked, did he recognize general uniformity in the sidereal system? And in what respect did his views at this stage differ from those which he subsequently adopted?

It is easy to reply to these questions, when once the scope of Herschel's series of researches has been recognized. It is manifest that at this early period he regarded the sidereal system as presenting a general uniformity of *structure* within its irregular boundary, such uniformity arising, not from a general uniformity of stellar distribution, but from a general uniformity in the distribution of the stars, star-clusters, and nebulæ within the system. He believed, in fact, in what may be termed regular irregularity; and one may present his theory on this point in some such manner as this: "If any two very large portions of the sidereal system be compared with each other, the number of stars, star-clusters, and nebulæ, in these several portions, will be proportional (or nearly so) to the volume of those portions respectively." That this was his view is not only clear from the passages I have cited, but is strikingly manifested by his applying to our sidereal system the term "Milky Way," as inclusive of the whole, and his use of the same term for external systems, all those nebulæ which he regarded as external, being at this stage of his labours called indifferently external systems, galaxies, or Milky Ways. But he also, even more distinctly, shews that he believed the sidereal system to be regularly constituted, when regarded as a whole, in the following remarkable passage, which presents more clearly than any other I have met with his true views at this time :—" The rich parts of the Milky Way, as well as those in the distant broad part of the stratum, consist of a mixture of stars of all possible sizes, that are seemingly placed without any apparent order. Perhaps we might recollect that a greater condensation towards the centre of the system than towards the borders of it should be taken into consideration ; but with a nebula of the third form, containing such various and extensive combinations as I have found to take place in ours, this circumstance, which in one of the first form would be of considerable moment, may, I think, be safely neglected."

But Sir W. Herschel by no means regarded this view of the sidereal system as demonstratively established, notwithstanding the fact that it was presented in company with the long list of star-gauges for which he is so justly celebrated. He knew perfectly well, what many of his admirers have overlooked, that a hypothesis cannot be established by the observations which it was devised to interpret. He reasoned thus :—Granting the truth of a certain hypothesis, a series of star-gauges, described in the paper of 1785, has a certain significance, and shews the sidereal system to have a certain shape: if the hypothesis be *not* true, they cannot be so interpreted.

This question, then (to be answered by other observations) remained for him,—"Is the sidereal system constituted as supposed in the hypothesis I have been employing?" If he had overlooked this question, he would not have been Herschel. No matter how great his skill as an observer, or how numerous his observations, he would not have been entitled to a higher position as a reasoner or as an interpreter of observations than any of his predecessors in the discussion of the stellar system, and not to so high a position as Wright, or Kant, or Lambert, or the ingenious Michell. But he was not thus negligent of cardinal considerations. He clearly recognized the weak point of the theory he was discussing (rather than advocating). "*I would not be understood,*" he says, (immediately after the words last quoted from the paper of 1785,) "*to lay a greater stress on these calculations than the principles on which they are founded will permit; and if, hereafter, we shall find reason, from experience and observation, to believe that there are parts of our system where the stars are not scattered in the manner here supposed, we ought then to make proper exceptions.*"

I propose now to describe how Herschel *did* "find reason, from experience and observation, to believe that" the Milky Way itself, which he had thus far regarded as not only resembling the rest of the sidereal system, but as being the sidereal system (the stars scattered over our skies being merely parts of the Milky Way stratum) is composed of stars quite differently arranged from those composing the rest of the sidereal system; I shall shew how he devised another mode of star-gauging differing essentially in plan and principle from that which he adopted in 1784, and first applied systematically in 1785; and then I shall endeavour to shew how the careful comparison of his results with others obtained since his time, suggests a method of star-gauging combining the principles of both Herschel's methods, advantageously applicable with every order of telescopic power, and promising, if patiently applied by a sufficient number of observers, to lift the veil from some at least of the mysteries of the stellar depths.

Let us pause, however, for a moment to notice that a new interest is given to Sir W. Herschel's researches when his earlier papers are correctly interpreted. We see him preparing in 1785 to deal with the most stupendous of all the problems of astronomy. A noble theory of the universe had presented itself to his mind, and already he had carried out a series of observations tending to indicate the proportions of the sidereal system, if that theory were true. But now he was preparing for labours of a more arduous kind, the thorough examination, in fact, of the stellar heavens so far as they were visible from his northern point of view. No celestial objects, except the members of our solar system, and the mysterious comets, were to be regarded as unimportant in this inquiry. The stars by their distribution in greater or less profusion, the nebulæ and clusters within our system as representing various stages of stellar aggregation, those external to it as indicating its more striking characteristics, and other orders of objects (not suspected when he began his labours), as affording new evidence respecting its structure,—all might throw light on the theory he had advanced, or might, when carefully studied, afford reason for abandoning or modifying that theory.

I apprehend, then, that had the notice of astronomers been attracted, at this early stage, to the work on which Herschel was entering, they could not but have awaited with extreme interest the result of his labours. It does not appear that this was actually the case. It may be that the difficulty and complexity of the problem he had taken in hand, or perchance the quiet and unobtrusive manner in which he presented it as it then appeared to him, or some other cause may have been in operation, but certain it is that very little notice was taken of Herschel's special work then, or during the remainder of his life. None helped him, though his researches were manifestly far beyond the strength of any single worker. No comments on his stellar observations, so far as they related to the great problem he was attacking, were made by contemporary astronomers.* It was alone, but confidently, that he advanced into the mysterious depths surrounding our solar system, seeking by the dim light which made

* To the general public Herschel was known as the discoverer of the Georgium Sidus, the observer of supposed volcanic eruptions on the moon, and for a variety of other such discoveries as are easily understood,—or misunderstood (which comes to the same thing so far as general fame is concerned).

the darkness visible, to determine, if it might be, the forms dimly discernible within those gloomy wildernesses of space.

Many years passed before he again addressed the scientific world on the great subject which he had taken as the "ultimate object of his observations." Eleven years * after the enunciation of the theory described in the former part of this essay, we find him pointing out, as the result of his researches during that long period, that the hypothesis of a general uniformity of structure in the galaxy " is too far removed from the truth to be depended upon." And although this does not imply a definite withdrawal from the theory of 1785, yet the stress now laid by Herschel on probable varieties of structure is a novel feature in his theoretical treatment of the subject.

But it was in 1802, (seventeen years, be it noticed, after the theory had appeared which is so commonly referred to as though it were the *result* of Herschel's observations instead of the occasion of them,) that Herschel first began to present an entirely new view of the general structure of the universe. In the essay of that year he described the results to which he had been led by the study of double stars. As Struve has well pointed out, there was much in Herschel's work in this direction which naturally suggested the adoption of new views on the wider subject

* The paper of 1789 contained a list of 1000 nebulæ discovered by Herschel, and was prefaced by a remarkable essay on the gradual development of stellar nebulæ. The reasoning does not readily admit of condensation, and this part of the paper is too long to be quoted in full.

of the sidereal universe itself. He had begun to observe double stars, not with the idea of recognising any connection between the components of these objects, but on the contrary, in the belief that double stars are simply stars which, though really at enormous distances from each other, chance to lie nearly in the same direction as seen by the terrestrial observer. He conceived (independently, we may suppose, though Galileo and Christian Huyghens had anticipated him), the idea of determining the distance of the brighter, and presumably the nearer, member of such a pair of stars, by noticing how much the orbital motion of the earth caused the brighter star to shift in position with respect to the fainter (necessarily much less affected by the earth's motion if really much farther away than the brighter). It would be interesting to note how the prosecution of this task, begun long before 1784, gradually led Herschel to the conception of binary systems, and later to the certain assurance that there are many systems of this class in the celestial depths. Still more interesting would be the history of the steps by which he was led from the same starting-point, but on another course, to the discovery of the motion of our sun through space, and therefore to the recognition of that most stupendous of the phenomena presented by the heavens to us,—the motion of all the suns accompanied by their attendant systems through the interstellar regions. But these matters, full of interest though they are, must here be touched on only incidentally, in their relation to the processes of star-gauging, by which Herschel hoped in a more direct manner to ascertain the structure of the universe.

It was natural that the recognition of binary stars,—that is, of pairs of stars not merely connected by an optical relation, but specially associated by the bonds of their mutual attraction, should suggest to Herschel the conception of other and more complicated systems, and that he should be prepared thenceforth to find in the star-depths other relations than those which the analogy of our sun had suggested. Our sun is an insulated star, the components of a "binary" are associated stars. May not higher orders of association exist, affecting other stars than those manifestly belonging to clusters or nebulæ? For note that, although the conception of associated stars had already (as I have shewn) been abundantly recognised by Herschel in the paper of 1785, yet the cases in which it had been recognized were those in which it was obvious at a single view; the study of double stars had led to the conclusion that stars not obviously associated, stars to which the method of star-gauging would have been applied without any suspicion, might be so near as to be bound together, (and, as it were, separated from other stars) by their mutual attraction. Herschel never applied his first method of star-gauging to any field of view containing a cluster of stars, in such sort as to infer from the large number of stars in the cluster an enormous extension of the sidereal system in the direction of that field of view. He himself pointed out the objection to such an inference—the fact, namely, that a cluster is manifestly a rounded group of stars, not a region of the sky which is rich because of enormous extension in the line of sight. But until many double stars had been proved to be 'binaries,' or pairs of stars 'whereof the one more bright is circled by the other,' he would not have thought of excluding fields in which double, triple, and multiple stars were numerous. Now however (in 1802), that he has to describe the recognition of binary stars, we find him for the first time drawing a distinction between insulated stars and all orders of multiple stars.

It is worthy of notice, especially by those who know what interest Sir W. Herschel took in the subject of life in other worlds,* that he regarded the insulated suns as alone, in all probability, the centres of planetary systems resembling our own. 'The question will arise,' he says, 'whether every insulated star be a sun like ours, attended with planets, satellites, and numerous comets? And here, as nothing appears against the supposition, we may from analogy admit the probability of it. But, were we to extend this argument to other sidereal constructions, or still further to every star of the heavens, as has been done frequently, I should not only hesitate, but even think that, from what will be said of stars which enter into complicated sidereal systems, the contrary is far more likely to be the case; and that probably we can only look for solar systems among insulated stars.'

* His discussion of the question whether life can exist in our own sun, is, perhaps, the strongest extant proof of the interest which this subject had for him.

Observing, then, that in 1802 Herschel first presented the distinction between insulated stars and 'those which enter into complicated sidereal systems,' a capital interest attaches to whatever he might at that time say about the Milky Way. In 1785, he had so fully believed the Milky Way to be only the richer part of our sidereal system, that he took the name Milky Way as a convenient title for the whole system, and called those nebulæ which he believed to be external sidereal systems, 'Milky Ways,' as adequately distinguishing them from the clusters and nebulæ which form parts of our stellar system. Let us see whether in 1802 he so viewed the Milky Way—for we may be assured that if he did, his views in 1802 were in the main very much like those he had held in 1785, whereas if he did not, we may be sure his views were greatly altered. His words are decisive on this all-important point :—

"The stars we consider as insulated are also surrounded by a magnificent collection of innumerable stars, called the Milky Way, which must occasion a very powerful balance of opposite attractions to hold the intermediate stars in a state of rest. For though our sun and all the stars we see, may truly be said to be in the plane of the Milky Way, yet *I am now convinced by a long inspection and continued examination of it, that the Milky Way itself consists of stars very differently scattered from those which are immediately about us.*"

So much as to the general and more important view of the question. It is clear that by the words, 'a long inspection and continued examination of the Milky Way,' Herschel refers to the seventeen years of observation which had followed the enunciation of the views he held in 1785. It is clear also from the words, 'I am *now* convinced' that he had changed his views, apart from the proof of the fact which I have deduced from the comparison of his statements in 1785, with the results to which he had been led in 1802. I mean, that no nice analysis of his words is required to shew that in 1802 he came before the scientific world with entirely new ideas as to the construction of the universe; since he says as much very plainly—*almost* as plainly as (we shall presently see) he stated the fact nine years later in the preface to the remarkable paper of 1811.

But let us see in what the change of view consisted :—

'On a very slight examination,'* he says, speaking of the Milky Way, 'it will appear that this immense starry aggregation is by no means uniform. The stars of which it is composed are very unequally scattered, and show evident marks of clustering together into many separate allotments. By referring to some one of these clustering collections in the heavens, what will be said of them will be much better understood than if we were to treat of them in a general way.' He selects the fine portion of

---

* One might pause here to ask whether, speaking as he does here of a 'very slight examination,' Herschel can be referring to results to which he had been led 'by a long inspection and continued examination.' But I think we need not find any difficulty in this, since results acquired with great labour may need but a very slight examination to indicate highly significant truths.

the Milky Way which occupies the lower half of the 'Cross' in the constellation Cygnus (a group which may be fairly called the Northern Cross). Here, he says, 'the stars are clustering with a kind of division between them, so that we may suppose them to be clustering towards two different regions. By a computation founded on observations which ascertain the number of stars in different fields of view, it appears that our space 'in Cygnus,'* taking an average breadth of about five degrees of it, contains more than 331,000 stars ;† and admitting them to be clustering two different ways, we have 165,000 stars for each clustering collection. Now the above-mentioned milky appearances deserve the name of clustering collections,‡ as they are certainly much brighter about the middle, and fainter near their undefined borders. For in my sweeps of the heavens it has been fully ascertained that the brightness of the Milky Way arises only from stars, and that their compression increases according to the brightness of the Milky Way.'

It is not easy to overrate the importance of the results embodied in the reasoning here quoted. Here are two rich

* That is the selected portion of the Milky Way.

† More stars in this small space, as viewed by Herschel's 18-inch reflector, than in the whole northern heavens, including this space as viewed with Argelander's $2\frac{3}{4}$-inch telescope. And yet my chart of Argelander's results presents 324,000 stars as a collection bewildering in its richness.

‡ The reader's attention is specially directed to the fact that the clustering collections here spoken of are not telescopic small clusters. They are two of the cloudlike masses which the Milky Way presents to ordinary vision on any dark, clear night.

regions of the Milky Way (which, according to the theory of 1785, indicated two projecting regions of the stellar system), now viewed as clustering collections, and selected as typical instances of want of uniformity in the structure of the Milky Way. They are not clustering collections in appearance only—that of course would have been no new fact, and would not have been worth announcing to the scientific world; but they are real aggregations of stars, surrounded on all sides by relatively vacant space. Between us, therefore, and these rich clustering regions, there lies a vast space not so richly filled with stars. The continuity of structure within the sidereal system, which constituted the very basis of the first method of star-gauging, is accordingly disproved. Thus the *first method of star-gauging is shewn to be inapplicable in this case and in all similar cases. Moreover the case being typical of the general want of uniformity in the structure of the Milky Way, the first method of star-gauging fails for the Milky Way itself, to interpret the nature of which it had been originally devised.*

If any doubt remain in the reader's mind as to Herschel's real meaning—if, for instance, it be supposed possible that Herschel may after all have referred to aggregation in particular parts of the heavens, as distinguished from aggregation in particular regions of space—then what Herschel proceeds to say respecting the great rich regions in Cygnus, can scarcely fail to remove all question as to his meaning. Yet, before quoting his words, I must premise that again we have to deal with a passage which, though really unmistakable, requires careful attention before its real import can be apprehended :—

'We may indeed,' he says (as if expressing hesitation, though really about to render his inferences more certain), 'partly ascribe the increase both of brightness and of apparent compression' in those clustering regions, 'to a greater depth of the space which contains the stars, but this will equally tend to shew their clustering condition ; for since the increase of brightness is gradual, *the space containing the clustering stars must tend to a spherical form,* if the gradual increase of brightness is to be explained by the situation of the stars.' In other words, whether we consider the greater central richness as due to the clustering of the stars towards the central parts of these groups, or to the shape of the groups themselves, or partly consider both causes of central aggregation, we are still led to the conclusion that the groups are roughly spherical in shape.

As the whole theory of 1785 was concerned in the reasoning here presented, I cannot too specially invite the reader's attention to the result to which Herschel had been led. I may illustrate the distinction between Herschel's views in 1802 and those which he held in 1785 in the following manner: We know that when a moderately thick low-lying mist covers a level plain, an observer placed on the plain sees through the mist above him, while near the direction of his horizon it is impenetrable, because the line of sight extends so much farther through it in such a direction. Now, let us suppose the case of a being—a visitant, let us say, from another world—not familiar as we all are with the appearances commonly presented by clouds, mists, or fogs, and introduced gradually to their various forms. If placed on a plain in the circumstances above described, he would readily convince himself that the impenetrability of the air towards the horizon was due to the fact that a mist within which he was himself placed had the shape of a flat stratum, so that where he looked along or nearly along the direction of the stratum's extension, the line of sight passed through a much greater range of mist. And we may conceive him attempting to determine the shape (the relative thickness and extension) of the misty stratum, by a method analogous to Sir W. Herschel's first method of star-gauging, estimating the extension of the mist in different directions by the apparent density of the mist in those directions. But now, suppose our observer introduced to a new state of things. Conceive him placed on a level plain, with mist enough low down to hide all terrestrial objects which otherwise might guide his eye, and that the sky for a considerable distance from the horizon is wholly cloud-laden, but not mist-enshrouded, the sky overhead being visible, with occasional cloud masses suspended there, while more and more clouds are in view the farther the line of sight is directed from the point overhead. We can readily conceive that the first interpretation he would assign to the observed appearances would correspond with the result of his former observations. He would suppose that towards the horizon there was a great extension of mist-laden air, and that there was also a great extension of misty matter towards those parts of the upper sky which shewed an impenetrable cloudiness. He would not at first be prepared to conceive a state of things unlike that which he had formerly recognised, or to suppose there was not, as in that case, a *continuity of mist-laden air* between himself and those regions where he perceived dense cloudiness. Gradually, however, the idea would present itself that the round-looking cloudy regions were really round in shape,—not bounded merely by an apparent outline on the sky, but by a rounded surface, *outside* of which he, the observer, was placed. A variety of observations so familiar to us that we hardly recognise the process of reasoning by which the mind becomes satisfied with their significance, would before long satisfy our observer of the justice of this conclusion. He would soon see reason to believe that not only the clouds seen separately overhead, but those confusedly intermixed towards the horizon through the effects of foreshortening, were in reality rounded masses of mist-laden air. Now, *just as markedly as the groups of clouds which are seen on a summer's day differ from a low-lying mist (so far as their relation to the observer is concerned) so completely does the system of great stellar clusterings recognized in the Milky Way by Herschel in* 1802, *differ from the stratum of stars, small clusters, and nebulæ, of which in* 1785 *he supposed the Milky Way to be the fore-shortened, and the stars of our constellations to be the transverse view.*

But it does not follow that Herschel in giving up the most striking result to which his first method of star-gauging had seemed to lead, was bound to give up also the method itself. It had failed for certain cases, simply because the principle on which it was based was not applicable to those cases; but wherever there was any approach to the uniformity of scattering on which the method depends, there the method might still be applied. Precisely as our imagined observer might still continue to test the shape and extension of a mist in which he found himself involved, by noting its apparent density towards different directions, abandoning that method only where he had reason to believe that cloudiness was due to mist within which he was *not* placed, so Herschel might still refer the richness of many of his star-gauges to great extension of stars in the corresponding directions, abandoning such inferences only where he had reason to believe that he was analysing the wealth of great clustering aggregations outside the bounds of which our solar system is situated.

But although after 1802 Herschel still occasionally referred to his first series of star-gauges, we do not find that he any longer regarded them in the same light as in 1785.

As my subject now is star-gauging according to the two methods devised by Herschel, I scarcely feel justified in entering at any length into another striking feature of the paper of 1802. And yet it may be well to notice how markedly Herschel's whole conception of the constitution of the universe changed at that epoch. Not only did he in 1802 advance his proof of the association between double and multiple stars, deducing thence and otherwise illustrating his inferences respecting wider laws of association, but he also selected this occasion to abandon the theory that, the great irresolvable nebulæ are composed of stars. He now regarded some among them as 'possessing the quality of self-luminous, milky luminosity, and possibly at no great distance from us.' *

* It is worthy of notice how readily a logically trained mind recognizes incongruities in result apparently presented with the highest possible authority. It is well known that Humboldt, quoting Arago's account of the results of Herschel's labours—so that the combined weight of these three names seemed to authorise the statement—presents our sidereal system as a "starry island, or nebula," forming a 'lens-shaped, flattened, and everywhere detached stratum.' Herbert Spencer, reasoning on the relations presented by Humboldt, shews the incongruity and absurdity of the statements (1) that this our island nebula has such and such proportions, and (2) that the nebulæ are remote sidereal systems, whether we assume, with Humboldt and Arago, that the differences of star magnitude are due to differences of distance, or reject this assumption. In a letter written to a weekly journal on Jan. 31, 1870, Mr Spencer, after quoting the passages in which he had shewn this, remarks that 'when they were written spectrum analysis had not yielded the conclusive proof which we now possess, that many nebulæ consist of matter in a diffused form. But quite apart from the evidence yielded by spectrum analysis, it seems to me that the incongruities and contradictions which may be evolved from the hypothesis that nebulæ are remote sidereal systems, amply suffice to shew that hypothesis to be untenable.' Thus, in this case Spencer was led by abstract reasoning to reject a conclusion which, so far as his authority could be trusted, had the combined weight in its favour of Sir W. Herschel's opinion, Arago's, and Humboldt's, and which astronomical authorities had never been at the pains to question. Yet the conclusion to which Spencer was thus led on the comparatively slight evidence he possessed was, in reality, the same which Sir W. Herschel had adopted in 1802, after a score of years of persistent study

In 1811, Herschel published another remarkable essay, mainly relating to the milky luminosity which he had now recognized, not only in nebulous patches, but spread thinly of the heavens. Comparing the value of Spencer's abstract reasoning with that of the enormous mass of observed facts which astronomers had been collecting during a half-century since Herschel's day—so long as these facts remained unsifted—we find a curious illustration of the mistake made by those who would divorce observation from theory. In the same paper by Mr Spencer, there occurs the following passage :—
'"The spaces which precede or follow simple nebulæ," says Arago, "and, à fortiori, groups of nebulæ, contain generally few stars. Herschel found this rule to be invariable. Thus every time that, during a short interval, no star approached, in virtue of the diurnal motion, to place itself in the field of his motionless telescope, he was accustomed to say to the secretary who assisted him, 'Prepare to write; nebulæ are about to arrive.'" How does this fact consist with the hypothesis that nebulæ are remote galaxies? If there were but one nebula, it would be a curious coincidence were this one nebula so placed in the distant regions of space as to agree in direction with a starless spot in our own sidereal system. If there were but two nebulæ, and both were so placed, the coincidence would be excessively strange. What, then, shall we say on finding that they are habitually so placed? (the last five words replace some that are possibly a little too strong). . . . When to the fact that the general mass of nebulæ are antithetical in position to the general mass of stars, we add the fact that local regions of nebulæ are regions where stars are scarce, and the further fact that single nebulæ are habitually found in comparatively starless spots, does not the proof of a physical connection become overwhelming?" Here Mr Spencer has deduced from the same facts which Arago and other astronomers have quoted in favour of the theory of external nebulæ, the inference which Sir W. Herschel arrived at, as we may see from the two passages quoted in an earlier part of this essay (see page 253). It is singular, however, how little weight the argument, from the improbability of repeated coincidences, here correctly applied by Spencer, has with ordinary minds. Michell employed this argument skilfully more than a century ago, in effect demonstrating the laws of association between certain groups of stars: but it was not till Sir W. Herschel had actually watched one star circling around another that even

over large parts of the heavens, and had learned to distinguish it from the milky light produced by multitudes of distant stars. His observations and deductions are full of interest, and especially interesting are his ideas as to the evolution of stars from the matter producing milky nebulous light. However, except in so far as they indicate his changed views respecting the constitution of the universe, these matters, worthy of study though they are in themselves, do not here concern us. There is one passage, however, from the essay of 1811, which cannot be too carefully studied by those who would rightly apprehend the nature and results of Herschel's work during the twenty-six years which had now elapsed since he enunciated the stratum theory of the sidereal system:—"I must freely confess," he says, "that by continuing my sweeps of the heavens, my opinion of the arrangement of the stars and their magnitudes, and of some other particulars has undergone a gradual change; and indeed, when the novelty of the subject is considered we cannot be surprised that many things formerly taken for granted should, on examination, prove to be different from what they were generally but incautiously supposed to be. For instance, an equal scattering of the stars may be admitted in certain calculations; but when we examine the Milky Way or the closely compressed clusters of stars, of which my catalogues

astronomers began to believe in such systems; and a third of a century later still, the idea was not accepted save by a few astronomers. Abstract reasoning must be strong indeed (and easy to follow, also) to overcome the inertia of slow apprehension.

have recorded so many instances, this supposed equality of scattering must be given up. We may also have supposed nebulæ to be no other than clusters of stars disguised by their very great distance; but a longer experience and a better acquaintance with the nature of nebulæ, will not allow a general admission of such a principle; although undoubtedly a cluster of stars may assume a nebular appearance when it is too remote for us to discern the stars of which it is composed."

It will be observed that in this passage Herschel abandons two of the principles on which his views in 1785 had been founded,* the general uniformity of stellar distribution, and the theory that all nebulæ, whether components of our system or external, are formed of stars. Each of the two principles here given up was essential to that theory (in its entirety), while the first of the two principles was cardinal even as respects the general relations of the theory. Two links of the chain of ideas enunciated by Herschel in 1785 were now rejected (as in fact broken under the strain of observation). One of these, at least, had to bear so large a part of the theory, that with its failure the theory itself came to the ground.

It must have been, then, at about this time, certainly not later, that the necessity for a new method of star-gauging presented itself to Herschel's mind. He was, however, too busily engaged in observing nebulæ and in endeavouring to detect the law of their development, to

---

* Compare the italicized passage in the quotation at page 256 of the present Essay.

enter on any scheme of observation for determining the constitution of the universe. It is necessary to notice, however, before we pass to the new attack made by Herschel on the wider subject, that he now recognised a much more complete series of celestial objects than he had imagined in 1785. Then, and in the remarkable paper of 1789, he pictured various degrees of stellar aggregation, from uniformly scattered stars to the most compressed clusters. Now, he placed at the lower extremity of the scale of celestial objects the widely spread luminosity first noticed in the paper of 1802. He passed from this irregularly diffused nebulosity through all the orders of gaseous nebulæ—irregular nebulæ, planetary nebulæ, nebulous stars—formed by the gradual condensation of the gaseous matter, until the star itself is formed; then, and then only, he entered on the part of the series earlier recognised, passing on to the various orders of stellar aggregation,—diffused clusters, ordinary stellar nebulæ, and more and more condensed stars, up to the richest clusters. He no longer speaks of external nebulæ. The paper of 1814 begins with these words:—"The observations contained in this paper are intended to display the sidereal part of the heavens, and also to show the intimate connection between the two opposite extremes, one of which is the immensity of the widely diffused and seemingly chaotic nebulous matter; and the other the highly complicated and most artificially constructed globular clusters of compressed stars. The proof of an intimate connection between these extremes will greatly support the probability of the conversion of one into the other."

For much that relates to the sidereal heavens, Herschel refers in this paper of 1814 to the paper of 1785, and it may be that such reference has prevented most of his commentators from noticing how completely his views had changed. In reality it is only where he is speaking of insulated stars that he quotes the earlier paper. So soon as he deals with aggregations of stars, though he refers to the star-gauges of 1785 he no longer explains them as of yore. He dwells afresh on what he had written in 1802 respecting the clustering condition of portions of the stellar heavens. He explains that his expression "forming clusters" was "used to denote that some peculiar arrangement of stars in lines making different angles, directed to a certain aggregation of a few central stars, suggested the idea that they" (the former) "might be in a state of progressive approach to them" (the latter).* "This tendency to clustering seems chiefly to be visible in places extremely rich in stars. In order, therefore, to investigate the existence of a clustering power, we may expect its effects to be most visible in and near the Milky Way." I would invite the reader's special attention to the circumstance that the Milky Way is here pointedly referred to as a stellar region distinct in its characteristics from the region of the stars forming our constellations. In studying

* We may notice here, again, a certain inexactness in Herschel's manner of writing, accounting, perhaps, for the extent to which he has too often been misinterpreted.

Herschel's papers we have continually to be on the watch for indications of the sort, and although this particular view is not new, since he had expressed the same opinion in 1802, yet as Herschel was now very near the close of his observing career, it is important to notice that in this critical respect he retained the views which he had adopted in 1802.

Thirty years had now passed since Herschel had enunciated his first method of star-gauging, and as yet we have found no indication of a second method. But at the close of this paper of 1814 he mentions a new mode of research, by which he hoped to determine the laws according to which the stellar universe is constructed. "The extended views I have taken," he says, "in this and my former papers, of the various parts that enter into the construction of the heavens, have prepared the way for a final investigation of the universal arrangement of all these celestial bodies in space; but *as I am still engaged in a series of observations for ascertaining a scale whereby the extent of the universe, as far as it is possible for us to penetrate into space, may be fathomed,* I shall conclude this paper by pointing out some inferences which the continuation of the action of the clustering power enables us to draw from the observations that have been given."

We find Herschel, then, in 1814, preparing a scale whereby to gauge the extent of the universe, "as far as it is possible for us to penetrate into space."

But in 1814, Herschel reached his seventy-sixth year, and itw as scarcely to be anticipated that he would live to complete in its entirety the task he had entered upon so late in his career—the most stupendous task which any astronomer had ever thought of undertaking. In 1784 and 1785 he believed that he had something finite to deal with; his telescopes reached, as he supposed, to the limits of the galaxy; he had but to gauge, by counting stars in field after field, to ascertain the shape of the sidereal system. Moreover he was then in the prime of life. Now, in his old age, the stellar system had widened on his view. Infinitely more complex than he had supposed, unfathomable (in parts at least of its extent) even with his mightiest instruments—how was he to hope in the few years remaining to him, to solve the mighty problem with which he alone of all men who had ever lived had dared to grapple?

There was no shrinking on his part, however, from the tremendous task which lay before him. He did not even allow himself to attack the work hurriedly. Thoughtfully he prepared the scale (the new method of gauging of which he had spoken in 1814), and not until 1817 did he describe the plan in detail and with illustrative instances of its application.

The reader may be prepared, after what has been said at the beginning of this paper, to find the new method differing little from the method of 1784. He may think that, since the two methods have been confounded together by many, perhaps the second is the same as the first, but applied on a larger scale and with higher powers, or if different from the other is still closely related to it.

So far, however, is this from being the case, that the methods may be described as not only unlike, but even antithetical to each other.

In the first method the same telescope was to be applied successively to different parts of the heavens; in the second the same part of the heavens was to be examined successively with different telescopes. In the first method the stars in each field were to be counted; in the second, the observer was to note simply to what degree the telescopes successively employed separated from each other the component stars brought into view,—or, in technical terms, to what degree the telescope effected the resolution of the stars in each field.

It seems to me tolerably clear that up to the year 1814, and possibly for a year or two longer, Herschel had been steadily advancing towards new and wider truths respecting the universe, and that the new method of star-gauging, as it first presented itself to his mind, was a well-considered means of attacking the great problem in the enlarged form to which it had grown. It is manifest that the higher the telescopic power we employ, the farther do we penetrate into the spaces surrounding us on all sides. It is, of course, probable (or rather it is certain) that many objects visible with a lower telescopic power may lie farther away than others brought into view with a higher power, because a very large star is visible from beyond depths which suffice to hide smaller but nearer orbs. Yet unless we assume that there are limits beyond which none of the larger stars exist, it is clear that each increase of telescopic power, by bringing into view new members of these larger orders, must carry our vision beyond the limits which it had before reached. And if we wish to form just conceptions of the structure of the universe, it seems manifest that our best, in fact our only available first step towards such knowledge, is to ascertain the aspect of the space surrounding us, as viewed with gradually increasing powers of vision. This, as I judge, was what Herschel proposed when, in 1814, he spoke of "fathoming the extent of the universe, so far as it is possible for us to penetrate into space."

But it is certain that the plan, as he began to carry it out in 1817 and 1818, does not correspond with this description. Nor does Herschel appear, in my judgment, to have worked in these years with his former skill and acumen. Power was not wanting, but there is no longer the elasticity which hitherto had been so marked a characteristic of Herschel's mind. I think, too, that it will become manifest to anyone who carefully studies the whole series of Herschel's papers, that when he wrote these last two, the great array of facts which he had been so long engaged in gathering together was no longer present in its entirety to his mind. It must not be held to involve irreverence towards the greatest astronomer the world has known, to suppose that in his seventy-ninth and eightieth years his mental powers were not so great as they had been, and especially that his memory began to fail for facts observed during the preceding ten or twelve years of his life. Assuredly no honest student of science should allow his respect for the work of Herschel's former years to cause him to overlook defects, if such exist, in the reasoning with which Herschel's latest observations were accompanied.

It is not difficult to show that his reasoning in 1817 and 1818 was no longer so sound as in former years. He was now applying, be it remembered, a process by which he hoped to determine the relative distances of star-groups. Supposing that a particular clustering aggregation began to be resolved into discrete stars with a certain telescopic power, and was entirely resolved when a certain higher power was employed, there would be *primâ facie* evidence as to the distance of the aggregation—because, given a group of stars of certain sizes and set at certain distances from each other, it is manifest that the farther away that group is placed the higher will be the telescopic powers required (1) to begin, and (2) to complete the resolution of that group into separate stars. But although such considerations may be reasonable enough when we are comparing two groups together, and even within certain limits when applied to different parts of the same group, there are circumstances under which their application to particular star-groups would be altogether incorrect, and which shew also how unsafe the general principle is on which this particular method of star-gauging depends.

In order to shew this, I will take as a typical instance a splendid pair of star-groups (not clusters properly so called) which adorn the uplifted hand of The Rescuer, quoting Prof. Nichol's account of Herschel's study of this

remarkable object:—'In the Milky Way,' he says,
'thronged all over with splendours, there is one portion
not unnoticed by the general observer, the spot in the
sword-hand of Perseus. That spot shews no stars to the
eye; the milky light, which glorifies it, comes from regions
to which unaided we cannot pierce. But to a telescope of
considerable power* the space appears lighted up with
unnumbered orbs; and these pass on through the depths
of the infinite, until, even to that penetrating glass, they
escape all scrutiny, withdrawing into regions unvisited
by its power. Shall we adventure into these deeper
retirements? Then, assume an instrument of higher
efficacy, and lo! the change is only repeated; those scarce
observed before appear as large orbs, and behind, a new
series begins, again shading gradually away, leading
towards farther mysteries! The illustrious Herschel
penetrated on one occasion into this spot, until he found
himself among depths whose light could not have reached
him in much less than four thousand years: no marvel
that he withdrew from the pursuit, conceiving that such
abysses must be endless!' The younger Herschel, speaking of instances such as these, where telescope after
telescope has been directed to the same spot without
apparently reaching its limits, says that here 'we are
compelled by the clearest evidence the telescope can afford
to believe that star-strewn vistas lie open, exhausting their
powers and stretching out beyond their utmost reach,
as is proved by infinite increase of number and diminu-

* A good opera-glass shows abundant stars in this wonderful group.

tion of magnitude, terminating in complete irresolvable nebulosity.'

It was thus that the elder Herschel interpreted these wondrously rich spots in the papers of 1817 and 1818. Followed as he has been in this interpretation by Sir John Herschel, Struve, Grant, Nichol, and others, it may seem incredible that an argument practically resistless opposes itself to such a conclusion. Yet there is such an argument; nor has its strength ever been impeached or even questioned.

Repeatedly in his earlier papers, Sir W. Herschel had noted the probability, rising almost to certainty in each individual case, and absolutely certain for many cases, that groups of stars which are rounded in appearance are roughly globular in reality, and that groups markedly distinct by their richness from *surrounding parts of the star-sphere* are really distinct as to richness from *surrounding parts of interstellar space*. If we consider the very group in Perseus which Herschel, as we have seen, regarded otherwise—or as a star-region extending away and away into space, along the track over which his telescopes of greater and greater power had carried him— we shall find abundant reason for that earlier interpretation. The group is much smaller in apparent size than the moon, but for the sake of argument imagine it as large. Conceive a cone having the eye as apex and just large enough to enclose the moon, extending out into space towards the great double cluster. Then, whatever else we may be in doubt about, we know quite certainly that the whole star region examined by Herschel is enclosed within that long tapering cone. If his later principle of interpretation is just, the brighter and, as he judged, the nearer stars of the cluster are so far away within this cone, that their light takes about a hundred years in reaching us—but say two hundred years to favour his interpretation (as will immediately appear) as far as possible. The farther parts, we have seen, he regarded, on the same principle, as so far away that their light takes 4000 years in reaching us, or twenty times as long. How much farther the star-region extends (on this interpretation) we do not know. But here we have the farthest known part, twenty times as far away as the nearest. Now, if any one will make a very taper cone of paper (it should be a yard high if its base is only a third of an inch in diameter, or three yards high for a one-inch base), and will cut off a twentieth part of its length, from the apex, the remaining part will show the shape of the region of space occupied, according to the interpretation of 1818, by the stars of the rich cluster. The paper frustum (still nearly a yard high, if the first of the above-mentioned sizes be adopted, and at its thickest part only a third of an inch wide), is, indeed, immensely exaggerated in width, long and slender though it seems. That wonderful group of stars, then, forms in reality, if rightly interpreted by Herschel in 1818, a long, thin, almost cylindrical array of stars, happening by a singular chance to have its length directed exactly towards our earth! As there are two clusters, indeed, there are two such enormously long and slender arrays, thus strangely adjusted! And all other similar cases—of which Herschel cites no less than ten, while many others were recognized by his son in the southern Milky Way—must be similarly interpreted.

The objections to such an inference are manifest; and in corresponding cases Sir W. Herschel had clearly recognized them. Note again, how Sir John Herschel disposes of such conceptions as being utterly improbable in the much less marked case of the two Magellanic Clouds. 'Were there but one such object,' he says, 'it might be maintained without utter improbability that its apparent sphericity is only an effect of foreshortening; but such an adjustment, improbable enough in one case, must be rejected as too much so for fair argument in two.' How much more, therefore, in the multitudinous instances presented by the clustering aggregations of the Milky Way.

The inference clearly is, then, that where Herschel had supposed (in 1817 and 1818) that he was fathoming, or attempting to fathom, the depths of stellar space, he was in reality only scrutinising more and more closely, as higher and higher powers were employed, one and the same region occupied by many orders of stars—from suns perhaps surpassing our own many times in volume, down to orbs which, large though they may be absolutely, must relatively be regarded as mere star-dust. I do not speak of this conclusion as doubtful, for it appears to me demonstrated. As the elder Herschel spoke of the two great clustering regions of Cygnus as spherical in shape, as the younger Herschel spoke similarly of the Magellanic Clouds, so may we justly say of these regions which had been regarded as the fathomless parts of our stellar system, that demonstrably they are 'island star-systems,' infinitely rich in stars, and infinitely varied in structure. We may indeed apply to them the very words which Sir John Herschel applied on sufficient but far weaker evidence to the Magellanic Clouds, 'it must be taken as a demonstrated fact that stars of the seventh and eighth magnitude, and irresolvable nebula' (not *nebulæ*) 'may coexist within limits of distance not differing more than as 9 to 10.' The caution which this discovery should inspire when we are dealing with other cases where the evidence is less simple, need hardly be insisted upon.

Both methods of star-gauging had been tried, then, when Herschel ceased from his labours, and in one sense both had failed. It had been at least demonstrated that the principles by which Herschel had hoped to be able to interpret either method, were unsound. He himself established the fact that the stars are not spread throughout our system with such an approach to uniformity that one can estimate the extension of the system in different directions by counting the stars which a single powerful telescope brings into view. He also collected the materials which prove that we cannot hope to estimate the distances of different parts of the system by testing with different telescopes the degree of stellar resolvability in those parts.

Is, then, the problem altogether hopeless? It seems to me that it is very far from being so, and that even where Herschel's methods seemed to fail they afford excellent promise of success. His first method, for example, had to be abandoned so far as his original purpose was concerned, because he found reason to believe that the great rich regions of the Milky Way are situated like great clouds of stars in space, and are not mere ranges of stars extending continuously from our own neighbourhood. But it was the method itself which taught this,—which, in fact, effected this capital discovery. The second method, again, cannot be interpreted as Herschel hoped. It cannot tell us how far off, relatively, are different star-groups. But this application of the method has to be abandoned simply because the use of the method itself has taught us that the architecture of the heavens is far too complex to be interpreted in so simple a manner. Here then is another great discovery effected by a method of star-gauging which, so far as its original purpose was concerned, has had to be rejected. We have learned, from the seeming failure of the two methods, two important and interesting facts—first, that the stars are gathered into certain regions of space, and segregated from others; and, secondly, that where stars are so gathered they exist in many orders of real magnitude, and are spread in different parts of such aggregations with very different degrees of profusion. Furthermore, over and above these valuable deductions, we have the observations themselves still available for use in other ways, still ready to reward whoever shall devote close and attentive scrutiny to them.

But it appears to me that so soon as we recognize the

success of both methods in one sense, and their failure in another, a method of research suggests itself which promises to combine all those qualities of each method which can really be trusted, and to be open to no objections. It was a grand idea of Herschel's to determine the varying richness of the heavens in different directions under the scrutiny of one powerful telescope. It was an equally noble occupation to watch the heavens "widening on man's view" with the widening pupil of the telescopic eye. Each method of research proved effective as used separately. But only by combining the two can the secret of the star-depths be mastered. We must not limit ourselves, however, to the study of a star-field here and a star-field there. With each telescopic power employed, the whole heavens must be surveyed. The results obtained with each power must be compared together, after being carefully indicated in suitable charts (since the most powerful intellect cannot grasp those results presented merely as statistics). Differential charts, shewing *by how much* each increase of power increases in each region of the heavens the number of stars brought into view, must also be constructed. No preconceived opinions must be suffered to mar the teaching thus obtained; but the architecture of the heavens so disclosed must be viewed precisely as it is presented to us by these results: because then, though it may be far too complex for our comprehension, we shall be less likely to be deceived than if we were prepared beforehand to recognize in it certain characteristic features.

This is a work in which almost every student of astronomy can help. Gaugings with small telescopes should by no means be neglected. Indeed, when we remember that the structure of the stellar universe is so complex and varied that some of the nearer parts cannot be analysed to their inmost recesses, even by the most powerful telescopes yet constructed, we see that our information about these parts can alone be brought near to completeness, and it is precisely about these parts that the smaller telescopes can give the most useful information.

I believe there is a great future for that noble domain of astronomy which Sir W. Herschel made the chief object of his study. By such methods of star-gauging as I have indicated—by the application of spectroscopy to distinguish the stars into their various orders as respects physical structure—by the careful analysis of stellar motions, in order to recognize the laws of association—and by other methods of research, the stupendous problem presented by the stellar heavens may be hopefully attacked; and even should the observations directed to its solution fail, so far as their main purpose is concerned, there can yet be no manner of doubt that the collected results will be full of value and interest.

SATURN AND THE SABBATH OF THE JEWS

In one of the most striking passages of his "Study of Sociology," Herbert Spencer considers what might be said of our age "by an independent observer living in the far future, supposing his statements translated into our cumbrous language."

"'In some respects,' says the future observer, 'their code of conduct seems not to have advanced beyond, but to have gone back from the code of a still more ancient people from whom their creed was derived . . . The relations of their creed to the creed of this ancient people are indeed difficult to understand. . . Not only did they, in the law of retaliation, outdo the Jews, instead of obeying the quite opposite principle of the teacher they worshipped as divine, but they obeyed the Jewish law, and disobeyed their divine teacher in other ways,—as in the rigid observance of every seventh day, which he had deliberately discountenanced . . . Their substantial adhesion to the creed they professedly repudiated, was clearly demonstrated by this, that in each of their temples they fixed up in some conspicuous place the Ten Commandments of the Jewish religion, while they rarely, if ever, fixed up the two Christian Commandments given instead of them. And yet,' says the reporter, after dilating on these strange facts, 'though the English were greatly given to missionary enterprises of all kinds, and though I sought diligently among the records of these, I could find no trace of a society for converting the English people from Judaism to Christianity.'"

It is, indeed, a strange circumstance that Christian teachings in our time respecting the observance of each seventh day, should be at variance, not only with what is known of the origin of the observance of Sunday, as distinguished from the Sabbath of the Jews, but even more emphatically with the teachings of Christ, both as to the purpose of a day of rest, and as to the manner in which the poor should be considered. Our Sunday is in fact, if not in origin, the Sabbath of the Jews, not the Lord's Day of the Apostles; it is regarded, not as a day set apart to refresh those who toil, but as though man were made for its observance; while the soul-wearying gloom of the day is so ordered as to affect chiefly the poorer classes, who want rest from work and anxiety, not rest from the routine of social amusements, which are unknown to them. But although the thoroughly non-Christian nature of our seventh day is remarkable in a country professedly Christian, and although it is a serious misfortune for us that an arrangement which might be most beneficial to the working classes is rendered mischievous by the way in which it is carried out, I certainly have no purpose here to discuss the vexed question of Sunday observance. There are some points, however, suggested by Spencer's reference to the origin of our weekly resting day, which are even more curious than those on which he touches. We take our law of weekly rest from Moses; we practically follow Jewish observances in this matter: but in this, except in so far as the contrast between Judaism and Christianity is concerned, there is nothing incongruous. For the Jewish nation was of old the sole Eastern nation whose priesthood taught the worship of one God, and resisted the tendency of their people to worship the gods of other nations. But the real origin of the Jewish Sabbath was far more singular. The observance was derived from an Egyptian, and primarily from a Chaldæan source. Moreover, an astrological origin may be recognized in the practice; rest being enjoined by Egyptian priests on the seventh day, simply because they regarded that day as a *dies infaustus*, when it was unlucky to undertake any work.

It needs no very elaborate reasoning to prove that the Jewish observance of the Sabbath began during the sojourn in Egypt. Without entering into the difficult question of the authorship and date of the Pentateuch, we can perceive that the history of Abraham, Isaac, and Jacob, in the Elohistic portion of the narrative, is introductory to the account of the Jews' sojourn in Egypt and exodus thence under their skilful and prudent commander, Moses. It is incredible that the person who combined these two accounts into one history, including an exact record of the rules for observing festivals, should have failed to add some reference to the seventh day of rest when quoting (from the Elohist) the ordinances which Abraham and the other patriarchs were so carefully enjoined to obey, if it really had been a point of duty in patriarchal times to keep holy the seventh day. In every injunction to the Israelites after they left Egypt, the duty of keeping the Sabbath is strongly dwelt upon. It not only became from this time one of the commandments, but "a sign between the Lord and the children of Israel for ever." In the patriarchal times, on the contrary, we find no mention of it: the test of righteousness was the worship of one God—the God of Abraham, Isaac, and Jacob. In the book of Job, again, no reference whatever is made to the observance of the Sabbath; and this is the more remarkable because Job makes "solemn protestation of his integrity" in several duties. He claims integrity in the worship of God; "If I beheld the sun when it shined," he says, "or the moon walking in brightness, and my heart hath been secretly enticed, or my mouth hath kissed my hand" (the token of worship), "this also were an iniquity to be punished by the judge: for I should have denied the God that is above." But he says no word about the observance which, after the exodus, is so specially associated with the worship of God.

It is, indeed, somewhat singular that the observance of the Sabbath should be derived from far remoter times, by those who insist on the literal exactness of the Bible record, seeing that the Bible distinctly assigns the exodus from Egypt as the epoch when the observance had its origin. For Moses, in solemnly reminding all Israel of the covenant in Horeb, says:—

"Remember that thou wast a servant in the land of Egypt, and that the Lord thy God brought thee out thence, through a mighty hand and by a stretched-out arm: therefore the Lord thy God commanded thee to keep the Sabbath-day."—(Deut. v. 15).

And these words occupy the position in the Fourth Commandment, which, in Exodus xx. 11, is occupied by the ords, 'For in six days the Lord made heaven and earth,' &c.

Assigning the origin of the first Jewish observance of the Sabbath to the time of the exodus, we are forced to the conclusion that the custom of keeping each seventh day as a day of rest was derived from the people amongst whom the Jews had been sojourning more than two hundred years. It is unreasonable to suppose that Moses would have added to the almost overwhelming difficulties which he had to encounter in dealing with the obstinate people he led from Egypt, the task of establishing a new festival. Such a task is at all times difficult, but at the time of the exodus it would have been hopeless to undertake it. The people were continually rebelling against Moses, because he sought to turn them from the worship of the gods of Egypt, in whom they were disposed to trust. It was no time to establish a new festival, unless one could be devised which should correspond with the customs they had learned in Egypt. Moses would seem indeed to have pursued a course of compromise.* Opposing man-

* There is a passage in Jeremiah which, as it seems to me, cannot otherwise be reconciled with the Pentateuch—viz., chapter vii. 21-23, where he says, "Thus saith the Lord of Hosts, the God of Israel; Put your burnt-offerings unto your sacrifices, and eat flesh. For I spake not unto your fathers, nor commanded them in the day that I brought them out of the land of Egypt, concerning burnt-offerings or sacrifices: but this thing commanded I them, saying, Obey my voice, and I will be your God, and ye shall be my people; and walk ye in all the ways that I have commanded you, that it may be well unto you." It seems plainly intimated here that (in Jeremiah's opinion, at any rate) the ordinances relating to burnt-offerings and sacrifices on the Sabbath and new moons were not commanded by God, however plainly the account in the Pentateuch may seem to suggest the contrary; and the two accounts can scarcely be reconciled except by supposing that the Mosaic laws on these points were intended to regulate and also to sanction an observance not originally instituted by Moses.

fully the worship of the Egyptian gods, he adopted, nevertheless, Egyptian ceremonies and festivals, only so far modifying them that (as he explained them) they ceased to be associated with the worship of false gods.

We have also historical evidence as to the non-Jewish origin of the observance of the seventh day, as decisive as the arguments I have been considering. For Philo-Judæus, Josephus, Clement of Alexandria, and others, speak plainly of the week as not of Jewish origin, but common to all the Oriental nations. I do not wish, however, to make use of such evidence here, important though it is—or rather because it is so important that it could not properly be dealt with in the space available to me. I wish to consider only the evidence which lies directly before us in the Bible pages, combining it with the astronomical, relations which are involved in the question. For it is to an astronomical or rather an astrological interpretation that we are led, so soon as we recognise the non-Jewish origin of the Sabbath. Beyond all doubt, the week is an astronomical period, and that in a two-fold sense; it is first a rough sub-division of the lunar month, and in the second place it is a period derived directly from the number of celestial bodies known to ancient astronomers as *moving* upon the sphere of the fixed stars.

The astronomical origin of the Sabbath is shown by the Mosaic laws as to festivals, illustrated by occasional passages in other parts of the Bible. In the 28th chapter of Numbers we find four forms of sacrifice to be offered at regular intervals—first the continual burnt-offering to be made at sunrise and at sunset (these epochs, be it noted, being important in the astrological system of the Egyptians); secondly, the offering on the Sabbath; thirdly, the offering in the time of the new moon; and fourthly, the offering at the luni-solar festival of the Passover. That is, we have daily, weekly, monthly, and yearly offerings. An attempt has been made to show that in the beginning of the Mosaic rule the months were not lunar; but, apart from all other evidence, repeated references to "Sabbaths and new moons" negative this view, and show that as Spencer (Rit. iii. 1) maintains, the Hebrews began their month when the new moon first appeared. It is also clear from the nature of the offerings made, that the festival of the new moon was held in equal esteem with the Sabbath; and although the observances were different, yet both days were strictly religious in character. For when the Shunammite woman said to her husband that she would "run to the man of God," he answers (supposing she went to hear the sacred books read), "Wherefore wilt thou go to him to-day? it is neither new moon nor Sabbath." And again, the new moon resembled the Sabbath in being a day when sale was prohibited. "Hear this," says Amos, "O ye that swallow up the needy, even to make the poor of the land to fail, saying, When will the new moon be gone, that we may sell corn? and the Sabbath, that we may set forth wheat?" It seems also, as Tirin has pointed out, that servile work was prohibited, for we read (1 Samuel xx. 18, 19) that Jonathan said to David, "To-morrow is the new moon:

and thou shalt be missed, because thy seat will be empty. And when thou hast stayed three days, then thou shalt go down quickly, and come to the place where thou didst hide thyself *when the business was in hand*," or as in the Douay translation, " in the day when it is lawful to work." *

We have evidence equally clear to show that the seven days of the week were connected with the seven planets, that is, with the seven celestial bodies which appear to move among the stars. It was by no mere accidental agreement between the number of the days and the number of planets that so many of the Oriental nations were led to name the days of the week after the planets. The arrangement of the nomenclature is indeed so peculiar that a common origin for the practice must be admitted, when we find the same arrangement adopted by nations otherwise diverse in character and habits. Moreover, the arrangement is manifestly associated with Sabaism on the one

---

* Tirin also asserts that the Jews observed the lunar system, and that their months consisted of 29 and 30 days alternately (29½ days, within about three-quarters of an hour, being the length of the mean lunar month). Hence the feast of the new moon came to be called the thirtieth Sabbath, that is, the Sabbath, of the thirtieth day. Thus Horace (Sat. I. ix.) "Hodie tricesima sabbata : vin' tu Curtis Judæis oppedere?" Macrobius mentions that the Greeks, Romans, Egyptians, Arabians, &c., worshipped the moon (Sat. I. xv.)? and it is probable that despite the care of Moses on this point, the Jews were prone to return to the moon-worship whence the feast of the new moon had its origin. We must not, however, infer this from the passage in Jeremiah vii. 17, 18, "Seest thou not what they do in the cities of Judah and in the streets of Jerusalem? The children gather wood, and the fathers kindle the fire, and the women knead their dough, to make cakes to the queen of heaven, and to pour out drink-offerings unto other gods." For the queen of heaven is Athor, parent of the universe.

hand, and with astrological superstitions on the other; and we find the clearest evidence in the Bible not only that Sabaism and astrology were known to the Jews, but that Moses had extreme difficulty in separating the observances he enjoined (or permitted?) from the worship of the Host of Heaven. He was learned, we know, in all the wisdom of the Egyptians (Acts vii. 22), and therefore he must have known those astronomical facts, and have been familiar with those astrological superstitions, which the Chaldæans had imparted to the Egyptians of the days of the Pharaohs.* It is noteworthy, too, that the first difficulties he met with in the exodus arose from the wish of the Jews to return to Sabaism. This is not manifest in the original narrative; but the real meaning of the account is evident from the following passage (Acts vii. 40), where Stephen, speaking of Moses, says, "This is he . . . whom our fathers would not obey, but thrust him from them, and in their hearts turned back again into Egypt, saying unto Aaron, Make us gods to go before us; for as for this Moses, which brought us out of the land of Egypt, we wot not what is become of him. And they made a calf in those days, and offered sacrifice unto the idol, and rejoiced in the works of their own hands. Then God turned, and

---

* He showed considerable skill, if Dr Beke was right, in his application of such knowledge (combined with special knowledge acquired during his stay in Midian) so that his people should cross a part of the Gulf of Suez during an exceptionally low tide. For though the Egyptians may have been acquainted with the general tidal motion in the Red Sea, it may well be believed that the army of Pharaoh would be less familiar than Moses with local peculiarities affecting (in his time) the movements of that sea.

gave them up to worship the host of heaven; as it is written in the book of the prophets . . . . Ye took up the tabernacle of Moloch, and the star of your god Remphan, figures which ye made to worship them."*

Now I might pass from what has here been shewn, to the direct inference that the Sabbath corresponded with the day which Oriental Sabaism consecrated to the planet Saturn; because we have the clearest possible evidence that all nations which adopted the week as a measure of time named the seven days after the same planets. But I prefer, at some risk of appearing to weaken

---

* This passage, and the passage from Amos, to which the protomartyr refers, are curious in connection with the special subject of this paper, as indicated by its title. For where Stephen says Remphan, Amos says Chiun. Now it is maintained by Grotius that Remphan is the same as Rimmon, whom Naaman worshipped, and Rimmon or Remmon signifies "elevated" (lit. a pomegranate), and is understood by Grotius to refer to Saturn, the highest of the planets. (The student of astronomy will remember Galileo's anagram on the words "*Altissimum planetam tergeminum observavi.*") Now Chiun, which denotes a "pedestal," is considered to be equivalent in this place to Chevan, or Kevan, the Saturn of the Arabians. (Parkhurst mentions that the Peruvians worshipped Choun. Moloch, of course, signifies king. Because children were sacrificed to Moloch, Bonfrére considers this god to be the same as Saturn, described as devouring his own children. If so, the words "tabernacle of Moloch and the star of Remphan" relate to the same special form of Sabaism—that, namely, which assigned to Saturn the chief place among the star-gods. I must remark, however, that this point is by no means essential for the main argument of this paper, which is in reality based on the unquestioned fact that amongst all the nations which used the week as a division of time, the seventh day was associated with the planet Saturn. It is necessary to call attention to this point, because not unfrequently it happens that some subsidiary matter, such as that touched on in this note, is dealt with as though the whole question at issue turned upon it.

the argument by introducing matters less certain, to consider the evidence we have as to the position of the god corresponding to the Latin Saturn in the Assyrian mythology.

Many years since, Colonel (then Major) Rawlinson, in a paper read before the Royal Asiatic Society, referring to an inscription beginning, " This the Palace of Sardanapalus, the humble worshipper of Assarach," made the following remarks :—

"There can be no doubt," he said, (I quote from a report not professing to be *verbatim*) " that this Assarach was the Nisroch mentioned in Scripture, in whose temple Sennacherib was slain. He was most probably the deified father of the tribes, the Assur of the Bible. This Assarach was styled in all the inscriptions as the king, the father, and the ruler of the gods, thus answering to the Greek god, Chronos, or Saturn, in Assyrio-Hellenic mythology."

Again Layard, speaking of Assyrian mythology, says—

" All we can now venture to infer is that the Assyrians worshipped one supreme God as the great national deity, under whose immediate and special protection they lived, and their empire existed. The name of this god appears to have been Asshur, as nearly as can be determined at present from the inscriptions. It was identified with that of the empire itself, always called 'the country of Asshur.' With Asshur, but apparently far inferior to him in the celestial hierarchy, although called the great gods, were associated twelve other deities . . These twelve gods may have presided over the twelve months of the year."—(*Nineveh and Babylon*, p. 637.)

In a note, Layard refers to doubts expressed by Colonel Rawlinson respecting the identity of Asshur and Nisroch, presumably removed by Rawlinson's later reading of the inscription referred to above. He remarks that this supreme god was represented sometimes under a triune form; and 'generally, if not always, typified by a winged figure in a circle.' Plate XIV. of my treatise on Saturn shews how these two descriptions are reconcilable; for there are shewn in it two figures of Nisroch, both winged and within a ring, but one only triune.*

Amongst the twelve great gods were included six corresponding to the remaining planets, though doubts exist as to the gods associated with the different celestial bodies. It seems probable that Shamash corresponded with the Sun; Ishtar (Astarte or Ashtar) with the Moon; Bel with Jupiter †; Merodach with Mars; Mylitta with Venus; and Nebo with Mercury. But the

---

* I do not here dwell on the curious coincidence—if, indeed, Chaldean astronomers had not discovered the ring of Saturn—that they shewed the god corresponding within a ring, and triple. Galileo's first view of Saturn, with feeble telescopic power, shewed the planet as triple (*tergeminus*); and very moderate optical knowledge, such indeed as we may fairly infer from the presence of optical instruments among Assyrian remains, might have led to the discovery of Saturn's ring and Jupiter's Moons. (Bel, the Assyrian Jupiter, was represented sometimes with four star-tipped wings.) But it is possible that these are mere coincidences. Saturn would naturally come to be regarded as the God of Time, on account of his slow motion round the ecliptic; and thus the ring (a natural emblem of time) might be expected to appear in figures of the god corresponding to this planet. It is curious, however, that the ring is flat, and proportioned like Saturn's.

† Layard associates Bel, "the father of the great gods," with Saturn, and Mylitta the consort of Bel with Venus, but without giving any reasons, and probably merely as a guess. He elsewhere remarks, however, that from Baal came the Belus of the Greeks, who was confounded with their own Zeus or Jupiter, and apart from the clear evidence associating Nisroch with Saturn, the evidence connecting Bel with

question would only be of importance in its bearing on my present subject, if we knew the Assyrian time-measurement, and especially their arrangement of the days of the week. Since we have to pass to other sources of information on this point, the only really important fact in the Assyrian mythology, for our purpose, is the nearly certain one that their supreme god Asshur or Nisroch corresponded to the 'highest' or outermost planet Saturn. He was also the Time God, thus corresponding to Chronos. But it is necessary to notice here that mythological relations must to some degree be separated from astrological considerations, in dealing with the connection between various Assyrio-Chaldæan deities and the planets. For instance, it is important in mythology to observe that the Greek god Chronos and the Latin god Saturn are unlike in many of their attributes, yet the association between the planet Saturn and the Assyrian deity Nisroch is not on that account brought into question, although we can only connect Nisroch with Saturn by means of the common relation of both to Chronos.

Many circumstances point to the Chaldæan origin of Egyptian astronomy. The Egyptian zodiac corresponded with the Dodecatemoria of the Chaldæans, and though some of the Chaldæan constellations were modified in Egyptian temples, yet sufficient general resemblance exists between the Egyptian arrangement and that which other

Jupiter is tolerably satisfactory. The point is not important, however, in relation to the subject of this paper. On etymological grounds, Yav, the fifth of the great gods, may perhaps be associated with Zeus, identical with the Sanscrit Dyaus, and the Latin root "Jov."

nations derived from the Chaldæans, to shew the real origin of the figures which adorn Egyptian zodiac temples.* The argument derived from astrological fancies is even stronger, for the whole system of astrological divination is so artificial and peculiar that it must of necessity be ascribed to one nation. To find the system prevailing

* In an essay on 'The Shield of Achilles' ('Light Science for Leisure Hours,' first series), I called attention, seven years ago, to the probability that the description of the Shield, a manifest interpolation, related originally to a zodiac temple, erected by star-worshippers long before Homer's time. Some of the Egyptian zodiac temples exist to his day, though probably they belong to a much later date, and were only copies (more or less perfect) of the ancient Chaldæan temples. That Homer, if he had visited such a temple, and had composed a poem descriptive of its sculptured dome, would have 'worked in' that description if he saw the opportunity when singing the Iliad, all Homeric students will be ready to admit. Like every improvisatore, the glorious old minstrel knew the advantage of the rest afforded by an occasional change from invention to recitation. In so using it, he appears to have pruned the description considerably; for in the 'Shield of Hercules' (manifestly taken from the same Homeric poem, though sometimes attributed to Hesiod) we find, along with much almost identical matter, several passages which are omitted from the Achillean description. Very curious evidence of the nature of the original poem is found in one of these passages. In a zodiac temple, the constellation of the Dragon (whatever the age of the temple) would occupy the boss or centre of the dome, for the north pole of the zodiac falls in the middle of that constellation. Now in the 'Shield of Hercules'—

> 'The scaly horror of a dragon coil'd
> Full in the central field, unspeakable
> With eyes oblique retorted, that aslant
> Shot gleaming flame.

(The very attitude, be it noted, of the Dragon of the Star sphere.) There is much more evidence of this kind to which, for want of space, I cannot here refer.

among any people is of itself a sufficient proof that they were taught by that nation. Nor can any question arise as to the nation which invented the system. The Egyptians themselves admitted the superiority of the Chaldæan astrologers, and the common consent of all the Oriental nations accorded with this view. We know that in Rome, although Armenians, Egyptians, and Jews were consulted as astronomers, Chaldæans were held to be the most proficient. 'Chaldæis sed major erit fiducia,' says Juvenal, of the Roman ladies, who consulted fortune-tellers: 'quicquid Dixerit astrologus, credent a fonte relatis Ammonis,'—whatever the Chaldæan astrologers may say, they trust as though it came from Jupiter Ammon. Another argument in favour of the Chaldæan origin of astronomy and astrology is derived from the fact that the systems of astronomy taught in Egypt, Babylon, Persepolis, and elsewhere, do not correspond with the latitude of these places; but this argument (which I have considered at some length in Appendix A. to my treatise on Saturn) need not detain us here. It is sufficient to observe that in Egypt the astrological system was early received and taught :—

'Egypt,' says a modern writer, 'a country noted for the loveliness of its nights, might well be the supporter of such a system . . To each planet was attributed a mystic influence, and to every heavenly body a supernatural agency, and all the stars that gem the sky were supposed to exert an influence, over the birth, and life, and destiny of man; hence arose the casting of nativities, prayers, incantations, and sacrifices,—of which we have traces even to the present day in those professors of astrology and divination, the gipsies, whose very name links them with the ancient country of such arts."*

One of the cardinal principles of astrology was this: that every hour and every day is ruled by its proper planet. Now, in the ancient Egyptian astronomy there were seven planets; two, the sun, and moon, circling round the earth, the rest circling round the sun. The period of circulation was apparently taken as the measure of each planet's dignity, probably because it was judged that the distance corresponded to the period. We know that some harmonious relation between the distances and periods was supposed to exist. When Kepler discovered the actual law, he conceived that he had in reality found out the mystery of Egyptian astronomy, or, as he expressed it, that he had "stolen the golden vases of the Egyptians." Whether they had clear ideas as to the nature of this relation or not, it is certain that they arranged the planets in order (beginning with the planet of longest period) as follows:—

1. Saturn.   5. Venus.
2. Jupiter.   6. Mercury.
3. Mars.   7. The Moon.
4. The Sun.

The hours were devoted in continuous succession to these bodies; and as there were twenty-four hours in each Chaldæan or Egyptian day, it follows that with whatever

* This may be questioned. It is said, however, that when the gipsies first made their appearance in Western Europe, about the year 1415, their leader called himself Duke of Lower Egypt.

planet the day began the cycle of seven planets (beginning with that one) was repeated three times, making twenty-one hours, and then the first three planets of the cycle completed the twenty-four hours, so that the fourth planet of the cycle (so begun) ruled the first hour of the next day. Suppose, for instance, the first hour of any day was ruled by the Sun—the cycle for the day would therefore be the Sun, Venus, Mercury, the Moon, Saturn, Jupiter, and Mars, which, repeated three times, would give twenty-one hours; the twenty-second, twenty-third and twenty-fourth hours would be ruled respectively by the Sun, Venus, and Mercury, and the first hour of the next day would be ruled by the Moon. Proceeding in the same way through this second day, we find that the first hour of the third day would be ruled by Mars. The first hour of the fourth day would be ruled by Mercury; the first hour of the fifth day by Jupiter; of the sixth by Venus; and of the seventh by Saturn. The seven days in order, being assigned to the planet ruling their first hour, would therefore be—

1. The Sun's day (Sunday).
2. The Moon's day (Monday, Lundi).
3. Mars' day (Tuesday, Mardi).
4. Mercury's day (Wednesday, Mercredi).
5. Jupiter's day (Thursday, Jeudi).
6. Venus's day (Friday, Veneris dies, Vendredi).
7. Saturn's day (Saturday; *Ital.* il Sabbato).

Dion Cassius, who wrote in the 3rd century of our era,

gives this explanation of the nature of the Egyptian week and of the method in which the arrangement was derived from their system of astronomy. It is a noteworthy point that neither the Greeks nor Romans in his time used the week, which was a period of strictly Oriental origin. The Romans only adopted the week in the time of Theodosius, towards the close of the fourth century, and the Greeks divided the month into periods of ten days; so that, for the origin of the arrangement connecting the days of the week with the planets, we must look to the source indicated by Dion Cassius. It is a curious illustration of the way in which traditions are handed down, not only from generation to generation, but from nation to nation, that the Latin and western nations receiving the week along with the doctrines of Christianity, should nevertheless have adopted the nomenclature in use among astrologers. It is impossible to say how widely the superstitions of astrology had spread, or how deeply they had penetrated, for the practices of astrologers were carried on in secret, wherever Sabaism was rejected as a form of religion; but that in some mysterious way these superstitions spread among nations professing faith in one God, and that even to this day they are secretly accepted in Mahometan and even Christian communities, cannot be disputed. How much more must such superstitions have affected the Jews, led out by Moses from the very temple of astrology? Knowing what we do of the influence of such superstitions in our own time, can we wonder if three thousand years ago Moses found it difficult to dispossess his followers of their belief in "the host of heaven," or if, a few generations later, even the reputed prophetess Deborah should have been found proclaiming that "the stars in their courses" had fought against the enemies of Israel.*

   * We are apt to overlook the Pagan origin of many ideas referred to in the Bible, as well as of many ceremonies which Moses at least *permitted*, if he did not enjoin. The description of the Ark of the Covenant, of the method of sacrifices, of the priestly vestments, &c., indicate in the clearest manner an Egyptian or Assyrian origin. The cherubim, for instance—figures which united, as Calmet has shewn, the body of the lion or ox with the wings of an eagle—are common in Assyrian scriptures. The oracle of the temple differed only from some of the chambers of Nimrod and Korsabad, in the substitution of 'palm trees' for the sacred tree of Assyrian scriptures, and open flowers for the Assyrian tulip-shaped ornament. Layard ('Nineveh and Babylon,' p. 643) states further that 'in the Assyrian halls, the winged human-headed bulls were on the side of the wall, and their wings, like those of the cherubim, 'touched one another in the midst of the house.' The dimensions of these figures were in some cases nearly the same—namely, fifteen feet square. The doors were also carved with cherubim and palm trees, and open flowers, and thus, with the other parts of the building, corresponded with those of the Assyrian palaces. On the walls at Nineveh, the only addition appears to have been. the introduction of the human form and the image of the king, which were an abomination to the Jews. The pomegranates and lilies of Solomon's temple must have been nearly identical with the usual Assyrian ornament, in which—and particularly at Khorsabad—the pomegranate frequently takes the place of the tulip and the cone.' After quoting the description given by Josephus of the interior of one of Solomon's houses, which even more closely corresponds with and illustrates the chambers in the palace of Nineveh, Layard makes the following remark : 'To complete the analogy between the two edifices, it would appear that Solomon was seven years building the temple, and Sennacherib about the same time building his great palace at Kouyunjik.' The introduction into the Ark of figures so remarkable as the cherubim can hardly be otherwise explained than by assuming that these figures corresponded with some objects which the Jews during their stay

That the Egyptians dedicated the seventh day of the week to the outermost or highest planet, Saturn, is certain; and it is presumable that this day was a day of rest in Egypt. It is not known, however, whether this was ordained in honour of the chief planet—that is their supreme deity,—or because it was held unlucky to work on that day. It by no means follows from the fact that Nisroch, or his Egyptian representative, was the chief deity, that he was therefore regarded as a beneficent ruler. Rather what we know of Oriental superstitions would lead us to infer that the chief deity in a system of several gods was one to be propitiated. And indeed, the little we know of Egyptian mythology suggests that the beneficent gods were those corresponding to the sun and moon,— later represented by Osiris and Isis (deities, however, which had other interpretations), Saturn, though superior

---

in Egypt had learned to associate with religious ceremonies. That the Egyptians used such figures, placing them at the entrance of their temples, is certain. Neither can it be doubted that the setting of dishes, spoons, bowls, shewbread, &c., on the table within the Ark, was derived from Egyptian ceremonials, though direct evidence on these points is not (so far as I know) available. We know, however, that meats of all kinds were set before Baal (see 'Apocrypha,' Bel and the Dragon). The remarkable breast-plate worn by the Jewish high priest was derived directly from the Egyptians. In the often-repeated picture of judgment the deceased Egyptian is seen conducted by the god Horus, while 'Anubis places on one of the balances a vase supposed to contain his good actions, and in the other is the emblem of truth, a representation of Thmèi, the goddess of Truth, which was also worn on the judicial breast-plate.' Wilkinson, in his 'Manners and Customs of the Ancient Egyptians,' shows that the Hebrew Thummim is a plural form of the word Thmèi. The symbolism of the breast-plate is referred to in the 'Apocrypha,' Book of Wisdom, lxviii. 24.

to the sun and moon, not only in the sense in which modern astronomers use the term superior, but also in the power attributed to him, was probably a maleficent if not a malignant deity. We may infer this from the qualities attributed to him by astrologers—

'If Saturn be predominant in any man's nativity, and cause melancholy in his temperature,' says Burton, in his 'Anatomy of Melancholy,' 'then he shall be very austere, sullen, churlish, black of colour, profound in his cogitations, full of cares, miseries, and discontents, sad and fearful, always silent and solitary.'

We may not unreasonably conclude, therefore, that either rest was enjoined on Saturn's day as a religious observance to propitiate this powerful but gloomy god, or else because bad fortune was expected to attend any enterprise begun on the day over which Saturn bore sway. The evil influence, as well as the great power attributed to Saturn, are indicated in the well-known lines of Chaucer:—

'. . . Quod Saturne,
My cors, that hath so wide for to turne,
Hath more power than wot any man;
*   *   *   *   *
'I do vengeaunce and pleine correction
While I dwell in the signe of the leon;
*   *   *   *   *
'Min ben also the maladies colde
The darke tresons, and the castes olde
My loking is the fader of pestilence.'

It is, however, possible that the idea of rest on the day dedicated to Saturn may have been suggested to Egyptian astrologers and priests by the slow motion of the planet in his orbit, whereby the circuit of the ecliptic is only completed in about twenty-nine years.

However this may be, we know certainly that on the Sabbath of the Jews rest was enjoined for a different reason. Moses adopted the Egyptian week and allowed the practice of a weekly day of rest to continue. But in order that the people whom he led and instructed might not fall into the worship of the host of heaven, he associated the observance of the seventh day with the worship of that one God in whom he enjoined them to believe, the God of their forefathers, Abraham, Isaac, and Jacob. So far as appears from the Bible narrative, there is no scriptural objection to this view. On the contrary, strong scriptural reasons exist for accepting it. If the account of the creation given in the first chapter of Genesis could be accepted as literally exact, it nevertheless would not follow that the seventh day of rest was enjoined before the time of exodus. And we have seen that the Bible account itself assigns the departure from Egypt as a reason for the observance, so that whatever view we form respecting the real origin of the seventh day of rest, we have no choice as to the time we must assign for the commencement of its observance by the Jews, unless Deuteronomy v. be rejected as not even historically trustworthy.

Nothing, therefore, that I have shewn in this paper need be regarded as necessarily opposed to the faith of those who honestly believe in the literal exactness of the reason assigned in Exodus xxxi. 17, for the observance of the Sabbath of the Jews. Such persons may accept the week as of Pagan origin, and the original observance of Saturn's day as of astrological significance, while believing in the reason given by Moses for the adoption of the practice by his followers, that 'in six days the Lord made heaven and earth, and on the seventh day he rested and was refreshed.' (The idea of rest, accepted literally, accords neither better nor worse with the conception of an Almighty Creator, than the idea of work.) But it seems to me that those who thus regard the Jewish Sabbath as a divinely instituted compromise between the worship of the seven planets as gods, and the worship of one only God the Creator of all things, may yet find in what I have here shewn a new reason for Christianising our seventh day of rest, even if we must still continue to miscall it the Sabbath. Since it was permissible for Moses to adopt a Pagan practice (to sanction, if not to sanctify, a superstition), it may well be believed that a greater than Moses was entitled to change the mode of observance of the seventh day of rest. We know that in Christ's time the Sabbath (of its very nature a convenient ceremonial substitute for true religion) had become a hideous tyranny; nay, that many, wanting real goodness, were eager to prove their virtue by inflicting the Sabbath on those who most needed 'to rest and be refreshed' on that day. Whether in the obedience to the teaching of Christ, who (we learn) rebuked those hypocrites, all this has been changed in our time, is a point which may be left to the reflection of the reader.

THOUGHTS ON ASTROLOGY.

We are apt to speak of astrology as though it were an altogether contemptible superstition, and to contemplate with pity those who believed in it in old times. And yet, if we consider the matter aright, we must concede, I think, that of all the errors into which men have fallen in their desire to penetrate into futurity, astrology is the most respectable, one may even say the most reasonable. Indeed, all other methods of divination of which I have ever heard, are not worthy to be mentioned in company with astrology, which, delusion though it was, had yet a foundation in thoughts well worthy of consideration. The heavenly bodies *do* rule the fates of men and nations in the most unmistakable manner, seeing that without the controlling and beneficent influences of the chief among those orbs—the sun—every living creature on the earth must perish. The ancients perceived that the moon has so potent an influence on our world that the waters of the ocean rise and fall in unison with her apparent circling motion around the earth. Seeing that two among the orbs which move upon the unchanging dome of the star-sphere are thus potent in terrestrial influences, was it not natural that the other moving bodies known to the ancients should be thought to possess also their special powers? The moon, seemingly less important than the sun, not merely by reason of her less degree of splendour, but also because she performs her circuit of the star sphere in a shorter interval of time, was seen to possess a powerful influence, but still an influence far less important than that exerted by the sun, or rather than the many influences manifestly emanating from him. But other bodies travelled in yet wider circuits if their distances could be inferred from their periods of revolution. Was it not reasonable to suppose that the influences exerted by those slowly moving bodies might be even more potent than those of the sun himself? Mars circling round the star-sphere in a period nearly twice as great as the sun's, Jupiter in twelve years, and Saturn in twenty-nine, might well be thought to be rulers of superior dignity to the sun, though less glorious in appearance; and since no obvious direct effects are produced by them as they change in position, it was natural to attribute to them influences more subtle, but not the less potent.

Thus was conceived the thought that the fortunes of every man born into the world depend on the position of the various planets at the moment of his birth. And if there was something artificial in the rules by which various influences were assigned to particular planets, or to particular aspects of the planets, it must be remembered that the system of astrology was formed gradually and perhaps tentatively. Some influences may have been inferred from observed events, the fate of this or that king or chief guiding astrologers in assigning particular influences to such planetary aspects as were presented at the time of his nativity. Others may have been invented, and afterwards have found general acceptance because confirmed by some curious coincidences. In the long run, indeed, any series of experimental predictions must have led to some very surprising fulfilments, that is, to fulfilments which would have been exceedingly surprising if the corresponding predictions had been the only ones made by astrologers. Such instances, carefully collected, may at first have been used solely to improve the system of prediction. The astrologer may have been careful to separate the fulfilled from the unfulfilled predictions, and thus to establish a safe rule. For it must be remembered, that admitting the cardinal principle of astrology, the astrologer had every reason to believe that he could experimentally determine a true method of prediction. If the planets really rule the fate of each man, then we have only to calculate their position at the known time of any man's birth, and to consider his fortunes, to have facts whence to infer the manner in which their influence is exerted. The study of one man's life would of course be altogether insufficient. But when the fortunes of many men were studied in this way, the astrologer (always supposing his first supposition right) would have materials from which to form a system of prediction.

Go a step further. Select a body of the ablest men in a country, and let them carry out continuous studies of the heavens, carefully calculate nativities for every person of note, or even for every soul born in their country, and compare the events of each person's life with the planetary relations presented at his birth. It is manifest that a trustworthy system of prediction would, in the long run, be deduced by them, if astrology have a real basis in fact.

I do not say that astrologers always proceeded in this experimental manner. Doubtless in those days, as now, men of science were variously constituted, some being disposed to trust chiefly to observation, while others were ready to generalize, and yet others evolved theories from the depths of their moral consciousness. Indeed, what we know of the development of astrology in later times, as well as the way in which other modes of divination have sprung into existence, shows that the natural tendency of astrologers would be to invent systems rather than to establish them by careful and long-continued observation. Within a very few years of the discovery of the spots on the sun, a tolerably complete system of divination was founded upon the appearance, formation, and motions of these objects. Certainly this system was not based on observation, nor will anyone suppose that the rules for 'reading the hand' had an observational origin, or that fortune-telling by means of cards was derived from a careful comparison of the result of shuffling, cutting and dealing, with the future fortunes of those for whose enlightenment these important processes were performed.

But we must not forget that astrology was originally a science, though a false one. Grant the truth of its cardinal idea, and it had every right to this position. No office could be more important than that of the astrologer, no services could be more useful than those he was capable of rendering according to his own belief as well as that of those who employed him. It is only necessary to mention the history of astrology to perceive the estimation in which it was held in ancient times.

As to the extreme antiquity of astrology it is perhaps needless to speak; indeed, its origin is so remote that we have only imperfect traditions respecting its earliest developments. Yet it may be worth while to mention some of these traditions, seeing that, whether true or not, they shew clearly enough the great antiquity attributed to astrology, even in times which to ourselves appear remote. Philo asserts that Terah, the father of Abraham, was skilled in all that relates to astrology; and, according to Josephus, the Chaldæan Berosus attributed to Abraham a profound knowledge of arithmetic, astrology, and astronomy, in which sciences he instructed the Egyptians. Diodorus Siculus says that the Heliadæ, or children of the sun (that is, men from the east,) excelled all other men in knowledge, particularly in the knowledge of the stars. One of this race, named Actis (a ray), built Heliopolis, and named it after his father, the sun. Thenceforward the Egyptians cultivated astrology with so much assiduity as to be considered its inventors. On the other hand Tatius says that the Egyptians taught the Chaldæans astrology. The people of Thebais, according to Diodorus Siculus, claimed the power of predicting every future event with the utmost certainty; they also asserted that they were of all races the most ancient.

However, we have, both in Egypt and in Assyria records far more satisfactory than these conflicting statements to prove the great antiquity of astrology, and the importance attached to it when it was regarded as a science. The great pyramid in Egypt was unquestionably an astronomical, that is (for in the science of the ancients the two terms are convertible,) an astrological building. The Birs Nimroud,* supposed to be built on the ruins of the tower of Babel, was also built for astrologers. The forms of these buildings testify to the astronomical purpose for which they were erected. The great pyramid, like the inferior buildings copied from it, was most carefully oriented, that is, the four sides were built facing exactly north, south, east, and west. The astronomical use of this arrangement is manifest. By looking along either of the two long straight sides lying east and west, the astronomer could tell the true east or west points of the horizon, and determine when the sun rose in the east †

---

* Every brick hitherto removed from this edifice bears the stamp of King Nebuchadnezzar. It affords a wonderful idea of the extent and grandeur of the building raised by the tyrants of old times, that the ruins of a single building on the site of Babylon (Rich's Kasr) has 'for ages been the mine from which the builders of cities rising after the fall of Babylon have obtained their materials.'—*Layard's* '*Nineveh.*'

† A good story is told about the rising of the sun in the east, the point of the joke being different, perhaps, to astronomers, than to others :—A certain baron was noted for never replying directly, even to the simplest questions, and a wager was laid that, if he were asked whether the sun rises in the east and sets in the west, he would not answer directly, even though told of the wager. The question was put, and he began—'The terms east and west, gentlemen, are conventional, but admitting that——,' the rest of the reply was lost, the wager

exactly, or set exactly in the west. By looking along the straight sides lying north and south, the astronomer could tell when the sun, or any other celestial body, was in the meridian. The figure of the pyramid has even been supposed to symbolize certain astronomical and mathematical relations; and a long slanting passage, opening in its northern slope, has been supposed to have been intended for the observation of the star Alpha of the Dragon, the pole star of about 2,000 years before the Christian era. Indeed, some go so far as to say that the builders of the great pyramid were instructed by a divine revelation in planning and building the pyramid. This idea, however, seems absurd on the face of it, seeing that the only conceivable object of such a revelation would be to preserve and render always available certain important astronomical relations; and the pyramid has not served this purpose, no one having understood it (according to those who have advanced this view) until now, when the building has lost the exactness of figure originally given to it. Far more probably, it symbolized such knowledge as the astrologers of Chaldæa and of ancient Egypt possessed, and was specially intended to advance the study of astrology, from which men expected to gain a complete knowledge of the future. Proclus informs us that the pyramids terminated at the

---

being won, which was all the enquirers cared for. If this worthy had answered simply 'Yes,' the wager would have been lost, but the reply would not have been correct; for the sun never has risen in the east and set in the west, exactly, at any place or on any day since the world began. If the sun rises due east on any day, he does not set due west, and *vice versâ*.

top in a platform, on which the priests made their celestial observations.

The figure of the Babylonian temple of astronomy was probably different, though it is possible that Nebuchadnezzar altogether modified the proportions of the original temple. We may infer the nature of the earlier use of such temples from later usages. We learn from Diodorus Siculus that, in the midst of Babylon, a great temple was erected by Semiramis, and dedicated to Belus or Jupiter, 'and that on its roof or summit the Chaldean astronomers contemplated, and exactly noted, the risings and settings of the stars.'

If we consider the manner in which the study of science, for its own sake, has always been viewed by Oriental nations, we must admit that these great buildings, and these elaborate and costly arrangements for continued observation, were not intended to advance the science of astronomy. Only the hope that results of extreme value would be obtained by observing the heavenly bodies could have led the monarchs of Assyria and of Older Egypt to make such lavish provision of money and labour for the erection and maintenance of astronomical observatories. So that, apart from the evidence we have of the astrological object of celestial observations in ancient times, we find in the very nature of the buildings erected for observing the stars the clearest proof that men in those times hoped to gain results of great value from such work. Now, we know that neither the improvement of navigation nor increased exactness in the surveying of the earth were aimed at by those who built those ancient observatories: the only conceivable object they can have had was the discovery of a perfectly trustworthy system of prediction from the study of the motions of the heavenly bodies. That this was their object is shewn with equal clearness by the fact that such a system, according to their belief, was deduced from these observations, and was for ages accepted without question.

Closely associated with astrological superstitions was the wide-spread form of religion called Sabaism, or the worship of the host of heaven (Sabaoth). It is not easy to determine whether the worship of the sun, moon, and planets, preceded or followed the study of the heavens as a means of divination. It is probable that the two forms of superstition sprang simultaneously into existence. The shepherds of Chaldæa, who

> 'Watched from the centres of their sleeping flocks
> Those radiant Mercuries, that seemed to move,
> Carrying through æther in perpetual round,
> Decrees and resolutions of the gods,

can hardly have regarded the planetary movements as *indicating*, without believing that those movements actually *influenced*, the fate of men and nations; in other words the idea of planetary power must from the very beginning, it would seem, have been associated with the idea of the significance of planetary motions. Be this as it may, it is certain that in the earliest times of which we have any historical record, belief in astrology was associated with the worship of the host of heaven. In the

Bible record we find the teachers and rulers of the Jewish nation compelled continually to struggle against the tendency of that people to follow surrounding nations in forsaking the worship of the God of Sabaoth for the worship of Sabaoth, turning from the Creator to the creature. They would seem even, as the only means of diverting the people from the worship of those false gods, to have adopted all the symbols of Sabaism, explaining them, however, with sole reference to the God of Sabaoth. Moses adopted in this way the four forms of sacrifice to which the Jewish people had become accustomed in Egypt —the offerings to the rising and setting sun (Numbers xxviii. 3, 4); the offerings on the day dedicated to the planet Saturn, chief of the seven star-gods (Numbers xxviii. 9); the offerings to the new moon (Numbers xxviii. 11); and the offerings for the luni-solar festival belonging to the first month of the sun's annual circuit of the zodiacal constellations (Numbers xxviii. 16, 17). All these offerings were in a sense sanctified by the manner in which he enjoined them, and the new meaning he attached to them; but that the original offerings were Sabaistic is scarcely open to question. The tenacity, indeed, with which astrological ceremonies and superstitions have maintained their position, even among nations utterly rejecting star-worship, and even in times when astronomy has altogether dispossessed astrology, indicates how wide and deep must have been the influence of those superstitions in remoter ages. Even now the hope on which astrological superstitions were based, the hope that we may one day learn to lift the veil concealing the future from our view, has not been altogether abandoned. The wiser reject it as a superstition, but even the wisest have at one time or other felt its delusive influence.

THE END.

www.ingramcontent.com/pod-product-compliance
Lightning Source LLC
Chambersburg PA
CBHW021207230426
43667CB00006B/601